ALBERT BALL VC

THE FIGHTER PILOT HERO
OF WORLD WAR ONE

Colin Pengelly

'*. . . Fierce fiery warriors fight upon the clouds*
In ranks and squadrons and right forms of war
The noise of battle hurtled in the air.'

Julius Caesar: Act 2, Scene 2
William Shakespeare

Pen & Sword
AVIATION

First published in Great Britain in 2010
Reprinted in this format in 2017
By Pen and Sword Aviation
an imprint of
Pen and Sword Books Ltd
47 Church Street
Barnsley
South Yorkshire
S70 2AS

ISBN 978 1 47389 355 9

A CIP record for this book is available from the British Library

Typeset in Palatino Light by S L Menzies-Earl

Printed and bound in Malta
by Gutenberg Press Ltd

Pen & Sword Books Ltd incorporates the imprints of
Pen & Sword Archaeology, Atlas, Aviation, Battleground, Discovery,
Family History, History, Maritime, Military, Naval, Politics, Railways,
Select, Social History, Transport, True Crime, Claymore Press,
Frontline Books, Leo Cooper, Praetorian Press, Remember When,
Seaforth Publishing and Wharncliffe.

For a complete list of Pen and Sword titles please contact
Pen and Sword Books Limited
47 Church Street, Barnsley, South Yorkshire, S70 2AS, England
E-mail: enquiries@pen-and-sword.co.uk
Website: www.pen-and-sword.co.uk

Contents

Acknowledgements 5

Introduction...6

Chapter 1   The Formative Years 12

Chapter 2   The Call to Arms 21

Chapter 3   Flying with No.13 Squadron...43

Chapter 4   Flying with No.11 Squadron
             The Ace in the Making..62

Chapter 5   The 'Rest Cure'
             Ball with No.8 Squadron 91

Chapter 6   The Rising Star
             Ball's Combats, August 1916 101

Chapter 7   The Consummate Fighter Pilot
             Combats, September to October 1916 114

Chapter 8   Leave and Home Establishment 132

Chapter 9   With No.56 Squadron
             February to March 1917 147

Chapter 10   Back to France, April 1917 158

Chapter 11   The Final Days, 1-7 May 1917 174

Chapter 12   The Last Patrol...189

Appendix 1   'The Wonderful Machine'...207

Appendix 2   The Austin-Ball Scout 209

Appendix 3   List of No.56 Squadron Pilots up to
             May 1917 217

Appendix 4   Victories List 219

Bibliography 221

Index 222

This book is dedicated to

Air Vice Marshal Raymond Collishaw
CB, DSO & Bar, OBE, DSC, DFC
Fighter Pilot, Historian and Friend
and my late feline friend "George" who sat with me
through much of the preparation of this book.

Acknowledgements

There have been many people who have been helpful in the preparation of this book. From the start of work Chris Weir and the staff at Nottingham Record Office were always helpful.

At the RAF Museum Guy Revell was always helpful in answering my queries and producing lists of relevant material for me. Norma Bulman checked the correspondence of Sir David Henderson. My copy editor, from Florida University Press, Ann Marlow, introduced me to Fred Libby's biography.

Of the individuals who have been helpful in the production of the manuscript, those who answered my original appeal in the *Nottingham Evening Post* were invaluable. Most particularly I must mention Brian Walker of the Nottingham Historical Film Society, and an aviation historian in his own right, who supplied me with many illustrations. In addition there was Kim Mycock of Trent College Archives. Gillian Lord, who did all the genealogical research for me never failed to produce the information I requested and left me full of admiration for her mastery of her sources.

Of those with a more direct connection with Albert Ball, I have managed to trace, through the efforts of Gillian Lord, the grandchildren of Flora Young and the daughter of Thelma White. All of them were happy to help in the supply of information and Thelma White (daughter of Albert Ball's Thelma) supplied personal photographs from her Mother's collection..

During the preparation of the book I had the benefit of corresponding with the late Chaz Bowyer who was helpful in supplying details from his own researches into Albert Ball and his family.

In the final stages of the book, when I was covering the period Ball was in 56 Squadron, I was glad to have the expertise and knowledge of Alex Revell, whose work on 56 Squadron and some of its personnel was invaluable. Alex agreed to read the manuscript through and made many suggestions for improvements, which I was glad to accept. Any mistakes which remain, are all my own work!

My wife, Evelyn, put up with my absences from home and the time I dedicated to writing, and deserves a mention for her understanding and tolerance.

Colin Pengelly
Weston-super-Mare, June 2009.

Introduction

The 7 May 2007 marked the 90th Anniversary of the death of Albert Ball. Ball was, at the time of his death, an iconic figure who represented the offensive spirit of the Royal Flying Corps (RFC) and whose loss was keenly felt. He is still remembered in his hometown of Nottingham and in Annoeullin where there is a College bearing his name. This book seeks to take a fresh look at his life and achievements.

As the last of the Great War veterans disappear and the War becomes a milestone in history rather than a living memory then I hope this book will stir interest in the War and keep in people's minds the sacrifices made by a whole generation of young people throughout the world for what they believed in. Albert Ball, like so many others, was dead before he reached twenty-one. He was a fighter-pilot in the first war in the air but he is fortunate that his deeds became famous when the equally important work of the rest of the aircrew of the air services of the great powers have largely become lost to memory, except for those who choose to look in their national archives.

The Star of Aviators was the title given to Albert Ball by a French News Agency when news of his death became known to the public of the Allied Countries[1]. Despite the wish of the British Army not to give publicity to the feats of their airmen, the name of Albert Ball had gradually become known throughout 1916. By the time he returned home for his last leave he was a national hero and celebrated as such, especially in Nottingham.

Albert Ball has been the subject of four previous biographies: two almost contemporary with his life, one in the 1930s by R. H. Kiernan which remained for many years the standard biography and, some thirty years ago, the late Chaz Bowyer produced a further biography, which was the first modern appraisal of Albert Ball and his achievements. Bowyer was still able at that time to talk to members of Ball's family and his fiancée as well as people who had flown with and known Ball as a friend or a squadron companion. This makes Bowyer's work important for the contribution it makes to the knowledge of the

---

1 *Captain Ball VC of the RFC* by W. Briscoe and H. Stannard (Herbert Jenkins 1918) p.308.

family background, which is now irreplaceable. An historian looking to reappraise Albert Ball has this basis of previous research and the private and official letters and correspondence to work from.

It is unfortunate that, after the appearance of Bowyer's book, the Ball family were prevailed upon to part with certain family papers, which were never returned. At some time Albert Ball's diary, which had been recovered by the family after his death, along with other papers, disappeared and is not held in the Ball Papers in the Nottingham Archives. The loss of the diary is particularly unfortunate for the biographer. The last biographer to see it was R. H. Kiernan in the 1930s who describes it as 'an honest record and in its sum reveals a love of fine motives, a realisation of frailties, a clean and manly heart'[2]. Ball himself told his father that if he ever went missing, 'You'll find my diary, from the day I joined the War – every day and every single thing'. It would be interesting to know his thoughts on various happenings of his career but this is now denied to us. The whereabouts of this document is no longer known and it seems to have gone missing before Chaz Bowyer completed his work for he confirmed to me that he never saw it during his research. One of the missing documents may have been the Albert Ball letter auctioned by a Swindon Saleroom in mid 2005. This was the last known letter to have been written by Ball and is partially quoted by Briscoe and Stannard in the work referred to earlier (see footnote 1). It was sold to a New Zealand buyer who has refused to let it be copied for the purposes of this work. This problem of 'historians' borrowing papers and photographs from well known pilots (or their families) of the Great War is not new. Air Commodore Fullard told me many years ago that he had suffered a similar loss of almost his entire set of records. The information available on which to construct a history of Albert Ball is therefore less full than might be desired. Most to be regretted is the fact that no letters to Ball seem to have survived, even from his first girlfriends and then his fiancée. The problem is of course familiar to all servicemen serving abroad, lack of space. My own experience is typical: while serving with the RAF in Kenya I wrote and received letters every week both from my parents and from girl friends. I had no space to keep all the letters I received and once replied to they were destroyed while my parents kept all my letters. I assume a similar

---

2 *Captain Albert Ball VC DSO* by R. H. Kiernan (John Hamilton 1933)

situation existed with Albert Ball who received and wrote many letters but only those sent by him now survive.

Albert Ball was a typical Englishman of his time. Deeply patriotic and deeply religious and with a strong love for his family, particularly his mother. Along with many others he felt it his duty to enlist and, with his newly discovered enthusiasm for flying, applied for a transfer to the RFC which he thought would get him into contact with the enemy more quickly. He was born into a middle-class family and was shaped by his upbringing and his education at a minor public school. Essentially, he was a 'loner', preferring whenever he could, to seek a billet to himself. To strangers he was reserved but polite but there is no element of the strain of snobbery, which is noticeable in the correspondence of his contemporary Arthur Rhys Davids. This probably indicates the difference in attitude brought about by the classical education, which Rhys Davids received at Eton, and the more practically based education which Ball received at Trent.

Ball was within ten days of his 18th birthday when war broke out. Like many others he was dead before he had reached twenty-one, but, unlike his anonymous contemporaries shot out of the skies in their vulnerable reconnaissance machines, killed fighting in the trenches or lost in the explosion of the Battle Cruisers at Jutland, he was not just mourned by his family, friends and companions. He had assumed the status of a national hero. His deeds were known throughout the Allied and Neutral countries and his loss was marked accordingly.

Air fighting had been gradually intensifying from the time of the introduction in 1915 of the German Fokker monoplanes equipped with the Anthony Fokker synchronising gear. Although the performance of the Fokker was moderate and was exceeded by some Allied designs, in the hands of two German pilots, Boelcke and Immelmann it was a deadly weapon and one which the British and French air services needed to counter.

Albert Ball's career had started with the BE2c (an aircraft for which Ball had no time), variants of which had been a common prey of the Fokker. The BE2c was not a machine that was easily able to defend itself because of the arrangement of the pilot in the rear seat and the observer in the front seat. Even with this unpromising equipment Ball's letters make it plain that, when flying the BE on operational patrols, he was looking to engage the enemy, though he recognised the deficiencies of the BE as an offensive weapon. It was when Ball was given his chance to fly single-seater scouts that his particular talents became plain.

He was not, according to Edward Baumann, his first flying instructor, a natural pilot, but as he progressed through training, particularly at the Central Flying School (CFS), his skills developed. Once he was given the chance to fly the Bristol Scout and later the Nieuport Scout it was apparent where his talent lay and it was with the latter plane that he began to make his name.

By the end of 1916, following the loss of Lanoe Hawker, Ball was indeed the 'guiding star' of the RFC. His deeds and prowess were known throughout the Corps and his example was contagious though few could emulate his method of fighting. A year later Captain Ira Jones of 74 Squadron, idoliser of Mannock though he was, was said to have a note pinned up in the cockpit of his SE5a: 'Remember Ball! They Must Fall!'

As with all the 'Aces' of the First World War the final score of Ball must remain a matter of doubt. He was essentially a lone fighter and consequently his successes were not always witnessed by anyone else. The later availability of the German records shows differences with the recorded victories of many 'Aces' and particular doubt has been cast on the record of Billy Bishop, another lone fighter. His (Bishop's) supporters have said that if Bishop's victories are to be decried then the same criterion should be applied to Ball. What is certain with Ball is that there is no doubt that he engaged in many combats with enemy aircraft in which he returned with moderate or even severe battle damage. There can be no doubt, at least not in my mind, that Ball was honest in what he claimed and that he did not put in claims for Enemy Aircraft (EA) which were fictitious or of which, in his own mind, he was not certain. That his final victory list may not tally with the German list is not surprising, many of the Allied pilots and particularly British and Commonwealth ones have this same doubt on their long accepted totals, but how much reliance is to be placed on German Records when Ball himself is shown in them as being shot down in a Sopwith Triplane? The German criteria for an aerial victory were more rigorous than that adopted by the Allies and in addition most of their victories fell on their own side of the lines. The 'scores' for any ace, British, French or German will always be a matter of discussion. An Appendix has been included which lists Albert Ball's victories in accordance with latest research.

Ever since the 1960s when John Terraine published his new biography of Sir Douglas Haig there has been a reassessment of the British performance in the ground war on the Western Front. These reassessments have produced new opinions on the character and quality of British tactics and leadership and the necessary 'learning curve' to the successful offensives of 1918. Until recently no such reassessment had taken place in respect of the aerial war, however, in his book *Bloody April. The Slaughter in the Skies over Arras, 1917*.[3] Peter Hart has quite rightly tied the efforts made by the RFC to the offensives undertaken by the Army. The work of Artillery Observation and Photographic Reconnaissance could be carried out by the RFC with an acceptable rate of loss during the time of the Somme Offensive but by the time the battles at Arras were underway aerial supremacy had been lost. The Germans, though outnumbered, had qualitative superiority and were able to exact a terrible price for the work which the British two-seater crews had to do. In his unremitting policy of the offensive, Sir Hugh Trenchard put his crews under a terrible strain in this period. Information had to be gathered on work done behind the German lines and as von Richthofen remarked, it was better, 'for customers to come to the shop' than to go and seek them.

The RFC had been providing such an essential service to the Army, that even when it became a lot more operationally hazardous to get these photos and carry out the 'Art-Obs' the effort was still made. The activities of the RFC were part of the Army as a whole and within that context the provision of artillery observation and photographic reconnaissance was essential. The crews of the RFC were, in part, made up of men who had volunteered from the trenches and they, above all others, appreciated the necessity for the RFC to support the Army on the ground. It was in this period, from the Somme to Arras, that Albert Ball came to the fore and by a combination of courage, luck and good shooting his successes began to mount.

Trenchard, and his successor Sir John Salmond, always remained committed to the offensive in the War in the air. Hugh Dowding, who commanded a Wing under Trenchard during the battle of the Somme, recommended a particular Squadron (No.60) be rested after a run of

---

3 Published by Weidenfield & Nicholson 2005.

heavy casualties. Trenchard accepted this recommendation and withdrew the squadron from the front temporarily but he soon dispensed with the services of Dowding and remained an enemy of the latter helping to secure his dismissal from Fighter Command in 1940. The 'offensive spirit' of the RAF, which was nurtured by Trenchard through a difficult period, manifested itself between the Wars by the concentration on an offensive-orientated bombing strategy which bore fruit as the bomber policy of Portal and Harris in the second war.

Ball, as with Billy Bishop, remained an individualist as far as air fighting was concerned. He was never happy as a patrol leader. His idea was to engage enemy formations by the method he had found successful, to dive into the middle of the formation, split them up and destroy his selected target. This method required courage and luck as well as good shooting. In the former quality Ball never gave up on his desire to attack the enemy but he knew that the strain was telling on him. His controversial request for a rest from operations while serving with No. 11 Squadron was a sign that he knew that there was a limit to what the human body and mind will stand. At this stage he had hardly begun his single-seater career having largely carried out the usual duties required of a BE pilot at that time. His luck remained good until that final moment when he emerged from the low clouds over Annoeullin with a stalled engine and his plane upside down. During the War many pilots survived horrendous crashes without any serious injury but two such crashes robbed the RFC and the RAF of two of its best fighting pilots, Albert Ball and James McCudden.

I have included an Appendix on a puzzling aspect of Albert Ball's career. What was the aeroplane, which he was reported to have plans of in mid-1916 and which he reckoned to be 'heaps' better than the Fokker? It was not, of course, the Austin Ball Scout. This was produced after Ball's death and represented Austin's attempt to design a fighter around a specification, which they had received from Ball himself.

In this book I have retold the story of Albert Ball and tried to give a 'warts and all' portrait of a young man, much of it in his own words, who never had a chance to grow into manhood.

CHAPTER ONE

The Formative Years

Albert Ball was born in the family home at 301 Lenton Boulevard (now numbered 245 Castle Boulevard) Nottingham on the 14 August 1896. He was the third child and first son of Albert and Harriet Ball. His father, who was born on 20 July 1863, was a dealer in land and property having changed from the original calling of being a plumber. He had been an ambitious man and from the time that he entered his father's plumbing business he prospered. The business expanded and in the trade directory for 1895 G. Ball and Son are shown as operating from three addresses. He had married Harriet Page in July 1886, the daughter of Henry Page from Oldbrook, Derbyshire. Their first child, Hilda, was born in August 1887 but lived only a few days. She was followed by a further daughter, Lois, born in 1892; Albert in 1896 and Cyril born in 1898. As his business prospered Albert Ball Senior moved gradually up the housing ladder into more opulent properties. From Lenton Boulevard he moved to Mettham Street soon after his son's birth; then to 60 Sherwin Road in 1900 and finally to Sedgeley House at 43 Lenton Road.

Albert Ball Senior had been born and bred a Nottingham man and was to devote a large part of his life to public service in the city. He served as a councillor, alderman, mayor and finally lord mayor in 1935. His services to the City were recognised by a knighthood and he became an accomplished public servant. Among the enterprises in which he took a special interest was the Gas Department. He had joined the Gas Committee in 1901, became Chairman in 1907 and remained in this post until 1945, a few months before his death. He was successful in re-establishing public trust in the Gas Department after the 'Gas Scandal' of 1930 in which the Chief Clerk was found guilty of fraudulent practices on a grand scale. Although he was successful in re-establishing trust in the operation of the gas service in

Nottingham, there were persistent rumours that he himself had been more deeply involved in the scandal than appeared to be the case. In his private business affairs there have been suggestions that he was involved in some sharp practice in his land deals. It is alleged that, due to his position on the Council, he became aware of properties and land which were likely to be purchased in the future and that he bought them and, when the time came he resold to the Council at a profit, something today which would be called 'insider trading'. Nothing, however, has come to light to show anything which was not strictly correct in his dealings and which was not in accordance with the conventions of the time.

Nottingham was a thriving and important centre for industry. The city was dominated by the imposing structure of the castle overlooking the city centre and it boasted the largest town square in Europe. The town was made a City in 1897 as part of Queen Victoria's Jubilee Celebrations. It was the home of the legendary figure of Robin Hood but in later years had become famous as a centre for the Lace Trade. Subsequently, as the Industrial Revolution gained momentum, although the manufacture of lace remained a major industry, the town became more industrialised and by the time Albert Ball was born in 1896 three major commercial enterprises, which were to become household names, had become established there. Jesse Boot had been born in Nottingham and, from inheriting his mother's herbal shop, had built up the trade and had opened a large store in Nottingham in 1884 (the first of the Boots Stores). Also based in Nottingham were Raleigh Bicycles, making the most of the Victorian enthusiasm for the pastime, and Players Tobacco. It was, therefore, a thriving and expanding town and this created opportunities for men like Albert Ball senior to make money from the buying and selling of property and land. By the end of the 1890s he had realised his ambition to enter local politics and in November 1899 he had been elected as a Councillor for the Castle Ward of Nottingham, the beginning of a long career of public service. Harriet Ball seems to have been a good mother and a well respected Lady Mayoress to her husband (and his brother) as he rose in social standing. For Harriet, family was everything and particularly her eldest son. Albert fully reciprocated her love and his surviving letters include many to his mother dashed off in moments of relaxation.

The family was enjoying the prosperity of late Victorian and

Edwardian Britain and was a happy and close knit group. Sedgeley House, where Albert's family moved to, was a large imposing house in the Park District. It had extensive gardens that allowed plenty of room for the Ball children to play. It was close to the castle and had views over the Nottingham Canal with the River Trent in the distance. Albert Ball developed a fascination for anything mechanical. He had a room at the top of the house, which was always kept as his so long as the family occupied the house.

Albert Ball senior enjoyed a close relationship with all his children but particularly with his eldest son. The two were very much alike and the son developed the same business acumen as his father. To Albert, the life and business achievements of his father were something to admire and emulate. Even while serving in France Albert Ball had his mind on the family business and completed deals with his squadron mates for cars, motor cycles and even plots of land in the Nottingham area.

Despite dabbling in many areas including kite flying and the newly founded Boy Scout movement, there was no doubt about his main interest in life, a passion for mechanical and engineering devices. In a shed in the garden, in which a radio receiver was installed, he received messages from abroad. The young Albert had an enquiring mind and he conducted various experiments with anything that interested him, particularly of a mechanical kind, and eventually he and his friends, could strip down and reassemble a petrol engine and get it to run again. This led to his first love for motorcycles and then for cars and this background, supplemented by his education at Trent College, would give him sufficient mechanical capability so that, when he joined the RFC, he was able to work on his own aircraft engine, a talent which he shared with James McCudden. Of equal use in his subsequent career as a fighter-pilot was his interest in shooting. At which he became increasingly expert. This was an interest his father encouraged him to follow.

Ball's adventurous spirit manifested itself on occasions. He was said to have decided to run away to sea, when he was allegedly at Trent College, but what drove him to this step, if it ever happened, is not recorded. If he had such an idea, and he was said to have got as far as boarding a steamer at Liverpool before he decided to return home, I have come across nothing in his correspondence to prove that this event ever happened. It is related in the first biography to be written of him by Walter Briscoe who, it must be assumed, spoke to members of his family while preparing his work, but the fact that Ball never mentioned it himself does make it of doubtful authenticity. The adventurous side of his nature and his lack of fear, a later feature of his aerial tactics, was shown when on his 16th birthday he joined a local steeple-jack in climbing to the top of a factory chimney and apparently feeling completely at home in what, to many people would have been considered a dangerous situation. However, if there was a desire to go to sea and explore the world it did not remain with him. When war came in 1914 he volunteered for the Army and not the Royal Navy.

Albert Ball's education began when he attended the local Church School in Lenton. He was later followed there, and, to his other schools, by his brother Cyril. From the Church School he moved on to Grantham Grammar School (a boarding school) and then to Nottingham High School in September 1907. Previous pupils at Nottingham High had included: J.D. Player (of Players Cigarette fame), Jessie Boot (of Boot's Chemists) and the novelist D.H. Lawrence who didn't enjoy the experience! When Ball joined the school the Headmaster was George Turpin, himself an old Boy, a science graduate from Cambridge who had been headmaster since 1901. The school offered the chance for pupils to become involved in areas other than academic; there were extensive sports facilities and in 1905 a rifle range had been opened of which, no doubt, Albert Ball made use.

Like most schools of its type Nottingham High had an Officer Training Corps (OTC). The school records show that Ball joined this organisation in January 1910 but seems to have attended only seven parades, two in October and five in November before leaving the school in December 1910. As an illustration of the toll which the Great War took on the manhood of Britain, the page which lists Balls name as a member of the OTC includes twenty-one other names of which at least four can be traced as having been killed during the War. Apart from Albert Ball there was one other Victoria Cross winner from the school, a former master, Theodore Hardy, who served as a Chaplain with the Lincolnshire Regiment and won the VC, DSO and MC but was killed on the 18 October 1918. His VC had been won for rescuing wounded men under fire without regard for his own safety.

From Nottingham High School the brothers moved to Trent College at Long Eaton, just outside Nottingham, in January 1911. Trent was a minor Public School which, with fees of £75 a year, was well within the reach of a man of such newly made wealth as Albert Ball senior and matched the aspirations he had for his eldest son. Apart from the influence of his father, Trent College was to be the other major factor in shaping the character of Albert Ball. He and his brother were allotted to F Dormitory and Albert was entered in Form VC where his form master was G.J. Thomas.[1]

When Albert and Cyril entered Trent College it had been open for nearly forty-three years, having been established for the sons of Church of England parents. The headmaster was the Reverend John Savile Tucker who had been in the post since 1895 and was to retire the year after the Ball brothers arrived at the school. The character of Tucker, a forbidding and remote man, was imprinted on the school and its pupils. The regime was austere and the day started with a wake up call at 6.25am and compulsory cold baths. Living conditions were Spartan with basic food (which many pupils supplemented with 'tuck' from outside sources) and ineffective central heating.

The school concentrated on bodies as well as minds and frequent long walks were organised by the school for masters and pupils which merit a mention in the letters home which Albert sent to report on his progress. He was not a natural athlete and did not take easily to sport, but did enter various internal school competitions. Punishments for misbehaviour varied from the task of writing lines for minor infringements up to a beating from the Head Master for anything of a serious nature. If there was one facet of his character which was formed by his time at Trent College it was his sense of duty, to family, college and finally to his country.

Book learning was something with which he struggled and he was never to achieve a really satisfactory level in the main subjects, which today would be called the 'core curriculum'. However, he did not like to be without a goal to strive for and in practical subjects he displayed an increasing ability and aptitude. One of his earliest letters, undated but presumably from some time in 1912 Ball told his parents that he was building a model electric launch which 'carries 48 lb and is looking very decent'. He also wrote that he had been studying technical drawing and was 'able to draw quite decently, and also understand a drawing'.

---

1 See *Albert Ball VC* by Chaz Bowyer (Kimber 1977). The information obtained by Bowyer on all aspects of Ball's childhood and education is invaluable.

In the middle of 1912 he began to consider the end of his time at Trent and what he was to do about his future career. He needed guidance and advice as to what his future career should be and what qualifications he would need to succeed in that career. He told his parents:

Well I have not got on especially well at Trent as regards knowledge, but I think that I have made a slight improvement. I have got a great love for my school and shall be very sorry in many ways to leave, but I think that if I get into a good business I shall be spending my life in a much more profitable way and bringing the best out of myself, I shall try my level best to be a good and straight forward business man, and follow to the best of my ability in my Father's footsteps.

I am anchious to know what I am going to be when I (grow up) (deleted) leave and I do hope Father is looking about well. I think there is still a lot of money to be made in the way of making small electric lighting plants for country-houses. Many people have invented these sets but they are all so large and need so much looking after. I should like to be placed in a large Electric Engineering factory where they make all kinds of Machinery from the Dynimo to the power to drive it.

I should like to have a chance to work my way up from the bottom and try to get to the top. I think that the place for me is where there is plenty of work and bussel so that I can keep my mind to it and not be troubling with other things.[2]

His parents advised him to seek an interview with the headmaster so that he could receive some guidance as to what subjects he would need to study in order to achieve his ambition. The headmaster was now Geoffrey Foxall Bell who had replaced Tucker earlier in the year, and Ball accepted the suggestions of his parents that he should seek an interview:

Well I shall think tomorrow about what I should like to be. I shall also consult the Head about the subjects I am to take. I shall then write to you another letter and tell you what my idea is if you agree I shall work hard until next Summer. Then try my luck if

2 Albert Ball letters. Letter 11/6/1912(?) Nottingham Archives DD1180/1-DD1180/6. All other quotations from this source will be listed as 'Ball Archive'. The spelling remains his own!

you will allow me. Of course it is a very important matter and has to be thought of . . .[3]

At the resulting interview with the headmaster he was told to do extra maths and drawing with a view to becoming an engineer.

He advised me to start at the practical end of engineering. Then after I have had a year at that I have then to take the theory. Then try to pass an exam. Well the Head thinks that Engineering is the right thing, so if it pleases you I will be an Electrical Engineer.

Well I shall try at School for 1 more year, and then see what I can do. Well I was 7 out of 15 this week 8 above Cyril.[4]

He reported to his father later that the master taking him for the extra maths was very pleased with his progress. His weak point remained his spelling, which remained a characteristic of his letters home. He was also puzzled by the meaning of some words and attributed this to 'slacking in the past'.

The extra year at Trent College meant a lot of hard work for Ball, but he was determined enough on his future to know that effort spent now would repay itself in later years. This final year also seems to have reawakened his interest in the OTC with which he had dabbled at Nottingham High School and he joined the corps at Trent. He was not naturally a boy who enjoyed the type of discipline and routine which being in the OTC called for but he felt he had to persevere for the sake of his duty to his parents. No doubt he did enjoy the opportunities for improving his shooting which being in the OTC presented.

The time finally came for him to complete his education and leave Trent College at the end of the summer term in 1913. The school had shaped the character and attitudes he was to show for the rest of his life as well as developing his mind and body. It had reinforced his sense of duty to family and country. It was this sense of duty which had sent him out to France for the last time in April 1917 and kept him there when his nerves were stretched to breaking point and in his heart wanted only to be home with Flora his fiancée. This willingness to continue to perform his duty to his country was not unique to Ball. It manifested itself in many men who found the war hell and almost unendurable but they did endure because they thought it was the 'right

---

3 Ball Archives, undated.
4 Ball Archives, 21/10/12

thing to do'. Albert Ball was now ready to join the 'real' world, which, to him, meant following his father's example and succeed in a business career. In the year left to him before the outbreak of war he proceeded with his intended career of becoming an electrical engineer.

Upon leaving Trent, parental influence secured for him a place at a small firm called Universal Engineering in Castle Boulevard, Nottingham. It was a small electrical and brass foundry concern and was an ideal place for the young Albert Ball to start his career. Because he was living at home no correspondence exists for this period but he appeared to very happy with his new world and immersed himself in the daily business of the firm, learning his trade and experimenting with his own ideas whenever he got the chance.

He had barely a year before his plans and dreams for the future were rudely interrupted by the declaration of war on Germany. The war, which was to shatter the old Europe and reshape the map of the world, arose from nationalist aspirations in the Balkans when Serbian extremists assassinated the Archduke Franz Ferdinand in Sarajevo on the 28 June. This event, which probably did not even register on the consciousness of Albert Ball, or many of his contemporaries, grew via the Austrian ultimatum to Serbia, the involvement of Russia in support of the Serbs, then the involvement of Germany in support of Austria, followed by the inclusion of France by means of her alliance with Russia. The involvement of Britain was caused by Germany violating the neutrality of Belgium, of which Britain was a guarantor. Although this was the ostensible cause for Britain entering the War the real reason remained, as it had always been over the centuries, the balance of power. The challenge represented by the industrial and military power of Germany was recognised by Britain and the likelihood was that unless Britain entered the war France would be defeated and Germany would become the dominant continental power and leave Britain with no allies with which to face her. However, despite the naval threat, war against Germany was considered unthinkable in some quarters. *The Times* wrote on 1 August that, 'We consider ourselves justified in protesting against being drawn into a struggle with a nation so near akin to our own, and with whom we have so much in common.'[5]

The 'Naval Race' between Britain and Germany and the pronouncements in Germany, which made it plain that the German

---

5 Quoted in *1914* by Malcolm Brown (London 2005) p17.

Navy was being built to rival that of Britain, had convinced many people that war with Germany was inevitable at some time. When it came it was warmly welcomed by the most of the population of Britain, and other countries, as an opportunity to 'match themselves with the hour'. Just over 60 years before the same sort of sentiments had possessed the population at the time of the declaration of war on Russia, the Crimean War. *The Times* printed some words on the 27 February 1854 which reflected the feelings of the British public when the opponent was Germany in August 1914:

> It is not our business to inquire very exactly into the character of this enthusiasm, or to ask how far everyone of the multitude, or even if the many gentlemen who were there, understands the question at issue. The prevalent feeling is an honourable and a just one. It is that England has bound herself to assist a weak neighbour against the violence of a strong one, and that, for one reason or another, she has, in effect been slow to fulfil her pledge, and has now to make up for that lost time. It is in fact the people's quarrel, and a just one. Whether that people might not have spoilt their cause ere this by over much zeal it matters little now, when all are agreed, and nothing remains but to fight it out . . . It is the whole nation that speaks in this way, and it is the whole nation that in heart and spirit goes with every regiment chosen for service . . . That nation, if not the most populous, is the most powerful, because the most determined . . . It never says what it does not mean, and never means what it does not carry out . . . It will certainly do its part, and will persevere in a noble cause to the utmost farthing, to the last inch of ground and the last drop of blood.[6]

Albert Ball's destiny was now shaped. He was beginning the path which was to leave him in the form in which he is known today, as a fighter-pilot and VC holder. That path was to be eagerly sought by Ball with his burning sense of patriotism and duty, and held to even in his darkest moments. The young man with the ambition to be an electrical engineer was to fulfil an entirely different destiny.

---

6 Quoted in *Crimea* by Trevor Royal (London 2000) pp121/122.

CHAPTER TWO

The Call to Arms

All over Britain in the days following the Declaration of War on Germany the young men of Britain, of all classes, thronged the recruiting centres. Rallies were held and prominent local and national personalities urged the youth of the country to 'join up' and fight for King and Country. The feeling of 1914 was the last expression of the patriotic and imperial feelings which had seen the British Empire cover a quarter of the globe. The final closing of that grand 'Edwardian Summer' into the autumn and winter of 1914 to 1918.

In 1914 there was no conscription in Britain. A pro-conscription movement had been started by Lord Roberts, but it had not brought public or political opinion round to the point of making conscription a fact of life. Britain had a small regular army and it was this which went to war in 1914. It was supplemented by the Territorial Army, which began to provide reinforcements and replacements during the last quarter of 1914. It was recognised by many, not least Lord Kitchener, the Secretary of State for War, that in a war with Germany a mass army would be required. Contrary to most public opinion, the most famous and influential soldier of the day thought that it would be a long war, lasting to at least 1917, and that Britain would have to raise a large army to fight it. It was Lord Kitchener's intention that the mass British Army he was raising would be fully deployed in 1917 by which time he reckoned that its intervention would be decisive and Britain would be able to dictate the terms of the peace. As conscription was not in force the army had to rely on volunteers to swell their numbers and these came in their hundreds of thousands as the weeks and months rolled by.

Among these enthusiastic young men was Albert Ball. He knew what he was fighting for and where his duty lay. Young men of his background were to form the basis of the officer corps of the services in the coming struggle. It is said[1] that he was one of the first to volunteer at a recruiting meeting addressed by the Duke of Portland and the Mayor of Nottingham, who was at that time his uncle Frederick Ball.

In the biography by Kiernan[2] Ball is said to have been the very first to join as he had given his name to the authorities before the meeting and this action was enthusiastically announced at the meeting as the son of a 'prominent citizen' having 'joined up'. The date of this meeting is not known but on the 21 September 1914 Albert Ball was enlisted in the 2/7th Battalion of the Nottingham and Derbyshire Regiment (familiarly known as the Sherwood Foresters or The Robin Hood Rifles). The 2/7th Battalion had been formed in Nottingham only two days previous to Ball's enlistment. It was a part of the 2nd Notts and Derby Brigade of the 2nd North Midland Division. Ball was allotted to 1st Platoon of A Company and was ready to begin his military career.

Because of his previous experience in the OTC at Trent he was promoted to the rank of Sergeant within a very few days of having enlisted. The recruits were undergoing basic training as a first stage in getting them to the standard of fighting soldiers fit for the front line. Rifle drill and training marches helped to provide the basics of discipline and fitness. Lectures on various aspects of army life, and the weapons they would have to use, formed the educational background in the drive to produce a great citizen army. The recruits came from all classes and not all were as adaptable to the life as Ball, though he was never one for the rigid disciplinary regime into which they were being moulded.

On 28 October Ball was commissioned as a Second Lieutenant, the commission to be effective from the following day. Because he was not far from home and could see his family regularly there are no letters from him to give an account of his feelings during this hectic period following the outbreak of war. Many believed that the war would be 'over by Christmas' and that only the fortunate few would be able to get to the front in time to strike a blow against the Germans. The days spent training were therefore days of frustration for many who saw their chance of action slipping away. As the Allies advanced after the Marne it seemed likely that these predictions of a short war would come true. Even as senior a general as Sir Henry Wilson regarded a quick victory as a certainty and discussed with a French Officer as to

---

1 Briscoe, p33.
2 *Captain Albert Ball VC DSO* by R.H. Kiernan, p.10.

how many months it would take to get to Berlin. They would have been shattered to have known then that the Allied Armies were never to drive the Germans back even as far as the Rhine let alone Berlin!

As the year of 1914 drew to a close the volunteers were all fully engaged in their training. With the British Expeditionary Force (BEF) fighting the ferocious battle of Ypres to hold off a German offensive it became increasingly obvious that the war was not going to be finished in 1914. Their services would still be required and it was just a matter of time before they would be called forward to active duty. Albert Ball was as frustrated as the rest so he thought of an idea which might improve his chances of getting into the fight quicker than merely sitting out his time with the Sherwood Foresters. He put in an application to be seconded to the North Midlands Divisional Cycle Company (NMDCC). On the 1 January 1915 the transfer was accomplished and he was soon posted to Bishops Stortford in Hertfordshire. He remained an officer of the Sherwood Foresters but on secondment. When he was further seconded to the RFC he was still registered as an officer of his original regiment. Why Ball believed this move improved his chances of getting to the fighting sooner is not known. It may have been to capitalise on his interest in all things connected with cars and motor cycles, both of which he could now drive with proficiency. He was well known in Nottingham for riding at high speeds through the streets on his motorcycle.

He arrived in Bishops Stortford on the 23 February and wrote a quick line to his mother that he had got 'a fairly decent house but shall move again as soon as I get the chance'. On the 24 February, after he had just sent a batch of men to France, he wrote to his parents a letter which indicated his eagerness to get to the front but must have given them a great deal to think about in the way in which it referred to the means of his getting moved to the fighting:

> Well Captain Black says that I shall go with the first draft of reserves which goes from here in 4 months time, I may go before if they kill enough of the men that are out at the front now. It is all very interesting and I watch every day with great interest the growing list of our men who are told off each day, it is suprising what a lot of the brave fellows are killed each day.
>
> I notice that it is mostly the best men who are killed in nearly every case.[3]

---

3 Ball Archives 24/2/15.

However, he was not to be in France within 4 months as he hoped. He was left with the vital task of training and waiting for the chance to come. He took upon himself the task of managing the Officers' Mess. He complained to his father that some officers had left unpaid bills behind but with no money to pay them! He also asked his father to get together all the bills which he had incurred in Nottingham in kitting himself out as an officer and pay them for him and he would reimburse him for the amount later. He was imminently expecting £20 to arrive after which he would be financially solvent! Ball was also incurring expense for his billet for he had opted to obtain a room for himself in the town rather than share with the other officers. This was to remain a characteristic of Ball that he preferred to live on his own whether in Britain or on duty in France.

On 8 March he was posted to Luton for his further training. He told his family that he and his platoon had marched 20 miles to Luton in snow and he was settled into lodgings at Luton with Mr Cooke at Hightown Road. At Luton he must have had a visit from his father and it is from this time that we get a first indication of his relationships with girls. He had become engaged to a girl called Dot (presumably short for Dorothy) Allbourne (he also uses the spelling Ellbourne). His father had thought that he was getting too serious about the matter for such a young man and persuaded him that he ought not to be too impatient and to let matters take their course for a while. After the visit of his father Ball wrote home a letter of effusive gratitude, full of good intentions:

> You have little idea what a happy son you have left behind, I will only promise to lead a better life, but with God's help I will do so. I trusted him in this matter and it has and will come out all right, if I try to do what is right.[4]
>
> I have written Dot and with her consent I shall keep on the engagement. I am then going to work hard and I will save in some way, it is hard to save on Army pay especially after my being such a fool, but I will do my best. (Dad it has put new life into me) I know you to well. I thought you would do the right thing and you have. I will please you now in all I can and I must say you deserve it.
>
> I shall stop smoking from tonight, please take note of the

---

4 Someone (?Lois) has written against these lines: *PS This was thinking of himself in love with a very nice girl, but he was so young that his father made him promise to wait a time, and of course he was pleased that he had done so.*

date, also please let me have my Pass Book from my private Bank
also a Credit Note Book (I will save to please you and provide for
Dot).[5]

Certain parts of this letter make one wonder just what the condition of
the relationship between Ball and Dot was. Do the words 'after my
being such a fool' and 'provide for Dot' mean that Dot was expecting his
child? If this was the case, no word of it appears in this or later
correspondence but, given the social mores of the time, this is not
surprising for it was not a thing for a middle class family to advertise.
Nothing can be proved in the matter either way so the words may just
mean that Ball realised he had been impetuous and that his
engagement should be a long term affair. His relationship with Dot,
however, was not to be of long standing for by the beginning of May
he had broken with her and was looking for further relationships.

At this time his father was a Director of the Austin Motor Company
and this connection was to prove useful to Ball in the future. During his
time in Bishops Stortford he was asked by his Commanding Officer if
he could use his influence with his father to obtain a couple of weeks
temporary work at Austin's for a Sergeant who was being forced to
take two weeks leave when he didn't want to. Rather than waste his
time he wanted to carry out a period of productive activity for which he
would not expect to be paid. In passing this request on to his father
Albert included the phrase 'Please get this through for me as it will help
me'. Help in establishing his status with his fellow officers as someone
to be cultivated perhaps shows that he was socially unsure of himself
at this time and felt he had to do something to increase his standing.

The obsession to get to France was still with him. It was made more
unendurable by the fact that he was daily witnessing other young men
like himself leaving for the front. He was under no illusion as to how
he might be called to the front, as he wrote to Lois, 'Nearly all the
cyclists who went from Bishops Stortford are either killed or wounded.
It will be fine when we go'.[6]

In April he was joined in the NMDCC by Cyril. This gave him some
companionship which, as he chose to live away from the other officers
he probably welcomed. He and Cyril had been close as brothers and
they had been together at Nottingham High and Trent College. Later
when Ball became famous and his deeds were the talk of the RFC there

5 Ball Archives 20/3/15.
6 Briscoe, p.40.

was certainly some feeling of resentment from Cyril at always being in the shadow of his famous brother. He felt an urge to emulate the deeds of Albert but he lacked the necessary qualities. As one of his Squadron Mates commented, Cyril felt he was as good an air fighter as his brother, but he wasn't. The same situation arose between James McCudden and his younger brother Anthony. The latter was in No.85 Squadron under the command of Sholto Douglas but despite all warnings he lacked the caution, as well as the experience of his brother and was shot down and killed before he had the time to develop either quality.

While at Bishops Stortford, Ball and his fellow officers used to obtain passes to spend time in London. Ball used these trips to take the opportunity to have the occasional meeting with Dot. In order to fill his time when off duty he asked his father to send his motorcycle to Bishops Stortford by rail. He promised his father that he would be careful, though he had a reputation for speeding!

By May his relationship with Dot had run into stormy waters and had run its course. He wrote to his father on the 9 May:

> . . . Well I think you wonder why I have given up Dot, I always seem to be doing very strange things, but do not ask for my reasons for this action. Mr Allbourne may write to you therefore I tell you that I have finished with Dot in every way. You will now know how things stand.[7]

By the end of the month there were the last rumblings of the affair from which it can be deduced that the break up between Ball and Dot had been an acrimonious affair rather than a parting by mutual agreement:

> I was not all pleased to get your letter, in fact it was a rotten letter, first of all you tell me that I have not written to you lately, then you say a lot of beastly things about Bishops Stortford.
>
> I sent you a letter on the 22nd enclosing £3 for my Bank and I do hope that you will receive it.
>
> Regarding Bishops Stortford I did send a rotten letter, but I was quite in order sending any kind of letter. I do not wish Dot to keep the ring, but if you think right let her keep the Pendant for that was a present.[8]

7 Ball Archives 9/5/15.
8 Ball Archives 26/5/15.

A note, presumably by Lois, has been added to this last paragraph:

> He used to tell his Father all his little escapades and then
> naturally as he was away from home, his father always talked to
> him, as he was anxious for his good.

If his romantic affairs were not going well at least he had his dabbling
in the motor trade to keep him occupied in his spare time. He had set
himself up as a sort of unofficial agent for the sale of motorcycles,
something he was to continue doing as long he was still based in
Britain. He had two motorcycles on order and reported a clear profit of
£5 on the sale of two further bikes.

In June he was posted again by the army to Perivale in Middlesex to
attend a further training course. Just to the north of where Ball was
camped at Perivale was Hendon Aerodrome, one of the cradles of
British Aviation. It may have been the sight of aircraft overhead that
gave Albert Ball the idea of learning to fly or he may have come across
the Hendon field as he was out on one of his motorcycle rides.
Whatever the inspiration, Ball decided to take the step of taking flying
lessons. There were several civilian flying schools at Hendon which
provided the basic tuition necessary to qualify for the Royal Aero Club
Certificate. This certificate, an indication of the holder's competence to
fly, was necessary before the holder could proceed with military or
naval service flying with either the RFC or the RNAS. The cost of taking
one of these courses varied from £75 to £100 and this had to be paid by
the person taking the course. If he was successful in passing for his
ticket then this cost was refunded by whichever service he joined.

The school at which Ball chose to enrol in was the Ruffy-Baumann
School. Edouard Baumann (Ball often anglicized it to Bowman in his
letters) was a Swiss citizen who had come to Britain before the war
and, with his brother Aime and with Felix Ruffi (usually spelt Ruffy),
they had founded the flying school at Hendon. The advertisements for
the school used the phrase 'The best system; a limited pupils' list which
prevents our school from assuming overcrowded proportions – a dire
condition for any educational establishment'. It was to this school that
Albert Ball entrusted his future as an airman.

Until he passed, and was accepted by the RFC, this pursuit of flying
tuition was a private matter which had to be fitted in to his spare time.
He was fortunate that it was now mid-summer and that there were

long days, hopefully fine, during which he would be learning. As he owned a Harley-Davidson motorcycle it was no problem for Ball to get up very early and be at Hendon by 4 a.m. This allowed him, weather permitting, to get in up to one hours instruction before having to return to Perivale to attend the first parade of the day at 6.45am. Sometimes there would be no flying because another pupil might very well have wrecked the machine on which instruction was taking place. The first mention of his new pursuit in his letters to his family was in a letter to his uncle (probably Frederick Ball):

> I go in for a little flying now and find it grand sport. I had a fall yesterday but I got straight again and went up on another machine. Please do not be very cross with me for flying, for it means that if the country is very short of pilots I shall be able to go.[9]

He was very enthusiastic over this new interest and told his father that he had had a 'ripping time' at Hendon. On one flight he had suffered an engine failure and crash landed in some trees but without injury to himself or his instructor. He made his way back to Hendon and went up again. He told his father:

> They say I am a ripping flyer and I must say I like it, and find that I can do anything with the machine.[10]

It is not known how his parents viewed this change of interests by their eldest son which took him into the then new world of aviation. They would have been well aware of his longing to get to the front and how frustrated he felt at having had to wait so long and that he viewed the question of learning to fly as another way of hastening that move. His father must have written something fairly encouraging to him for he replied from Perivale on the 6 July:

> Well you ask me to let you know about my flying, I am only to pleased to let you know for I am getting on fine. I go to Hendon every morning at 4 o'clock and I hope to pass for my ticket in a few weeks. If I pass I get £60 back from the RFC in the first place you have to pay £75. I have paid £10 to learn flying and as they are very short of pilots I may be a little good. I went up the other

---

9 Ball Archives 28/6/15.
10 Ball Archives undated.

day and got of sight of land then turned straight down to earth with the tail pointing straight up, the ground seemed to rush up to meet me, and my ears and nose seemed to be bleeding but it was ripping, I think that I shall make a good pilot.[11]

The sort of flying instruction which he received at this time was very basic. He had made a preliminary payment of £10 to Baumann and for this he was given instruction on the controls and handling of the aircraft and a few short flights. As he progressed the flights got longer, but then so did his journey. Once he moved from Perivale, when his army course was finished, he had a nearly a forty-mile round trip to Hendon from St. Albans in order to keep up his flying. To be able to do this, and still be back for the first parade of the morning, he used to get up at 3am full of enthusiasm. It must have been a good time for him for it saw a period when he was able to indulge his love of riding fast on motorcycles in order to get to his other love of flying! Life could not have been much better for him except that he still wanted to get to the front and into the fighting.

The aircraft used seem, from the photograph of the Ruffy-Baumann School to have been derivatives of the Caudron G.3. The G.3 has been described as '. . . the ultimate expression of the formula established by the earlier Caudron Types . . . being the quaintly characteristic combination of the fundamentally pusher configuration with a tractor engine installation.[12]

The G3, which saw limited service with the RFC, had anything from Rotary to Radial engines of from 70 hp to 100 hp. The Ruffy-Baumann School is said to have used a 50 hp or 60 hp (both rotary and radial) engines. This drop in power must have reduced the sea-level speed of 65/70 mph for the RFC version to probably less than 60 mph. Ball's first flying lessons were given by Clarence Winchester, a pre-war airman, and these introduced him to the element in which he was to make his name. He was not at first any more than an average ability pupil. It was not until later that he developed the flying skills which enabled him to succeed in aerial warfare. His progress towards receiving his 'ticket', however, was by no means as fast as he had anticipated and it was four months before he finally qualified for this very vital piece of paper. The low power of the machines meant that they were unable to fly if the wind was too high and the tight schedule on which Ball was operating

11 Ball Archives 6/7/15.
12 *The Aeroplanes of the Royal Flying Corps (Military Wing)* by J.M. Bruce (Putnam 1982) p.191.

meant that he was unable to wait around for the conditions to improve. This, together with the occasional loss of machines through crashes, all tended to extend the time it took Ball to pass his test for the Royal Aeronautical Club (R.Ae.C) Ticket.

While he did keep up with his other Army responsibilities, his contact with aeroplanes and motor bikes meant that he was in proximity to machines which spewed out oil and naturally his uniform became splashed by it. The commanding officer of his unit told him that he was not to appear on parade in future with an oil stained uniform. He was given a few days to sort this out and present himself on parade in a fit and proper condition. He thought this strange as he told his father, but, as everybody else was appearing smart he decided he had better make the effort too.

The detachment to Perivale finished at the beginning of August and he was then moved to Shaffords Farm near St. Albans thereby lengthening his trip to Hendon. The longer summer days meant that he was still able to fit in his flying but it was taking more of his time to do it. Usually rising early to be in time for the morning flights and often returning again after normal army work was finished for the day to try again in the evening.

He seems to have developed a good business in the purchase and sale of motorcycles at this time. He told his father that if he was thinking of buying a motorcycle for Cyril he had just the machine for him, a Rover motorcycle which he could have for £50 which was £8 under list price. Ball described it as a 'ripping motorcycle'. He was also eagerly anticipating the sale of two other motorcycles to some of his comrades for £5 profit each. In addition to his flying, his army duties and his private dealings in motor cycles he also took over the running of the canteen and asked his father if he could get some cheap cigarettes from Players. He was able to put the canteen on a sound financial footing, where it had been struggling before, and to make a profit out of the operation. It is no wonder that he wrote that he had very little time for flying at that time and that this was 'no good'!

Amidst all this hectic life he began again to think about his relationships with girls. On his 19th Birthday he wrote to his father:

> . . . about 2 years ago at Northchurch I met a ripping little girl, ever since then I have sent her one letter a week without saying anything to you also without really having any love for her. She

has always sent me ripping little letters telling me about how her brothers were going on at the front. I have gradually got to like her very much, but have not gone mad, as in most cases. I have visited her a few times and met her people at Northchurch(?) very often.

Now I look back on the last 2 years and see what a rotter I have been, I have fooled 2 girls that you know of, and of course I have made heaps of other girls think I liked them that you do not know of. I really do feel a bit of a rotter, but I really mean to stop now, in fact I will try.

All the time I knew Dot Elbourne and Thelma I was writing to this other girl but only as an ordinary friend. I still only write as a friend, she is very young and is very loving.

Now I am going on in this way and shall try to treat this other girl in a firm and proper way. I certainly like her in fact I love her but find that she is to good to fool, so I shall try to go in a slow way, so that if I find that I do not really like her I can still keep the same old friend and she the same old Bobs.

It seems strange that I should go steady, but I think I can for I have (?) to do without going round on girls, and I really think it is time I tried.

. . . Well Dad I will now dry up for I have said enough perhaps too much. I did not know how to tell you about Bobs, after what has happened with the others but I will play the man this time.[13]

This letter introduces for the first time the name of Thelma, a girl he was to be attached to for some months. Judging by the way the name is introduced in the letter it seems that his family were aware of his attachment to her. Thelma was very young, from the information in the 1901 Census only about 14 or 15 when Ball must have first met her. Her full name was Thelma Starr and her father was a domestic pottery manufacturer in Nottingham, making, it is believed, garden pots. It may have been because of her age that Ball's family were never happy with the relationship and were constantly trying to get him to give her up. The 'Bobs' mentioned in the letter is assumed to be the girl at Northchurch. The use of the nickname 'Bobs' is interesting. His last girl friend, Flora Young, he nicknamed 'Bobs'. Is this the same 'Bobs'? The girl referred to in this letter lived in Northchurch, a district of

___

13 Ball Archives 14/8/15.

Berkhamstead and Flora, when she first met Ball in 1917, lived in the St. Albans area two locations not too far apart. Could the meeting of 1917 be in fact a reunion of two people who had known each other before? The whole letter shows that Ball had the normal young man's feelings as regards the opposite sex. The impression that he remained more or less disinterested in girls until he met Flora Young is obviously wrong. It seems that he had a very susceptible heart and fell in love easily and that he in his turn had no difficulty in attracting girl friends. Where his male companions may have found him rather quiet and not inclined to social chat, women seem to have found him almost irresistible!

At the end of August he asked his father if he could spend two weeks at Austin's in a leave period which would enable him to expand his mechanical knowledge. Prior to going to Austin's he was going to spend some time at the Peter Hooker Works. This was the British Company which made the French designed Gnome aircraft engines, though the Hooker produced versions were found not to perform as well as the French originals. The Hooker works was situated within reach of Hendon and he told his father that he intended to fly each evening at Hendon at 5pm. He added a PS to his letter, 'Enclosed photo of myself and machine on which I hope to take my ticket.[14]

This is assumed to be the well known photograph of him standing in front of a Caudron type machine (and which he subsequently used for his identity photograph on his R.Ae.C Certificate) and which formed the cover of Chaz Bowyer's book and is reproduced in the present volume. It has been suggested that the photo was taken on the day he passed for his ticket but this letter proves it to have been taken slightly earlier.

By this time he had decided that his future lay with the RFC and fighting in the air. He had applied to the War Office for his transfer from the Sherwood Foresters but the important step in this was to pass his flying test for which he was impatiently waiting.

By September he was at the Peter Hooker works and billeted at The Old Welsh Harp at Hendon from which he was able to continue his flying morning and evening. Other, less welcome people, were also flying at that time and Ball told his father that, 'the Germans were making a mess of the place last night we could actually hear the beasts in the air but could do nothing.[15]

---

14 Ball Archives 31/8/15.
15 Ball Archives 12/9/15.

With his strong religious beliefs he was not, despite his hectic schedule, neglecting his attendance at church. As he explained to his father who must have asked whether he still practiced his faith:

> . . . your remarks about me going to Church made me laugh. I always go to Church and I like it very much for it is quite a change to be able to think quietly for a short time and I do like it and do miss it when I cannot go.[16]

By the end of September he was avidly looking forward to the day when he could pass for his Ticket and thereby secure his transfer to the RFC. He seems to have spent a few days at Folkestone but still continued flying and told his father that Baumann thought he wanted only five more days to be ready for his test. However, this was not to be for on the 6 October he was writing again that he hoped to take his test the following week, 'if all is well . . . Baumann says I shall get through about Tuesday'.

His family must have been living on their nerves by this time, even if Ball wasn't, for he regularly regaled them with tales of the various crashes which had taken place even the fatal ones! He told Lois that one pilot, 'a ripping boy' had had a serious smash and died of his injuries and then Albert asked his sister if she would like to go up for a flight anytime! On the 8 October he wrote to his father:

> Am now getting on fine.
> I had a ripping flight this morning at 6.30am but had a very near shave to a smash, however, I came off alright. I was caught in the backwash of another machine and it nearly turned me over. Yesterday one of the Beatty School men had a rotten smash, breaking his arm in three places, at the same time nearly getting burnt to death. However he is getting on much better today and will get over it. I shall finish one day next week and will let you know when. I am with the NMDCC I shall not be long with them for my transfer is nearly through.'[17]

Lois came down to Hendon a short time before he took his ticket and stayed until this feat was accomplished. Lois and her mother had been supplying Albert regularly with cakes as he told them that he loved to take a piece with him when he went flying.

Bad weather delayed his hoped for test. He turned up one morning

16 Ball Archives 16/9/15.
17 Ball Archives 8/10/15.

early at Hendon and waited while one of his companions took his test. When it came to Ball's turn the wind had got up and was considered too strong for flying. The rest of the day was also washed out and Ball had to hope that his turn would come the next day, but it was not in fact until the 15 October that he was finally able to complete his test:

> It is now Thursday morning, and through the wind blowing so much on Monday and Tuesday I have not got my ticket yet. I did some ripping flying by myself this morning, but now the wind is up again, but I shall stay on the ground all this afternoon, and if it drops for half an hour I am going up for my ticket. We went up to town yesterday, and I called at the War Office and was told that I was in the Flying Corps and should be told when to report in a few days. I have to send a Cheque for £1 10s.(£1.50) in order to be in the Royal Flying Corps. Please excuse short note as I am very excited.[18]

Having passed his test Ball was awarded Royal Aero Club Certificate No.1898 and thereby achieved the next step in his objective of flying in the RFC. He was not yet a member of the RFC, he would have to pass a satisfactory period of RFC training for that to be achieved. He was on secondment or probation pending the success of his further progress. If he succeeded he would then be awarded his 'wings' and become a fully qualified RFC pilot. The war was now nearly 15 months old but at last Albert Ball was making progress in his desire to get into the fighting. Within twelve months he would be one of the best known pilots in the RFC.

From the time he passed his test at Hendon Ball could begin to take to the air in earnest. On the 17 October he told his father, 'tomorrow I shall go over to the RFC' and that as soon as he passed for his wings he would get £1 a day extra flying pay. He felt so confident of his ability that he told his father that if and when Austin's got their flying ground finished he would be glad to test fly for them on the free Saturdays which he had!

A few days later he was posted to No. 9 Reserve Squadron at Mousehold Heath a few miles north of Norwich. He seems to have arrived penniless for he pleaded with his father to let him have some money to go on with. He was initially billeted at the Royal Hotel. As

---

18 Ball Archives 15/10/15.

previously, he preferred his own company and sought permission from the Commanding Officer (CO) to go into private billets in town. He was granted this permission provided that he arrived at the flying ground in time for the first parade and did not rely on the services of any of the RFC tenders. He found accommodation in a private house, 24 Riverside Road on the banks of the River Wensum. Having found this accommodation he soon became dissatisfied with it, disliking the food, his room and the other occupants of the house and he started to look for another billet. He found one, which seemed to be to his liking, at 68 Thorpe Road, Norwich but he soon found that all was not ideal and he quarrelled with his landlord about the quality of the food. The upshot was that he told his landlord that he would leave and seek other lodgings. His letters give no indication of his having actually found and lodged at another address for the duration of his time at Mousehold Heath, so he may well have decided that what he had was satisfactory enough for the duration of his time.

For his training for the RFC he was flying Maurice Farman Shorthorn and Longhorn, which had had brief operational careers with the RFC but were now used extensively as trainers. They were well suited to this role and fulfilled this purpose until the advent of the Avro 504 and the DH6. He found them very different to the machines that he had been flying at Hendon. They were much larger than anything he was used to and he called them 'huge' but he enjoyed the experience and said that his instructors were pleased with him. The first couple of weeks that he was at Mousehold Heath the weather was very bad with wind and heavy rain which effectively put a stop to all flying activities. In early November there came a chance for him to go to France much sooner than he would have expected. The War Office was seeking observers to go to France with No. 18 Squadron equipped with the Vickers FB5 (popularly known as the 'Gunbus').

The FB5 saw service with the RFC in France from February 1916 and two complete squadrons, Nos.5 and 11, were to be equipped with the type. It was not an operational success and was outclassed by the contemporary German aircraft.

No.18 Squadron needed a few Observers to make up its complement and all trainee pilots were circulated with the offer to go to France in this capacity. This offer was tempting to many, including Albert Ball, and to any trainee who was beginning to recognize that he would never make the grade as a pilot it would have warranted serious consideration. With Ball it did receive serious consideration but in the end he decided to stay on with the pilot training. As he put to his father '. . . as I have paid for my course at Hendon, I had better wait and go as a pilot'. Whether his life expectancy as an Observer in the FB5, or other machines, would have been different is doubtful. The FB5 in particular was underpowered and slow and no match for the German Fokkers.

In early December the day of his first RFC solo arrived. He had spent the previous night as Orderly Officer and on reporting to the flying field was told to take up Maurice Farman Longhorn No.418 solo. He had no qualms about this and made a good take-off climbing to 300ft. He then turned back to the field in order to land but either inexperience or nervousness made him do a bad landing. The instructor was, understandably, cross and sarcastically said he advised Ball to seek further basic training at a girls flying school. His outburst was understandable in a man who was in a profession where he lived on his nerves, and in many cases they themselves did not have many more hours flying than the people they were trying to teach. Ball replied in kind, as he too was 'wound up' by the excitement and tension of his first solo flight in the RFC and said that he had had only fifteen minutes dual instruction on the Longhorn and that if he was not to get good tuition then he would rather return to the NMDCC! Faced with Ball's indignation the instructor ordered that another Longhorn be wheeled out and made ready for flight. Ball then took it up and made a series of five good take-offs and landings, which satisfied the instructor that he was fully competent in his handling and control of the machine.

It must have been some time after this day that he wrote to his family about his flying activities in a letter home:

I started my day of success by flying for half an hour in the clouds. Well as you know when in the clouds you cannot see land or even sky, however, I stuck to the machine and flew it right through the cloud. I then did a right hand spiral and landed most rippingly in the middle of the flying ground. Well this surprised the officers and I think it more than surprised the Instructors.

. . . the afternoon came and I was told to go up first. The clouds were not very low in the afternoon so I was able to get up to 1,500 ft, put the nose down and did a left-hand spiral finishing up with a perfect landing. Of course every one at once came rushing up expecting to hear me told off in (?) by the instructor for spirals by pupils are not allowed. However, all he said was 'In future when you wish to try any tricks get well clear of the flying ground and for God's sake be careful'. The chaps could not believe their ears but this was not the end, before I left the ground Captain Cox came up and told me that next week I could have a flight in his 80 hp Machine. I was also told that if I wished I could go to another flying ground and learn to fly the very fast English Fighting Machines, so I look like having a lot of good sport.

Really you cannot guess how I love flying and how anxious I am to get on.[19]

It is not known to what type of machine Captain Cox was referring when he offered Ball a flight in an '80 hp machine' for both the Longhorn and the Shorthorn were commonly fitted with 80 hp Renault engines and would not be considered by Ball as something special to fly. It is possible that a Bristol Scout was meant although I can find no record to show that one was on the strength of No. 9 Reserve Squadron. The reference to his being offered the chance to go to another flying ground to learn to fly very fast 'fighting machines' is interesting. Again the type is not mentioned but the implication is that he was being offered the chance to fly single seaters. His flying skills must have been sufficiently high at that time for someone to consider him suitable for such duties. When he went to France to join No.13 Squadron in a few weeks time it might very well be the case that his record was endorsed with the recommendation that he was considered suitable to fly single seaters.

In his new life with the RFC, with all the excitement of eventually getting his wings, he still found time to seek relationships with girls despite his supposedly close relationship with Thelma. He wrote a letter to his parents confessing to his lapses from true fidelity:

Really I cannot say if you know what a job it is for me to be satisfied with just one girl, but it is a huge job. However I am making a good smack at it and am not making a bad show. I

19 Ball Archives 5/12/15.

have only had one little fall but it was nothing, only one of my Norwich friends came to see me but she soon went, but I did not know if I was pleased or not at the moment, for I am so lonely at my rotten billet. However, I was pleased I let her go without asking her to come to the Empire or anything after that style.

You know you two dears, I have got one of the sweetest nippers in my dear Pup Thelma, and I feel sure we do love each other real, but time will prove.

I sent her a letter a few days ago saying that the scarf her sister made for me was now worn out and today I received a ripper nearly half a yard wide and two yards long, she has made it all (?) for me.[20]

For the moment Thelma remained the main romantic interest in his life, but his trips to Norwich gave him a chance to socialize and he had no difficulty in making friends among the local girls. Once again he proved that he had the ability to be at ease with women while, except for a few intimates, he never achieved the same level of friendship with his male companions.

The fact that he was taking his training flights in the middle of winter meant that the weather was not always favourable. He told his parents that he had to fly in the wind and rain and got a 'lot of very bad bumps' one of which dropped him 300ft. As he was at 3,000ft he had time to correct the machine; his piloting skills now becoming more and more apparent. But, he longed to get to the Front:

. . . I shall go mad on the day I fly out to the Front, I simply long to have a smack, but my turn is really a long time coming.[21]

His 'turn' was rapidly approaching. He finished his time at Mousehold Heath in the middle of December. He was moving on to the Central Flying School (CFS) at Upavon in Wiltshire. This would be the final phase of his training, a final polish before he was sent on to a service Squadron. He arrived at Upavon on the 19 December but without his personal kit, which was to follow him later. Upavon had been a centre of flying excellence in Britain for some time and was situated on the windswept area of Salisbury Plain. The weather was cold and he was put in a hut which had no form of heating and in addition, having no mess kit, he was unable to socialize in the mess. Despite these

20 Ball Archives 9/12/15.
21 Ball Archives 9/12/15.

inconveniences his training continued with flying practice and lectures, until the establishment dispersed for the Christmas period. He had been impressed by what he saw of the CFS and told his parents that, 'progress here will be slow but sure for there is a proper system.'

The Christmas of 1915 was a rather disappointing one for Ball. His family, which had had a recent spell of poor health by Lois to cope with, had gone to Skegness, where they owned a property, to spend the holiday season. He seems to have to gone to Matlock where he said he had a 'good time' but wished that he had gone to Skegness instead. For some reason on returning from Matlock he did not join his family but spent the rest of his time in Nottingham. He looked up some of his old girl friends a fact which he felt he had to disclose to Thelma. 'so I shall be in for a good blowing up'. There seems to have been some coolness between Thelma and his sister Lois for he was very pleased when Thelma (for whom he now seems to have adopted the nickname 'Nipper') told him that she had seen Lois out riding and Lois had smiled at her. Previously it seems that on such occasions Thelma had been completely ignored, 'I am so pleased for it was rotten to have Lois going on in such a way!' He felt he had to defend his relationship with Thelma to his father as well as his activities over the Christmas period in looking up his old girl friends:

> You say in your letter that you hope I did not have too good a time when up in London, also that you are afraid (that) what I call love for Thelma is not real love.
>
> Now in the first place I had quite an ordinary time up in Town, also I am suprised that you look on me as being such a gay bird.
>
> Your second remark I do not like and shall be very pleased if you would explain yourself a little more. I suppose you have been told by some kind meaning friend, that during my stay in Nottingham I went out with a few of my girl friends. What would you do if you were by yourself in town? Would you walk about doing nothing all day? I do not think so, and even if you would, I would not. So I did meet a few people. However, Thelma knows about it, and although she did not like it, she was not very cross. Do please remember that it was Xmas time, also no one was at home.[22]

---

22 Ball Archives 3/1/16.

He was back in Upavon for the end of the year to continue his course but on the 5 January he told his father that he had had a crash. It seems to have been caused by rough weather as he says he, 'was thrown down 1,000ft the machine smashed into matchwood'. However, he was not seriously hurt and was unconscious for only a few seconds. He appears to have been very attached to this machine and was disappointed that it had been so badly damaged that it had to be written off. Four other machines were written off the same day but only one pilot was badly hurt, 'and he will get over it'. The incident seems to have upset him for it was probably his first serious crash and an indication of the dangers of his new profession. It appears not to have scared him but to have annoyed him, perhaps on the basis that he might have considered that he should have been able to avoid such situations by his own skill in flying. Accidents were common in flying training and he reported another pupil 'who lost his head' (not literally!) when flying at 1,500ft and crashed his machine. In addition to any other duties at Upavon each pilot had to spend a time as the emergency pilot in case any Zeppelin raid should come as far west as Wiltshire. The thought of having a go at intercepting a Zeppelin was very appealing to him and he was disappointed that no such emergency arose during his time.

His period at Upavon was coming to an end and to ensure his course had a satisfactory ending he gave up his periods of weekend leave and spent the time studying. He spent extra time in the engine workshops as he wanted to get as thorough a knowledge as possible of the 'mechanics' of flying; something which his natural aptitude for anything to do with engines would have lead him to. His Flight Commander told him that his flying was 'A1' and that he should be ready to pass for his 'wings' in three weeks. As he remarked to his parents, 'If I go for my wings in three weeks I shall be out at the front in four'.[23]

As a part of his final stage of his training he was asked to do a cross-country flight:

I have just come back from a cross-country flight to Calne. I had to make a forced landing at Calne, for my machine went wrong. However, I managed to put it right and with the help of the Villagers got off again. When I arrived back and handed in my report, my CO said that I was to go in for my final either this

23 Ball Archives 22/1/16.

week or next, so I shall at last be off. I shall visit home again before I go, for it may be one or even two years before I get back again.[24]

Finally on the 26 January he was able to send a telegram to his father that he had just got his 'wings' and was taking three days leave as well. He asked his father to wire him £10 as once again he found himself short of funds! He was now permanently transferred to the RFC with effect from the 29 January 1916. Having spent the end of January with his family in Nottingham he then proceeded to join No.22 Squadron at Fort Rowner at Gosport while they waited for their orders to come through. The Squadron was due to be equipped with the FE2b two-seaters. A pusher design, like the DH2 and FE.8 single-seaters, it was seen as another answer to the Fokker. The pusher layout of these three machines compensating for the lack of a successful interrupter gear. In its time, in the spring and summer of 1916, the FE was a successful fighting machine and one was credited with shooting down the German Fokker Ace Max Immelmann. It spent a long time at the Front, latterly as the re-engined FE2d with the more powerful Rolls Royce Eagle engine but it had long lost its effectiveness and suffered badly at the hands of the Albatros scout variants introduced in the autumn of 1916. However, in combats between F.E.2ds of No.20 Squadron and the Richthofen Circus some compensation was gained for their losses when the Ace Karl Schafer was shot down and killed and von Richthofen himself narrowly escaped death but suffered a serious head wound. The FE soldiered on to the end of the war but latterly in the guise of night bombers.

He spent the time instructing pupils on the Avro 504 trainers and occasionally flew a Martinsyde (probably the G100 'Elephant' which was just coming into service). While he waited for his move to France he was kept busy and at one time he flew with thirty pupils in one day and sent six of them solo.

At this time flying training was very much an ad hoc affair and many of the people doing the instructing had very little experience themselves and often had no aptitude for the task which, combined with a thorough distrust, almost amounting to hatred, for the 'Huns' (the nickname for pupils) they were instructing, did not make for a satisfactory situation. It was not until Major Smith-Barry the former commander of No.60 Squadron in France, realised that it was

---

24 Ball Archives 24/1/16.

necessary to 'professionalise' the system that matters began to improve. He was given a free hand and reorganized it from top to bottom to set up the Gosport System of flying training that matters began to improve. The work done by Smith-Barry was vital to the work of the RFC in the field and was copied worldwide.

On the 6 February Ball wrote to his parents:

> At last the sport is going to commence. I have just been told by the CO that I am the next for the EF (Expeditionary Force) so in a few days I shall be flying in France.[25]

He next wrote to them from London, a hastily scribbled note:

> Regents Palace Hotel, London
>
> 17th February 1916
>
> Dearest People
>
> Just a line and only a line, for I have only seconds in hand.
> I go to Boulogne by boat today, from there I get my machine and fly to the Front. It is strange to be leaving.[26]

His 'turn' had finally come after a wait of eighteen months and he was finally going to get 'into the war' and experience what life on active service was like. No doubt his parents did not view it with the same joy and anticipation that he did.

---

25 Ball Archives 6/2/16.
26 Ball Archives 17/2/16.

CHAPTER THREE

Flying with 13 Squadron

Despite his expectation that he would be able to fly to the front from Boulogne he was disappointed. He had to make the usual long dreary train journey with which all who went to France were so familiar. He found time to scribble a quick note on the way in which he anticipated a further nine hours train journey! He gave his address as 'BEF 13th Squadron; 3rd Wing' although he had not yet arrived at his destination. He told his parents that he was to fly a BE2c, 'so I do not consider my luck very good, however, I shall have a good smack'.

No.13 Squadron, to which he had been posted, had been formed for just over a year. It had been raised from a detachment from No.8 Squadron and was then commanded by Captain P.L.W. Herbert and equipped with the BE2c and 2d. The strength of the Squadron was later increased by a further detachment, from No.22 Squadron, and was then declared fit to fly to the front.

The Squadron arrived in France in October 1915 and first went to St. Omer and finally to Vert Galant where it deployed on 21 October, flying its first operation the next day. The realities of the war soon struck home on the 23 October when it suffered its first casualties with the loss of Lieutenant Marks and 2nd Lieutenant Lawson shot down behind the German Lines. Victories over German aircraft were to be few and far between but the first was achieved when a German two-seater was shot down on the 26 October. The reality was that the work undertaken by the artillery observation and reconnaissance squadrons was not intended to destroy enemy aircraft. Their job lay in cooperation with the Army and by that means they were responsible for inflicting casualties on the German Army. In the whole war the squadron only shot down fifteen German aircraft and in doing so lost forty-three of their own machines.

The equipment of the Squadron when Ball joined it at Marieux was the BE2c and it is indicative of the opinion of the pilots who had to fly it that he should have been so negative about it. The BE series of aircraft originated from the Royal Aircraft Factory, the first BE1 being designed by Geoffrey de Havilland in 1911. This aircraft flew satisfactorily acting as a sort of flying test bed for various modifications. The BE1 (of which only one was produced) was followed by an improved version, the BE2 which de Havilland flew in February 1912. This machine took part in the Military Aircraft trials of 1912 where it performed most satisfactorily. Although the Cody biplane was declared the winner this was considered impracticable as a military aeroplane and orders were placed for the BE.

The BE2 metamorphosed into the BE2a although the designs were not vastly different, but it was in this form that the type began to see squadron service, although the earlier types had also been taken on charge of the RFC. In this version the aircraft performed very satisfactorily before the war and promised to be a suitable vehicle for reconnaissance for the army, which was the main task envisaged for the RFC. The fact that you might have to fight for your information on enemy dispositions was not widely considered a probability. When war broke out a BE2a No.327 piloted by Captain F. Waldron and Air Mechanic Skerritt was the first British machine to land in France. The design was further advanced by the appearance of the BE2b in October 1914, with improved crew accommodation along with new flying controls and fuel system.

It was the crew positions which were to prove the Achilles heel of the design. From the original BE1 up to and including the BE2d the observer occupied the front seat and the pilot the rear. This layout proved perfectly satisfactory in pre-war exercises and in the early operations in France when reconnaissances were not likely to be seriously opposed by enemy aircraft. The design variation, which became the BE2c, was also modified in testing to produce an inherently stable machine and this end was largely achieved. When it was undergoing tests and trials in 1914 the idea of aerial combat was not seriously considered and the existing crew arrangement continued. It was only when the Fokker monoplane, equipped with a machine gun to fire through the propeller, began to make its appearance in the middle of 1915 that the deficiencies of the BE2c, and other reconnaissance aircraft of the Allies, became glaringly obvious. Situated in the front seat the Observer could not operate his Lewis Gun satisfactorily (Lewis guns had now replaced the rifle as the weapon of choice for aircraft defence). In the case of the aircraft of No.13 Squadron it is said that twin Lewis guns were fitted, at least on some aircraft, but the increased firepower was of no use if the Observer's field of fire was obstructed by the struts, wires and wings.

The Fokkers were initially issued by the Germans on the same basis as the British issued their single-seaters, just one or two to a unit. However, a tactical rethink in the German Air Force saw the formation of small fighting units of three or four Fokkers which were given the task of seeking out and destroying the Allied two-seaters. Their success in this role led to the RFC Headquarters issuing an instruction in January 1916 stating that, until the RFC was in possession of a superior machine to the Fokker, each reconnaissance or photographic machine was to be accompanied by three others as escort. Flying in close formation was to be practised by all squadrons. The directive as to formation flying for mutual protection was amended later when HQ RFC suggested a formation of six machines flying in a particular formation as the best for self-defence. This suggestion brought a response from Major Marsh as Officer Commanding No.13 Squadron:

> With reference to the formation of six machines when on reconnaissance, vide 3B/14 dated 2/3/16, this is not at all favoured by my pilots. It appears to have the disadvantage of masking the fire of the various machines. My pilots prefer, and the last two days have been practising, a fan-shaped formation. May permission be obtained for its adoption by this squadron.[1]

This correspondence continued with Major Marsh contending that the fan-shaped formation which he had proposed was 'more elastic and gives greater volume of fire for most directions' and could be manoeuvred more readily. Experience on the squadron, he said, had shown that formation flying required a great deal of practice in order to be well done. Time which might be hard to find in a normal operational environment.

Losses of the BE machines became so severe that they were referred to as 'Fokker Fodder' and Noel Pemberton-Billing, an MP who was also

---

1 AIR1/1636/204/90/43

an aircraft constructor, made reference in Parliament to the 'murder' of RFC crews because of the failings of the BE and its use by the High Command.

The other machine which Ball was to fly with his squadron, was the Bristol Scout, examples of which were with various squadrons. They were for experienced pilots, who were thought to have the aptitude to handle them. About the time that Ball was doing his first patrols with the squadron, orders were issued for the squadron (along with Nos.8 and 12 Squadrons) to maintain Bristol Scout patrols over the lines in the region Gommecourt-Arras-Souchez. The No.13 Squadron Bristol was to be over the front from 9.15-10.30 a.m. and 1.00-2.30pm. These patrols were to be maintained until the 23 March after which the schedules would be reissued.[2]

The Bristol Scout was a pre-war design by Frank Barnwell. The first example had gone for trials in February 1914. It was an advanced machine for the time, as Barnwell was a forward looking designer who was later to be responsible for one of the great icons of the war, the Bristol F2b Fighter and one of the great 'maybes' with the Bristol M1C monoplane. The former was a great success while the latter suffered (allegedly) from official prejudice against monoplanes, but also was short on endurance. The Monoplane was highly regarded by flying instructors at fighting schools as an excellent fighting aeroplane. However, in the Middle East, where it saw its only active service, it was not highly regarded for its manoeuvrability. With the Bristol Scout, however, Barnwell produced a neat little single-seater which, using an 80hp Gnome Rotary, had a top speed of 95 mph at ground level, which earned it the nickname of the Bristol 'Bullet'.

Throughout its service career attempts were made to arm the Bristol and in the early stages of his career Ball himself flew one which had been fitted with a Vickers machine gun with the Vickers-Challenger interrupter gear. Although of earlier derivation than the DH2 it had a comparable performance but never achieved the fighting success of the pusher scout. It had its moment of glory with the VC winning exploit of Lanoe Hawker on the 27 July 1915 when he shot down one Albatros two-seater in flames, forced another to land with a damaged engine and drove down a third. Hawker was awarded the VC for this exploit.

We have looked at the aircraft with which No.13 Squadron was equipped and with which Ball began his operational career. It is

---

2 AIR1/1636/204/90/43

instructive therefore to look at the German machines which would be facing him and his companions as they carried out their various operations. The Fokker monoplane has been mentioned above but two other aircraft are also mentioned in the combat reports: the Aviatik and Albatros two seaters.

The Fokker Monoplane went through various designations during its operational career from the M5 of pre-war vintage to the unsuccessful EIV of 1916. The equipment which raised the status of an otherwise undistinguished aircraft series, was the fitting of the first mechanical interrupter gear. The French had been first in the field (in 1914) with a practicable working interrupter gear developed by Raymond Saulnier and Louis Peyret of the Morane-Saulnier company. The device worked but trouble with the ammunition of the Hotchkiss gun meant that it was not developed further and a cruder device, deflector plates, was fitted instead. A Morane fitted in this way and flown by Roland Garros had operational success but Garros was shot down by ground fire and the secret of his aircraft was then in the hands of the Germans. The Germans copied the device initially but Anthony Fokker, having been given the airscrew of the Garros Morane, eventually developed a mechanical interrupter gear. The first production machines to be fitted with the device were the Fokker E1 which entered service in July 1915. This began the era of the Fokker aces: Immelmann, Boelcke, Althaus and others. On 1 August 1915 Immelmann shot down his first British aircraft and from then on until his death just under a year later, became a successful predator of the British reconnaissance machines. Moving through various models, the EII and EIII and culminating in the EIV, the Fokker and its pilots struck fear into the hearts of their opponents and enjoyed a period of superiority which forced the RFC to more desperate measures to get its work done. By the beginning of 1916 the Allies were beginning to deliver the antidote to the Fokker, the Nieuport 11 and the DH2. In April 1916 a captured Fokker was tested against a Morane Scout by the RFC and the inferiority of performance was soon seen for the Morane was obviously superior in all aspects.

The two seaters with which Ball and his companions clashed on their patrols were the Aviatik and the Albatros. The Aviatiks were probably the CI or CIII, either of which might have been in service at the period and as with the BEs their roots lay in a pre-war design. As with their BE opponents the CI retained the front seat position for the Observer and had been in service since 1915. It was more likely that the Allied pilots' opponent was the CIII, which was designed on the same crew arrangement, but eventually changed to the more practical layout and was powered by a 160 hp Mercedes engine. When the Germans attempted a bombing raid on Paris in April 1916 it was Aviatik 2-seaters which made up the formation which attempted the attack. With a maximum speed of 82 mph at sea level and a ceiling of 11,500ft it outperformed the BE2c.

The Albatros works produced a series of two seaters for the German Air Service which were used throughout the War. In 1914 the designer for the Albatros Company was Ernst Heinkel who was later to go on to form his own company. The BI which was produced just before the War and saw early service at the front was later superseded by the improved BII, which set a height record before the outbreak of the war of 14,764ft and was widely used, along with the BIIa, up to early 1916. It can be assumed that this is the machine which Ball designated the Albatros Type B. The Albatros C series was an improvement on the B series and the CIII was one of the most widely used of the German two-seaters. It came into service in 1916 and remained until early 1917 as the mainstay of the German reconnaissance and bomber squadrons. With a top speed of 87.5 mph and a service ceiling of 12,000ft it was also superior to the BE2c.

By the time Albert Ball arrived in France the answer to the Fokker menace had reached the front. The DH2, manufactured by the Aircraft Manufacturing Company and designed by Geoffrey de Havilland, had begun to appear in Squadron service. The DH2 design had been started in February 1915 and the prototype had flown in June of that year so its origins were not as an answer to the Fokker. The first models had reached France in January 1916 and in accordance with the usual practice they were scattered about among the various squadrons. The first squadron to be completely equipped with the type, and therefore the first fighter squadron ever, was No.24 Squadron which arrived in France on 7 February 1916 under the command of Lanoe Hawker VC, at that time the foremost fighting airman in the RFC. It was Hawker who gave the pilots of the squadron the confidence and ability to handle the DH2 after some initial spinning accidents. The maximum speed of the DH2 at sea level was not exceptional at 92mph but the aircraft proved to be part of the answer to the Fokker, which in itself was not a good design, but it was the synchronised machine-gun which made the Fokker formidable. No. 24 Squadron was to be joined by other DH2 squadrons and F.E.2b squadrons which all helped to turn the tide of the war in the air back in favour of the Allies.

When Ball joined No.13 Squadron it was in a state of flux and was imminently expecting to move from its temporary resting place at Marieux. Command of the squadron had been taken over by Major A.C. Marsh at the beginning of the year.[3]

It was the tail-end of the winter of 1915/16 when Ball arrived and it was still very cold with frequent snow showers. He made his first flight with the squadron when he took up BE2c 4352 for an half hour flight on the 20 February to familiarise himself with the local area. The BE was by far the largest machine he had ever flown and this experience would have enabled him to get some idea of its flying and handling qualities. On the 21st Ball carried out his first operational flight, with Lieutenant Green as his Observer. Leaving the airfield at 9.56am, they proceeded over the German lines where their machine was subject to German anti-aircraft fire but they continued with their task. This fire (which the British crews had nicknamed 'Archie') did no serious damage to the machine. When three Fokkers appeared Ball had to break-off his work and dive for the safety of the British lines. Before their full task was completed the BE suffered engine trouble and made a forced landing just behind the British lines. He and Lieutenant Green, spent a cold night by the machine in heavy snow. They managed to restart the engine the following morning and return to the airfield in short hops because several times they were forced down by further snow showers. Major Marsh was surprised to see them for he had written them off as another casualty. His initial impression of Ball had not been favourable and he had thought of sending him back for further training. However, the determination which Ball had shown in getting his machine back to the squadron, impressed Marsh and he kept Ball with the squadron.

Ball wrote to his parents about his arrival at the squadron and his first experiences of operational flying:

> I am now billeted in a hut and it is very cold. For the past two days it has been snowing hard and even now it is coming down fairly fast . . .

---

3 All activities of 13 Squadron are found in AIR1/1625/90/2 the Squadron Record Book.

On Sunday we moved to a new flying ground and I had to fly
one of the machines. We spent the remainder of the day putting
things in order.

On Monday I was sent on some work over the Hun lines. Oh
it was sport! The Archie guns were firing at us all the time but we
were not hit, but I am sorry to say that one of our flight machines
was hit and brought down by a Focker Machine. The Pilot and
Observer were killed.

On the way back from the lines my engine went wrong and I
had to land. I spent nearly all night with the machine, but got it
right in the end and started back at 8 am on Tuesday. It started
to snow and I could not see a thing so I had to land. Each time
the snow stopped I started up and flew a few miles and in the
end arrived back at 4.15. The Major was very pleased for he did
not expect me to bring the machine back in the snow.[4]

After this incident things went better for him as he settled into the
routine work of the Squadron. The bad weather continued and snow
continued to fall thereby affecting operations. A bombing raid planned
for the 27 February was cancelled because of heavy snowfalls. Later
that day Ball flew, with Lt. Gregory as his Observer, on an 'Artillery
Patrol' as he called it. Low cloud forced them down to 2,000ft and they
were subject to ground fire whilst over the German Trenches but
suffered no damage or injury. On the 28th with Lieutenant Gregory
again, he completed a successful artillery shoot without interference
from the German Fokkers or engine trouble. On the 29th he was flying
BE2c 4352 under the new rules put out by HQ RFC as 'escort' to
another of the Squadron's machines on a reconnaissance mission.
During this mission he started in pursuit of a German machine which
he spotted in the vicinity but was restrained by his Observer,
Lieutenant Gregory again, who persuaded him that their duty was as
escort to their squadron charges and not seeking combat with enemy
aircraft which were not trying to interfere with their mission. This
eagerness to come to grips with the enemy was an early manifestation
of Ball's natural aggressive instinct and which was to play such a large
part in his success. With the end of the month he could consider
himself well and truly initiated into the operational routine of the
squadron. Flying BE4352 he had flown five operational flights varying

---

4 Ball Archives 23/2/16

from artillery observation to escort duties as well as numerous lesser flights to test various aspects of his machine.

On the 1 March he had a more eventful day to report to his family, though from squadron records it is difficult to identify on which date this incident took place. The only operational flight he undertook on the 1 March was in BE 4076 was with Air Mechanic Parkes when they flew as escort to other machines, in the early afternoon:

> I was five miles over the Hun lines on a Patrol to inspect a station and report on the trains. I got there alright but on the way back I had a rotten time. The Archie guns shot at us from three sides and to make it worse the old fools sent rockets up to try and set my machine on fire. We had got nearly back over our lines when an Hun Focker attacked us. My observer let fly with the gun but after two shots the beastly thing went whonkey. I then pulled out my Revolver but this also stuck. However by this time we were over our own lines and the Focker did a bunk.[5]

In this letter he said that the squadron was preparing to move to a new landing ground. This proved to be Izel-le-Hameau which at the time was occupied by a French squadron but was to be handed over to the British. The squadron moved over a period of a few days, the stores and personal kit moved first, the flying crew moved last, though flying was severely restricted because of heavy snow. Ball only had to survive in this restricted state for a short time though and he told his parents, 'all I have is a big cake and a little brilliantine.' He did manage one patrol in the conditions, but his effectiveness was restricted by the continuing snow and low clouds. Flying from Izel Le-Hameau Ball went up in BE 4105 with Lieutenant Joel as his Observer. They were airborne for just over an hour and were to try and cooperate with the Artillery. The weather proved too much for them, low clouds making cooperation with the British batteries unsuccessful. This flight took place on the 9 March and the squadron records show that Ball did not fly again until the 16th when he and Lieutenant Villiers in BE 4352 were once again on escort duty, but in a letter home of the 12 March he told his parents that despite the snow he flew on the 11 March.[6]

He was sent to patrol the lines and he called it 'a rum go'. On arriving over the lines he immediately became lost in a thick cloud and when he

---

5 Ball Archives 3/3/16

emerged he found that he was well over the lines at only 500ft. According to Ball his observer was so scared by this situation that he forgot to work his machine gun. They were under heavy rifle fire from the German trenches and looking over the side he could make out the faces of the German soldiers. He found that the Germans ceased fire when he put his nose down, Ball assumed that they thought they had hit him and that he was going to land. He took advantage of this cessation of fire to zoom into the cloud again and to try and make his way back to the British side. On returning home he reported to Major Marsh who reprimanded him for being over the German lines at that height when squadron procedure was not to cross under 7,000ft. Marsh asked Ball what good he thought he was doing. Ball replied that he was doing no particular good but he had caused every German in that trench to wet his trousers and to waste a hundred rounds on him! Ball admitted to his parents that it was a mad thing to do, 'but it was sport'!

The photograph of the group of No.13 Squadron pilots, which is reproduced in this book, was taken on the 13 March at Izel-le-Hameau. The machine in the background is Ball's own BE No. 4352 which he flew on a regular, though not exclusive, basis. He sent a copy of the photograph home to his parents and asked his sister to get six copies made and posted back as soon as possible.

The squadron was only a week at Izel-le-Hameau before they moved yet again, this time to Savy. Algernon Insall who flew from Savy with No. 11 Squadron has left a description of the aerodrome:

> Savy was quite a good aerodrome. You climbed up to it from the straggling little string of Farm buildings constituting the village, where the sluggish Scarpe meandered eastwards towards the line which it crossed below Fampoux. The French in their customary way, had installed themselves in 'bake-house' hutments tightly grouped at the top of the muddy twisting lane that led up to the edge of the almost infinite landing ground . . .[7].

Ball flew in 4352 with Air Mechanic Dale, from Le Hameau to Savy on the 19 March. It was from this airfield that Albert Ball operated for several months to come and established his reputation as a fighting pilot.

The following day, on his first flight from Savy, with Lieutenant

6 Ball Archives 12/3/1916
7 *Observer* by A. J. Insall (Kimber 1970) p113

Villiers as Observer, he had his first serious crash since he had been in France. He took off just after 7am for an artillery observation flight in 4352. But the machine suffered an engine failure and crashed after having only gained a little height. Ball was unable to take any action to correct the fall and the machine was wrecked beyond repair. Ball and Villiers were trapped in the wreckage. Fortunately for them the wreckage did not catch fire and they escaped without serious injury.

In one of his letters home to his parents he describes this crash as having been due to the damage sustained by anti-aircraft fire, though the squadron records do not support this and ascribe the crash solely to engine failure on take-off. The crash did not seem to affect Ball too much for a few hours later he was flying another mission with Lieutenant Joel as his Observer in BE No 4173.

On the 27 March he was in fact shot down by anti-aircraft fire when flying BE2c No.4200 with Lieutenant Gregory as Observer. The machine was hit by AA fire and the engine damaged. He was forced to crash land, managing to put the machine down near Aubigny without injury to either himself or Gregory.

His letters at this time are often on the subject of Thelma. He was very keen for the family to get to know her and her parents. He particularly wanted his mother to visit the Starr family and told her that he had told Mrs Starr that his mother would one day call round for tea. His family, however, never accepted Thelma as a suitable girl friend for their son and Ball pressed for a rapprochement between the two families in vain. It is almost certain that it was Thelma's age which caused the doubt about her suitability. At only just over fifteen, she was certainly very young, perhaps too young to be a serious girl friend for Ball, with long term intentions of marrying and settling down.

The weather still continued generally bad which had an effect on the number of operations the squadron could fly. On many occasions the clouds remained low which was an effectual bar to cooperation with artillery. On his being ordered to collect a new BE from the depot at Candas the weather deteriorated on his return trip and he was forced to land and to continue the flight next day.

Ball had now been with No.13 Squadron for about a month. Long enough for him to have time to correct the first impressions which Major Marsh had formed of him. He had been under fire from both enemy ground fire and from aircraft, but he had yet to engage an enemy in combat. This chance came on the 30 March when, with Lieutenant Villiers in BE 4200, he was sent off for an artillery shoot. This intention was foiled by the weather, low clouds preventing any satisfactory view of the target. With his original intention frustrated he remained on patrol 'looking for trouble' and spotted a German two-seater between Vimy and Givenchy. He dived in to attack and from the front seat Villiers fired one and a half drums of Lewis ammunition at the enemy. The front seat position of the Observer in the BE did not make for easy shooting and of course there was no question of firing directly ahead. The attack being unsuccessful they had no chance to take further action against their original target for they were immediately attacked themselves by a second German aircraft coming down on them from the rear. The fire from this second aircraft, possibly part of a planned decoy operation, did no serious damage to Ball's BE but before he could turn to engage it the two Germans had dived away behind their own lines. This action is ascribed by Chaz Bowyer to the 29 March and BE 4070, but the Combat Report[8] for this incident, completed by Villiers, is held in the squadron records and confirms the above details:

> Date 30 March 1916
> Pilot 2nd Lt A. Ball
> Observer: 2nd Lt S. Villiers
> Machine: BE2c 4200
> Armament: Lewis Machine Guns (2)
> Location: Vimy-Givenchy
> Height: 8,000ft
> Time: 9.10am
>
> Remarks on Hostile Machines:
> Two Aviatiks, machine guns, speed about 85 mph

> While going northward west of Vimy a hostile machine was sighted coming from the direction of Givenchy. We were at 8,000ft and the hostile machine was about 2,000ft below. We dived at him and fired while doing so. The hostile machine dived when we fired, towards his own lines and went out of sight. During the operation another hostile machine of the same type which was 1,000ft above us, kept up a strong fire on us. One and

---

8 AIR1/1219/204/2634/13

a half drums were emptied into the first machine, but none at the second as it made off when we turned to meet it. Our right hand rafwire was severed by a bullet.

S. A. Villiers 2nd Lt
RFA

The realities of operational flying were forcing upon Ball the nature of his new profession and the fact that like others in the squadron he might soon become an empty chair in the mess. He still referred to his activities as 'sport' in his letters home but was no longer eager for his brother Cyril to join him. He told his father, 'Tell Cyril that perhaps he had better stick to his regiment. I like this job, but nerves do not last long, and you soon want a rest.' And later he wrote, 'Do please ask him to keep out of the RFC. I shall send him a long letter the first chance I get in fact I will start tonight.' His mother had written to him that she expected that though he had left for France as a boy he would come back a man. Ball disagreed with this idea saying that he had gone out as a boy and would come back as a boy, 'I am younger every day and it will take many years to lose my boyhood.' Boyish pranks were certainly a part of his life with the squadron:

> Have just been having a mud and water fight with Lieutenant Villiers. You will think this very strange but we often do strange things over here, in fact we are strange people. Villiers and myself are great pals. He is one of B Flight Observers and comes up with me very often.[9]

On the 31 March he was flying in BE 4200 with Lt. Gregory, engaged in artillery registration, when they met and engaged an Albatros 2-seater over Gavrelle at 9,000ft. The Albatros two-seater was some 2,000ft lower than the BE. Ball was again flying with the BE fitted with two Lewis guns. Gregory fired from the right-hand mounting as Ball dived and banked to the right. Both machines exchanged bursts of machine-gun fire but neither side caused any serious damage to their opponent in this brief engagement and it ended indecisively. Ball reported the BE as suffering minor damage to the centre section.

When not in the air he was often to be found exploring the local area. On the 31 March he went with Major Marsh on a goodwill visit

---

9 Ball Archives 5/4/16

to the artillery batteries with which they worked. He told his father that he and Villiers visited a large town (probably Arras) behind the lines and 'looted the ruins'. Keen churchgoer that he was Ball was particularly struck by the ruins of a church which he came across. He makes no mention at this time of his attending any religious services but given his attitude to religion he would no doubt have been anxious to do so.

Mail from home was always eagerly anticipated. He waited avidly for the letters and parcels to arrive and chided Lois in being slow in getting the copies of the squadron photograph back to him. A letter from Thelma was always welcome and the relationship between them was still strong. He always felt it a duty to write frequently to his family and Thelma and his surviving correspondence is full of hastily written letters of just a few lines to let those who cared for him know that he was alright. He had a large circle of people with whom he kept in contact and who in turn sent letters to him. He once wrote to his father that he had over twenty letters to reply to.

The weather in early April was still poor and flying was restricted. It seems that at this time Ball was billeted in a hayloft, which, he told Lois, he was trying to make as comfortable as possible. He had a stove installed and curtains at the windows and Lois was asked to send him some photographs to put round the walls. Later in the year he was to begin to construct a hut for himself out on the airfield to enable him to get the privacy which he preferred. He did not reject the company of other officers, and Villiers and he were very close friends, but he seems to have had a preference for his own company as far as living accommodation was concerned.

His hut did in fact come to be a meeting place for the pilots and observers of the squadron who seemed to drop in chat when the day's flying was done. He seems to have been active in his dealings with his fellow pilots and at one time asked his father about the possibility of buying land near Nottingham.

It may have been in these idle days, when flying was restricted, that the genesis of the proposed counter to the Fokker threat came about, with he and Villiers talking together, most likely about flying and the Fokker which presented the greatest threat to their existence. The question is discussed in Appendix 1, but lacking further documentary proof no satisfactory conclusion can be reached. As mentioned in the Appendix, I believe Villiers to be a likely candidate for the origin of the design. In the same letter quoted below, in which he makes mention of the plans in his possession, he also says that Villiers was going for a pilot's course and that he, 'was clever and knows a lot about flying'. And asked his father to enquire about a job for his friend at Austin's after the War. He wrote to his father about the plans:

> I also want to know if Austins would take on a job. I have managed to get the plans of a most wonderful machine. It would be heaps better than the Hun Focker. I have been to the Major and he has given me full permission to fly it, if I get one out. I know that it would be a fine thing, What do you think.[10]

The whole episode is very mysterious and raises all sorts of questions, but lacking any copies of replies from his father none of these can be answered satisfactorily.

Despite any strain that Ball may have been feeling from his operational flying, this did not curb his aggressive tendencies. On 10 April in BE 4200 he was involved in escort duty with Villiers. With the mission accomplished Ball and Villiers were on their way home when they saw a German observation balloon. Ball and Villiers decided to attack the balloon. Even at this stage of the war the task of attacking such a target was not to be undertaken lightly. Balloons were usually well ringed with gun defences but the two friends defied this obstacle and opened fire on their target. The balloon was hastily hauled down by its ground crew while the BE, although unable to destroy it, escaped unscathed from the protective ground fire. At every suitable opportunity Ball was using the BE2c in an aggressive manner but he had no illusions about the suitability of the BE as a fighting machine. Around this time he received a letter from his father asking if he could get hold of a German souvenir. In his reply he made his opinion of the BE2c quite clear:

> We are the Wireless Squadron now, and have to register the gun shoots. It is a most important job, but we do not get many chances to do in Huns. However, luck may come. For one thing you see a BE2c is not a fighting machine.'[11]

It was this dissatisfaction with the BE2c which led Ball to cast envious eyes over the Bristol Scout which was attached to the squadron. He wanted to fly and fight alone without the responsibility of an Observer. He asked Major Marsh on several occasions whether he could fly the

10 Ball Archives 14/4/16
11 Ball Archives 17/4/16

Bristol but the Major declined each time. Towards the end of April things changed as he related in a letter to his father:

> You know that I do not like BE machines. Well each day I have asked the Major to let me fly the Scout. He always said no but today I hear that I am going to a certain Aerodrome to fly a new Morane Scout Bullet. If all is well, I shall be back at No.13 in about a month's time, and my mount will be a Morane which will do 120mph. This will be great sport, and at least I shall have the chance I wish for.[12]

The Morane Scout which Ball was referring to in this letter was the Morane Type N which was commonly known in the RFC as the Morane 'Bullet'. Despite Ball's optimistic claim for a speed of 120 mph the Type N Morane could only achieve about 90 mph at sea level with the 80 hp Le Rhone engine. This was roughly the same speed as the Bristol Scout Type D. The first examples of the type had been delivered to the RFC in September 1915 but these had only been fitted with the primitive deflector plates on the airscrew. Further deliveries of the Type N began in March 1916 and altogether five Moranes were on the strength of the RFC before the battle of the Somme. These early deliveries were made to No.3 Squadron but it was not to this unit that Ball went to try out the Morane. One example of the type had been retained temporarily at No 1 AD (Aircraft Depot) at Candas and it was to this unit that Ball went. He was not gone for a month, however, as he was back with the squadron by the 27 April. There is no mention in any of his letters as to how he got on with the Morane or his opinion of it. It is likely that he was not impressed as the aircraft was generally reckoned to be difficult to fly due to its wing warping rather than ailerons and 'all flying' tail surfaces and it remained unpopular throughout its brief operational career.[13]

On 29 April Albert Ball gained his first positive aerial success. He took off at shortly after 6.00am in BE No 4070 with Villiers. They were scheduled for an artillery shoot and were engaged in this over the Oppy-Rouvroy area when a formation of five German Albatros two-seaters approached. The artillery registration was forgotten and Ball turned towards the formation but, perhaps fortunately, the Germans turned away and his aggressive intentions were frustrated. Shortly

12 Ball Archives 23/4/16
13 Bruce *The Aeroplanes of the RFC etc..* pp296-302

afterwards another German two-seater appeared on the scene and immediately moved towards the British machine. The combat report takes up the story:

> At 6.45 am hostile machine sighted NW of Oppy. Height 8,000ft. BE2c dived until level and fired one drum when within twenty yards. Albatros (B) opened fire almost simultaneously but was silenced almost immediately; the Observer was apparently hit as gun was dropped and he fell back into fuselage. At this point both machines turned, the Albatros passing a very few feet under BE2c
>
> The Albatros then climbed about 100ft passing in rear. BE2c then fired again with rear mounting and then turned to chase. Albatros then dived and appeared to make a good landing SE of Rouvroy.[14]

The report shows the genesis of his later successes: getting in close to his opponent before opening fire. He wrote in a letter home that they were close enough to the German machine to see the faces of their opponents. This Combat Report again presents a clash of dates for in his letter to his parents of the 28 April, in which he reported his return from Candas, he describes the combat as having taken place on that day.[15]

Dedicated as Ball was in his application to the routine squadron duties he longed to fly the single-seater Bristol scout. On the same day as the combat with the Albatros two-seater he took up the Bristol No. 5316 for a short familiarisation flight. He was airborne for half an hour from 12.15-12.45pm. This is probably not his first flight in a Bristol for, as we have seen, he was promised a flight in an '80 hp machine' during his training. That he was now allowed to fly the No.13 squadron Bristol was an indication as to how much he had improved as a pilot and perhaps to the aggressive tendencies he had shown during his work on the BE2c. He wrote to his parents that he had flown a Bristol 'so I shall get a few better chances'. He said that he would still fly the BE for 'wireless jobs'.

There is a mysterious reference at the end of this letter to the aeroplane design that he had mentioned earlier in the year to his father. He had been sent some plans by his father, but he had not yet

14 AIR1/1219/204/5/2634/13
15 Ball Archives 28/4/16

had a chance to look at them. He hoped to have some spare time in a few days. This leads to the possibility that Ball sent home an outline sketch of the aircraft which his father had had drawn up into a technical drawing, by an Austin Draughtsman. There is a note, undated, but assumed to be a few days later, in which he said that he will return the plans in a few days. There is also a reference to Lieutenant Villiers in the note which appears to strengthen the possibility that Villiers may have been responsible for the outline design. Ball describes his friend as:

> clever with Mechanics and will be a pilot before long. He knows a lot (? about) Mechanics and Chemistry. Before the War he was at college. Age 19.[16]

There is one final reference to these plans in a letter to his father of the 6 May:

> Re plans for new machine. We cannot send plans by post so I should bring them when I come home on leave. The Major thinks it is a topping brain wave.[17]

The Bristol test flight was followed that evening by a patrol over the lines. He flew the Bristol for nearly an hour and a half but no hostile aircraft were seen. It is reported that the armament fitted to the Bristol when Ball flew it was one of the early models of the Vickers Challenger Interrupter gear. The taste of freedom, which the Bristol had given him, was repeated on the 5 May when he flew Bristol 5313 on an offensive patrol. In the period between this flight and the previous one, Bristol 5316 had been written off by another pilot and a replacement had been flown in from Candas Aircraft Depot.

As Ball climbed to his patrol height over the lines he fired a burst from his Vickers to warm up the mechanism and prevent possible freezing to which guns were prone in the cold upper air. The patrol was uneventful and he had no further occasion to fire his gun, for the few rounds which he had fired had almost severed a blade of the propeller due to the timing mechanism being faulty. As he wrote home, if he had lost his propeller he would have been forced to land behind the German lines for he could not have made it back to Savy. After returning with the Bristol he flew another mission in the BE2c but the

16 Ball Archives. Letter to father undated.
17 Ball Archives 6/5/16

engine failed just as he left the ground and he had to crash land. As he remarked to his father 'that was enough for one day!'

The Squadron had been visited by Brigadier General Higgins[18] who congratulated Ball on his work and told him that a new Morane Bullet was expected to be delivered and that he was to fly it.

Ball's time at No.13 squadron was now coming to an end and he flew his last missions with the squadron on the 6 and 7 May. On the 6th he flew BE No.4070 to Candas and brought back No.2644. On the 7 May he flew an early morning patrol with Major Dore as passenger in 2644 looking for German troop movements. This ended his time in No.13 Squadron and he prepared to transfer to No.11 Squadron. It is a coincidence that the 7 May should be the date of his move. A year later it was to have a different significance. Ball was one of a number of pilots of two-seater machines who had been selected to fly scouts in No.11 squadron on account of their aggressive tendencies.

Despite the operational pressures to which he had been subjected Ball's commercial instincts were not dormant. In the last few days in the squadron he sold a motorcycle to Lieutenant Joel and a plot of land in Beeston to another, unnamed, colleague.

Whether he regretted his move from No.13 Squadron is not known. He would still be on the same airfield and able to keep in touch with such friends as Villiers. What he must have rejoiced in was the letter he was carrying in his pocket for he must have been aware of the contents. In this letter from Major Marsh to the Commanding Officer of No.11 Squadron, Major T. O'B Hubbard, Ball was commended, ('A keen and conscientious young man . . .') despite his relative youth and lack of experience, as a suitable pilot for flying in single seat scouts. This was to be the real beginning of his fighting career.

---

18 John Frederick Andrew Higgins(1875-1948) entered the Royal Artillery 1895. He fought in the Boer War 1899-1902 in which he was wounded and awarded the DSO. AOC in Iraq 1924-26; Air Member for Supply & Research 1926-30; Retired 1930. Recalled as AOC India 1939-40.

CHAPTER FOUR

Flying with No.11 Squadron
The Ace in the Making

There is a verse from an RFC song which was sung to the tune of *Do you Ken John Peel!* which included the refrain 'We hadn't got a notion what to do . . . So we hadn't got a hope in the morning'. However, by the time Albert Ball was transferred from No.13 Squadron to No.11 Squadron it was very far from the case that RFC pilots were left in ignorance of fighting procedures. There was widespread discussion, both in the squadrons, and at home, even spreading as far as the Air Board, a body which was largely concerned with the various aspects of production and the allocation to either the RFC or RNAS of airframes and engines, than operational matters.

From the rather makeshift alternatives of the haphazard days of 1914, both sides were feeling their way in aerial combat. The problem of mounting a machine-gun had been settled, the gun could be synchronised to fire through the propeller arc and more than one could be carried. The use of fighters in squadrons rather than as individual machines was coming to be accepted by both sides. The questions on combat tactics and manoeuvres were being asked and answered, with the Germans probably leading the way with their use of the Fokker Monoplanes and the way such pilots as Boelcke and Immelman handled them. The 'Immelman Turn' became a recognised fighting tactic used by both sides and increasingly the use of spinning as a means of getting out of a fight when things were going badly.

That a veneer of chivalry still clung to the air war is shown by both Nos.13 and 11 Squadrons having the idea of dropping a note over the German lines in November 1915 which read:

A British officer pilot is anxious to meet the redoubtable Captain Immelman in fair fight. The suggested rendezvous is a point above the first line trenches just east of HEBUTERNE. The

British Officer will be there from 10am to 11am daily from November 15th till November 30th, weather permitting. It is to be understood that only one aeroplane can be sent to meet this challenge, and that no anti-aircraft guns may fire at either combatant.[1]

The proposal was said to have arisen with Major Dawes, the Commanding Officer of No.11 Squadron. Presumably, rather tongue in cheek, he put the idea up to Wing who then forwarded it to RFC Headquarters. The proposal received the approval of HQ and this was passed down to the squadron. There is no indication of the name of the Officer offering the challenge, though in his memoirs A.J. Insall states that the selected officer was Captain Patrick Playfair[2] with whom he often flew as observer.[3]

It is not known whether the message was actually dropped or not. Insall is of the opinion that it was not, but does say that shortly afterwards, during the interrogation of a captured British crew they were asked whether they knew the identity of the British pilot nominated for the duel.

The air war was, however, 'hotting up' and pilots of both sides were under increased pressure as the fight for either survival or success became harder. The time of the mass use of fighters was yet to be evolved, it was still largely a case of small groups or singleton pilots who contested air supremacy and in this scenario Albert Ball flew and fought with growing success. As a part of his successful fighting tactics Ball eschewed the use of any ideas of chivalry. He soon realised that surprise was the best weapon he possessed to carry out his chosen form of fighting. Good eyesight, coupled with experience, gave some pilots the ability to see enemy aircraft before they themselves were seen. This quality Ball had, or developed, and combined with his unquestioned nerve and courage, brought him to the point where he wished to engage, as close to the enemy as he could get, often in the centre of their formation. From there he had his undoubted shooting ability to try and down his opponent before they had recovered from the shock of his attack. With No.11 Squadron Ball was to begin his career as a single-seat pilot and develop the fighting skills necessary.

By the time he came to leave No.13 Squadron Ball was due for home leave. There is no doubt that he was feeling the strain of nearly

1 AIR1/1219/204/5/2634/11.
2 Later Air Marshal Sir Patrick Playfair (1889-1974). Joined army 1909; RFC 1912; Commanded No.8 Squadron 1/1916-8/1916. Commanded 13th Wing 1916/18. Commanded CFS 1919. Various inter-war appointments. Commanded Advanced Air Striking Force 1939/40; AOC in C India 1940. Retired 1942.
3 See Insall pp74-75.

3 months of operational flying. His letters home contain admissions that he was feeling what we would now call 'combat stress' and he admitted 'I really do want a rest from all this work', and his advice to Cyril was not to join the RFC. His leave, however, was postponed. He told his parents of the move to No.11 Squadron saying that his luck had gone a 'bit wonkey' but he had been told that he was to fly a new French machine so this would mean the end of his leave.[4]

Also, the great British offensive on the Somme was in preparation and every effort had to be made in the air to win and maintain air supremacy and the benefits arising from it. This alone affected his prospects of leave, but on the personal front he was looking forward to flying the Nieuport 16, which his note from Major Marsh to Major Hubbard recommended, and for this reason he may have been more willing to forgo his leave. The Nieuport was a far better fighting prospect than the Bristol Scout and it was to be the marque on which he made his name.

No.11 Squadron had been formed in February 1915 and had proceeded to France in July 1915, equipped solely with the Vickers FB5 'Gun-bus' two-seat pusher. It was the first RFC squadron to be equipped with one type of aircraft and was allotted the role of 'fighting duties'. By the time Ball joined the squadron, this exclusivity of the Vickers pusher had been lost. A Bristol Scout was attached to the squadron as well as the Nieuport 16. The Vickers was to be phased out over the next couple of months. It had never been satisfactory as a fighting machine but had been popular with its crews. Because of its poor performance it had been unable to force combat on unwilling adversaries. It was now being replaced by the more substantial, and effective, FE2b. This had an improved performance over the Vickers, and was to remain, in its FE2b and 2d versions, a formidable addition to the RFC. By the time of the start of the battle of the Somme only four Vickers were left on the strength. Ball was more interested in flying the Nieuport 16, the best fighting scout which the RFC had and superior to both the Fokker and the DH2.

The Nieuport 16 was a development of the earlier Nieuport 11 and was powered by the 110hp Le Rhone Rotary engine. This gave it a speed of 103 mph at 6,500ft and a climb rate of 5 minutes 50 seconds to 6,500ft and a ceiling of 15,700ft. The use of the Nieuport by the RFC was entirely by the courtesy of the RNAS. The latter service had placed

4 Ball Archives 7/5/16.

an order for the Nieuport but subsequently agreed to transfer them to the RFC. The first of these transferred aircraft was at the Aircraft Depot at St. Omer on the 18 March 1916 and was soon followed by two further aircraft. In the first instance the Nieuports were allocated to squadrons as single aircraft and Nos 1 and 11 Squadrons received early examples. Later in the year No.60 Squadron was completely equipped with the type; the first RFC Squadron to be so equipped.[5]

Among his fellow officers in the squadron was Lieutenant A.J. Insall an Observer. Insall was the brother of Lieutenant G.S.M. Insall who had won the VC with the squadron the previous year. Over 50 years later Insall recorded his impressions of Ball in those early weeks in the squadron.[6]

He considered Ball 'a bright young fellow, inclined to rather more self confidence than the run of pilots of his flying hours . . . and more self assurance than his experience justified'. This initial impression was later modified as he came to know and talk to Ball. He came to recognise that in Ball he had found someone who was thinking seriously about his profession and with a will to succeed. He also noted in Ball the desire, which he had shown earlier, to be on his own as much as possible rather than joining in the full social life of the squadron. He was dedicated to his work and flew as often as he was allowed, but when operational flying was finished for the day he did not remain long in the mess but disappeared to his own quarters.

The keenness of Ball to come to grips with the enemy and to practice his skills soon became apparent. The day following his arrival on the squadron he took out one of the Bristol Scouts and made a familiarisation flight. Insall and Ball struck up an acquaintanceship, not really a close friendship, for, as with many others, Insall found the young man was not looking for companionship, but was willing to talk on professional matters and to be polite but not effusive on personal relations.

In the conversations they had together Ball admired the Colt revolver which Insall was carrying and disclosed his own interest in pistol shooting from his pre-war days in the garden of Sedgely House. He promised that one evening he would join the rat hunting expeditions which Insall and Captain Burdon took to the River Scarpe in the evenings, but he always seemed to be too busy, particularly with setting up the Lewis Gun on his Nieuport. He had realised the

---

5 The story of the introduction of the Nieuport Scout to RFC service is well set out in J.M. Bruce's *The Aeroplanes of the Royal Flying Corps* (Military Wing) (Putnam 1982). See also the Cross & Cockade Monograph on the Nieuport.
6 A.J. Insall. pp114-117.

necessity for success as a fighting pilot of paying attention to the details of his profession and among these was care of his gun and getting the alignment of the sight right for the range at which he wished to fight. This trait was symptomatic of the successful pilot, perhaps none more so than James McCudden who took great pains over his guns and ammunition, inspecting the individual rounds which went into the belts and ammunition drums of his machine.

When Ball transferred to No.11 Squadron at least one of his ground crew went with him. Frederick Lang had enlisted in October 1914 and after training in England had been sent to join No.13 Squadron and been designated as Albert Ball's mechanic. According to Lang in his recollections, which were recorded in 1978 and published in 2006[7], he got on very well with Ball and Ball often treated them to an exhibition of aerobatics. When they got to No.11 Squadron Lang had the job of looking after Ball's Nieuport and fitted the tubes for the Le Prieur rockets which Ball used in his attack on the German Balloon line on the 25 June, and Lang took part in the celebrations on Ball's successful return to the airfield.

The relationship with Lang was very close and they even had the occasional drink together which was unusual even for the RFC. Lang recognised the privacy which Ball wanted and did not go to Ball's hut. If Lang was wanted by Ball the latter would come to him, Lang would never go to the hut. Ball took an interest in Lang's career and worked to get him promoted. The last words that Ball spoke to Lang were to the effect that he deserved promotion and he would be posted away soon to Hythe School of Aerial Gunnery. This duly happened and additionally Lang was promoted to Sergeant and later Flight Sergeant, all, he believed, due to Ball's interest in him.

Ball had been billeted in the village of Aubigny close by and was not pleased with the house to which he had been allotted. He considered it to be dirty and not fit to live in and his suggested solution was to live on the aerodrome. He had a tent erected on the airfield, near to the aircraft hangars, and had an area around it wired off so that he could convert it into a garden. He asked his parents to send him packets of seeds, both flowers and vegetables, which he could plant. The project got under way one wet morning when flying was impossible. Instead of going to the mess to pass the time until operations could resume, he started to prepare his garden and in three hours had dug over a

---

7 See Malinovska & Joslyn pp142/147.

sizeable area and planted peas. The tent was soon to be replaced by a hut, which he constructed himself, but the garden remained as his form of relaxation from the perils and stresses of combat flying.

It was more than a week before Ball had his first success with the squadron. His combat reports seem to be missing from the squadron records in the National Archives so we have to rely mainly on his letters home for details of his success. Writing to Cyril and Lois on the 16 May he described the actions of the previous day which brought both sadness and joy:

> Do please excuse me not writing two letters, but really things are desparate just now, and my mind is full of poo-poo thoughts. I have just lost such a dear pal, Captain Lucas. He was brought down by a Fokker last night about 5 pm. Now don't show Mother and Dad this letter, and I will tell you about the fights.
>
> The Fokker came up behind the BE from the rear. It opened fire and at once hit Captain Lucas who was the Observer. Lieutenant Wright was the pilot, and such a fine chap. He kept at his job, although he was hit in the shoulder. Fifty shots the Fokker fired but Lieutenant Wright got over our side and landed, walked out a few yards and then fell down. Captain Lucas died in a few hours. The machine was brought back this morning, and I am not exaggerating when I say it was soaked in blood, and full of holes. No. 11, my squadron, lost six machines yesterday, and one crashed today. Only one of our Flight is missing, and he was such a topping chap.
>
> Now for a bit of cheerful news. I was on patrol yesterday morning on Bristol Scout. I was at 12,000ft and saw a Hun at 5,000. It started off and I went after it, catching it up when 20 miles over its own lines. It took 120 shots to do it in, but in the end it went down upside down. I got back but was archied badly. In the afternoon I received orders to fly a new French machine. Did well on it so they are now getting one for me. This means I shall be on one of the best machines England and France can give a pilot, so I hope for a good run.[8]

Captain Lucas and Lieutenant Wright were former colleagues from No.13 Squadron. His own combat took place while he was flying Bristol Scout 5313 (believed to have been fitted with a synchronised

---

8 Ball Archive 17/5/16.

Vickers gun). The Albatros two-seater is credited to Ball as 'Out of Control' and recorded in the RFC Communiqué of 16 May. The location of the engagement is given as Givenchy-Beaumont. There is some confusion over this victory. No combat record exists for the action so we have to rely on the letter from Ball of the 16 May in which he talks of being on patrol 'yesterday morning'. This can be construed, of course, as meaning the 15 May. In the entry against Ball in *Above the Trenches* an identical combat is recorded for the 16 May an entry which has been supported by RFC Communiqués. The likely explanation is that Ball either misdated his letter or that it was written in two parts, the second part describing his own combat and written on the 17 May.[9]

His opponent on this occasion was an Albatros two-seater (type is uncertain but probably a CIII) from *Kampfgeschwader 17*. Ball had spotted the EA over Givenchy, flying at a lower level than his Bristol and pursued it towards Beaumont. He had not yet adopted his later characteristic fighting style of the dive and zoom into the underneath position and on this occasion he did not have the wing mounted Lewis gun which made such a tactic more effective. This time he dived on the Albatros from above and fired as he approached. He continued firing until he was at close range, when he broke off his attack. The burst had been accurate and the German Observer was wounded. The Albatros aircraft fell away steeply, but probably under control, as the pilot was later able to recover control and land his aircraft near a field hospital for his Observer to be taken care of. Ball last saw it at about 2000ft, no longer diving, but on its back. As his own engine was running erratically Ball did not stay around to watch the fate of the Albatros and he turned for home.

The Albatros was later credited to Ball as 'driven down' though 'out of control' would have been equally applicable. The fact that Ball dived and engaged the German aircraft from above and behind has an element of risk. The lesson he learnt from this engagement was not to open fire too soon. If the German Observer had been fully alert, and there is no record of his having fired any return shots, then the approach would have exposed Ball to a certain amount of danger. His later tactic of diving and engaging from underneath was preferable giving him much more chance of success with less risk. It is said that

9 Chaz Bowyer has accepted the Ball letter as placing the combat on the 15 May and ascribing it to Ball in Bristol Scout 5313. The later research for *Over the Trenches* goes for the 16 May and Bristol No. 5312. The description and location of the combat are identical from both sources and I am inclined to support the idea of the combat taking place on the 16 May though I have not yet found proof in Squadron records for either date.

during their respective home leaves Albert Ball met James McCudden. Ball would have been at the height of his fame while McCudden was just starting his fighting career but they talked tactics together. Ball explained his methods to McCudden and the latter immediately saw the sense in it and often adopted it for his own engagements with two-seaters.[10]

At the time of Ball's posting to No.11 Squadron it had two Nieuport Scouts attached to it. The first 5173 (which was one of the first two Nieuports to be handed over to the RFC from the RNAS) had been delivered to the unit on 29 March and the second, A126, had been taken on charge on 26 April it was these aircraft which Ball meant by 'a new French machine'. Ball was later given 5173 as his own personal aircraft and only made one more operational flight on the Bristol. Ball was very enthusiastic about the Nieuport:

> You will be pleased to know that at last I am flying one of the best machines England or France can give a pilot.
>
> I flew it for the first time yesterday afternoon, and did very well. When it lands it hits the ground at 80mph so you can guess what speed it goes in the air. It is a single seater, with a 110hp engine, so I have no Observer to keep safe.[11]

Possibly to reassure his parents he told them that 'No Nieuport Machine has been brought down since the war commenced, and my latest new one is a Nieuport'. This is, of course, a palpably false claim, but was obviously to put their minds at rest that he would not be in any greater danger as a result of his new role.

The Nieuport 16 was vastly superior to the Fokker monoplane, but it was not without its problems. It required far more sensitive handling than any machine that Ball had previously flown, far more so than the Bristol scout. The light weight of the aircraft made it much more difficult to land and in one of his early flights Ball made a rough landing at Savy and broke the lower wing as he bounced over the ground.

RFC experience with the Nieuport showed it to have a weakness in the lower wing, which could break away in an extended dive. However, in the middle of 1916 it was the best fighting scout which the RFC had and over the period in which it saw service (in different variants) as a front line aircraft it established a good fighting record. Three RFC pilots

10 See *McCudden VC* by Christopher Cole (Kimber 1967)p.89.
11 Ball Archives 17 & 18/5/16.

had great success on the Nieuport, exploiting its manoeuvrability and rate of climb as well as its wing mounted Lewis gun: Ball, Phillip Fullard and Billy Bishop.

The top-wing mounted Lewis gun was mounted initially on a short swivelling pillar mounting. It could be pulled down to change the ammunition drums, but this type of mounting was soon replaced in No.11 Squadron by that devised by Sergeant R.G. Foster. This consisted of a curved rail on which the gun could be pulled down to change the ammunition drum but it could also be held in that position and fired upwards which made possible the underneath attack position which Ball found so successful. The Foster mounting was so successful on the Nieuports of the squadron that it was adopted as standard fitting on all the Nieuports of the RFC and on the later SE5 & 5a scouts. The actual process of pulling the gun down, either to secure an upwards shot or to change the drum, could not have been easy especially in the heat of combat. The physical effort required must have been considerable but it was obviously considered worthwhile as the method was retained for the later SE5 and 5a as well as the Sopwith Dolphin.

Flying Nieuport A126 Ball had his first successful combat in the type on the 22 May when he attacked a pair of two-seaters, an Albatros and an LVG. His fire forced both aircraft to seek safety by landing, proof that he had engaged both of them over the German side of the lines. The machines were not destroyed but they were credited to Ball in the records as 'driven down'.

It was the following day, when, as he got out of his aircraft after an evening patrol, he was handed a leave warrant for the next day. The thought of going home and seeing his family overjoyed Ball and the night must have been spent in happy anticipation. The next morning, however, he saw Major Hubbard who told him that his leave would have to be deferred. He was told by Hubbard that, as one of only two pilots flying the Nieuport, he could not be spared in the critical time of preparation for the Somme Offensive. The decision was momentarily shattering to Ball, who had been counting the days to when he would see his family again. However, a moment's reflection, and some consoling words from Hubbard that he would try and get him some leave as soon as possible, convinced him that the decision was right and he would have to accept it.

On the 29 May Ball was again up in Nieuport 5173 on a morning patrol. Climbing to 10,000ft at 8am he sighted and chased an LVG two-seater over Beaumont. The German was at about 6,000ft and Ball dived and closed on the LVG. This time he did not open fire early but held his fire until he was within 30 yards when half a drum was emptied into the cockpit area of his opponent. The LVG went into a vertical dive and Ball eventually lost sight of it as it fell away. It was credited to Ball as 'Out of Control'.

He continued his patrol and in the area of Oppy he saw an LVG escorted by two Fokkers. Deciding that the odds were too great for him he followed the trio of German aircraft, waiting for a chance to attack one of them without the others being able to interfere. Two other Fokkers then appeared but did not join forces with the formation which Ball was stalking. His wait was rewarded when the LVG parted company from the two Fokkers. Ball immediately went into the attack closed to fifty yards and fired the remainder of the ammunition drum at the two-seater. He turned away to put on a fresh drum and attacked again. The LVG dived away, with the Observer firing at Ball from the rear cockpit and scoring some hits on the Nieuport. Ball followed it down and eventually had the satisfaction of seeing it land. He made no attempt to attack the LVG or its crew while it was on the ground but made for home, suffering some damage from ground fire. He told his parents that in all this combat only eight bullets had hit his machine, though one of these had gone very close to his back.

These two combats marked the end of Albert Ball's fighting for the month of May. In the short period in which he had been with No.11 Squadron he had established a reputation as someone who was rapidly learning the art of fighting in the air. The strain was there, but despite this he was happy that in the Nieuport he now had an aircraft which was equal to the efforts which he wished to make. During May he had written a long letter to his parents which gives us an indication of his attitude and his state of mind during this time:

Well, now I have tons to say, but am very tired, for I was at work at 3.30 this morning. However, I am now sitting under a hedge resting, at the same time writing. So do excuse pencil. I will commence from yesterday afternoon. General Higgins came over, he sent for me and congratulated me on my work, also for bringing the Hun down. He also said that a machine called a Bullet[12] was coming in a few days, and I am to fly it. This will make the third fighting scout I have been given to fly. I have not brought any other machine down on my latest machine yet, but I have chased a lot; however, they ran away.

Now, for today's news. I was told to be on the 4.15 patrol, so I got up at 3.30. On getting out I saw our AA guns firing at two Huns nearly over our aerodrome. Naturally, I got very excited, for they do not often come over now. My Nieuport was got ready and I went up. Got up 10,000ft in 10 minutes, and got ready to chase. My gun (Bowden)cable smashed, and I had to return. My Bristol was next got out and I went up again, but this machine is much slower. However, I got up to them and chased them over their lines, but was unable to get near enough to fire. On turning to come back I found that I could not see the ground, also I was about forty miles from the aerodrome. I got back in about two hours.

The Major met me and told me to get off to bed, for I am to fly again from 5 – 7. Oh! We have got a topping Major. Well, I have not gone to bed, but am resting and writing.

Re leave, I must say that although my nerves are quite good, I really do want a rest from all this work. I can stand a lot, but, really I have been coming on in leaps and bounds in the last few days, and it is just beginning to tell on me. I always feel tired.

I have struck a topping lot of chaps in this squadron, and they look after me fine, but they all think me young and call me John. Well, this is no hardship, and I am very happy.

Now I think I will close and have an hours sleep, so that I shall be in working order tonight.

PS – Garden going topping, and such a real pleasure.[13]

This letter, although existing records do not support it, shows that Ball may have flown the Morane 'Bullet' on at least one operational flight over the lines. The general opinion of those who had to fly it was that the Morane, with its wing warping system, was difficult to fly and it was never popular. To someone used to the Nieuport it would have felt very different in handling qualities and with no advantages in speed.

On 1 June Ball was airborne again in Nieuport 5173. He had decided on a plan to strike the Fokkers in their own nest. He set course for Douai, the aerodrome known as the base from which Fokkers

12 The Morane Type N Monoplane. Known in the RFC as the Morane 'Bullet'. There is no record of one being allocated to No.11 Squadron.
13 Ball Archives. 30/5/16.

operated. Before 10am he was over the aerodrome at 10,000ft and waiting for the first German planes to come up. After half an hour's wait he was rewarded by the sight of an Albatros CIII and a Fokker taking off together. He selected the Albatros as his target and dived into the attack when the two-seater had reached 10,000ft.

A short burst from his Lewis gun persuaded the Albatros pilot to put his nose down and return to land on the aerodrome. This left the Fokker which was closing on him. Ball waited until the Fokker opened fire before he reversed the situation and by a sharp turn out manoeuvred his opponent and dived on the German plane, firing short bursts from his Lewis gun. The Fokker pilot, seeing Ball had the advantage of height, also dived away to the aerodrome and landed, apparently undamaged. Of these two opponents only the Fokker was credited to Ball as 'forced to land'. The action had shown in Ball a considered approach, which was not to be the hallmark of his fighting career. General Higgins was on the aerodrome when Ball landed and once again congratulated him on his work.

On the 12 June he left for home for his delayed leave. It would be the first time that he had seen his parents for four months and his joy in this and the release from the strain of operational flying, was obvious. He had been well aware that he had been 'stretched' physically and mentally by his period in France, and had recognised that he could become a casualty. He had promised his parents that, 'I will be careful, as you wish'. Being 'careful' did not really describe the method of fighting which he had begun to adopt and which became his creed. From wishing his brother to hurry up and join him, he had now begun to write again that Cyril should avoid the RFC, *as nerves do not last long*.

Prior to his leave Ball told his mother that he expected to be in Nottingham on Monday or Tuesday 'if all goes well'. He warned her, however, that his leave could still be cancelled even at this late stage, . . . *for leave goes not on greased wheels for me*. The fellow officer he was going home with, as he pointed out to his mother, had only been out about two months. He consoled himself with the thought that he was lucky in other ways he flew a Nieuport and had more fights than any other pilot in either Nos.11 or 13 Squadrons over the last three months and was the only pilot of the scout group to have brought down a German plane.[14]

His period at home did Ball good and gave him the ease of mind and

---

14 Ball Archives 7/6/16.

body of which he was in need. We do not know what he did, no doubt he did get in some of the fishing which he had been looking forward to, but it was the close friendship of his family circle which sustained him. He would almost certainly have seen Thelma on this leave but no record of this survives although the two had exchanged long letters just prior to his coming home. His thoughts on leaving home again are well expressed in a short letter he wrote to his parents from Folkestone while waiting for the boat to cross to France:

> Just a line before leaving dear old England again. You have been dears during my leave. Well now, dears, I will not attempt a long letter, for the boat goes soon. I shall do my best during the time I am away, also when I come back, shall try, with God's help, to repay your dear love.[15]

The subject of Thelma must have come up during his leave for, apart from his fond farewells to his mother and father, he replied with a firm 'no' to some suggestion which his parents had made to him about the relationship, though he does not elaborate on what that suggestion was. He stressed that he loved Thelma very much and included these words in support of his relationship with her:

> ... However, I know she is a bit full of life but I think she will cut down for me. I have written her a long letter.
> Now if you ever get to know anything, do always tell me. I trust my Nipper but I know even the strongest love has weak moments, and she is not of the strongest. Nor am I. However, she has tons of good.[16]

Ball returned to No.11 Squadron on the 23 June and in his refreshed state he got ready again to fight his type of war. While he had been away there had been tangible evidence that the time of the Fokkers was over. In a combat on the 18 June with FE2bs of No.25 Squadron the German Ace Max Immelman had been shot down and killed by Lieutenant Alan McCubbin and Corporal J. Waller. The superiority of the British answer to the Fokkers had been proved and for the next couple of months the British were to establish and retain air superiority over the Somme battlefront. The pendulum would swing again, with a vengeance, and the introduction of improved German types from

15 Ball archives 22/6/16.
16 Ball Archives 22/6/16.

August/September onwards initiated a period of pressure on the RFC from which it was only just beginning to recover by the time of Albert Ball's own death.

While he had been away his Nieuport, 5173, had been flown by other pilots and on the 21 June Captain H.A. Cooper, having just come back from leave, had been shot down and killed in what Ball called 'my machine'. Two other pilots were also reported by Ball to be out of action throwing extra work on to those who remained. It seems that 5173 was not a complete write off for it had been recovered and made serviceable and Ball flew it on a Balloon strafing operation on 25 June.

Sometime prior to the battle of the Somme, a remarkable new officer joined the squadron. His name was Frederick Libby, an American from Platte Valley Colorado. He had been born and raised as a cowboy, but tiring of that life had decided to travel, and the outbreak of war found him in Canada, where he joined the Canadian Army. He eventually transferred to France and after a period serving with a motor transport unit behind the lines he volunteered to join the RFC as an observer. He had flown with No.23 Squadron and on his first trip over the lines, in an FE2b, he had shot down an Ago two-seater. This standard was to be kept up, and with No.11 Squadron he shot down a further nine enemy aircraft, including three single-seaters. In his autobiography he describes his arrival at Savy airfield:

> Arriving at Savoy (sic) airfield, which is Eleven Squadron headquarters, I find almost the same kind of field as at Twenty-third. Our quarters are in the woods and there is a hedge around and in front of the hangars. To reach the landing field the ships are wheeled out through an opening in the hedge. Coming through the opening towards the headquarters to report, I am spotted by three fellows beating a shuttlecock attached by a long string to a pole. They are in shirt sleeves and really giving themselves a work-out. Quitting their game. They give me a welcome greeting, telling me they are glad I am to be a member of Number Eleven and that Major Hubbard is expecting me, that Price (his pilot who had also transferred from 23 Squadron) is in the air but will be back for dinner. They are Lieutenant Ball, Lieutenant Foot and Captain Quested.[17]

In his autobiography, Libby professes a great admiration for Albert

---

17 Libby *Horses don't Fly* p161.

Ball and how the appearance of Ball in his Nieuport was always a welcome sight when Libby and his pilot Captain Price were hard pressed over the German side of the lines. There is no doubt that Libby was a very effective Observer and had the natural ability of being a good shot. By the time he left No.11 Squadron his success had been such that his fighting record must have been second only to Ball.

With the opening of the battle of the Somme approaching the British made every effort to 'blind' the Germans as to what was happening on their side and put a stop to their counter battery work. The work of the German two-seaters was already being made difficult by the activities of the now superior British fighters. However, the Germans still maintained their line of observation balloons and various squadrons were ordered to destroy them.

According to Andrew Boyle[18], Trenchard, the commander of the RFC, placed a bet that the British planes would bring down more balloons than the French. The operation took place on the 25 June on the front of all four British Armies. Twenty-three observation balloons had been spotted from the British side of which fifteen were attacked.

Albert Ball was one of those ordered to attack. For his attempt he was flying Nieuport 5173 which had racks fitted to carry 40lb Phosphor Bombs. Ball reached the Balloon line and made his attack under severe anti-aircraft fire but he was unsuccessful in securing a hit. On return to the aerodrome he asked Major Hubbard for permission to try again and Hubbard agreed.

For this second attack his Nieuport (now A134) had been fitted with Le Prieur Rockets. These were mounted in tubes on the interplane struts and fired electrically. There could be no attempt at aiming your weapon, like the Congreve Rockets of the previous century the Le Prieur Rockets were notoriously inaccurate. A pilot could do no more than point his aircraft in the direction of the target and the nearer he got the better his chance of securing a hit.

At 4 p.m. Ball took off again and flew towards the German Balloon line. This time he closed the distance to his target and was successful in hitting and destroying the German balloon with a fusillade of rockets. The anti-aircraft fire was by now very intense and as he turned for home Ball's Nieuport was hit in the engine. The engine immediately lost power and at the resultant low altitude and reduced speed Ball was

---

18 Trenchard. *Man of Vision* pp182.

a much easier target for the ground gunners. He flew the 8 miles back to the British lines and received even more damage. One bullet, which he kept as a souvenir, had passed though an induction pipe, the engine bearer and other parts of the structure. Ball, however, remained unscathed.

He wrote home telling his parents of the success of the operation:

> You will have seen in the papers that on the 26th (sic) five German Balloons were brought down.
>
> I brought one of them down. And at night a wire came from General Trenchard and General Higgins congratulating me. Oh! It was rotten for I only just got back.
>
> Three of us were sent from this squadron. The first time we did no good, so I asked for another chance. We all set out again.
>
> I went for my Balloon and set it on fire but my engine was badly hit and I had to come back all the eight miles over Hun land at half speed and only a few feet up. My machine was hit badly. I have enclosed one of the bullets. This bullet went through my Induction Pipe, Engine Bearer, Plane and three inches of wood. Not so bad is it. I have also enclosed the Wires.
>
> The Induction Pipe I am sending to Thelma.
>
> The other chaps were not very successful. One crashed his machine and the other did no good.[19]

It was chiefly for this action, returning again to attack the balloon, that he was awarded the Military Cross. The citation in the *London Gazette* of the 27 July read:

> For conspicuous skill and gallantry on many occasions, notably when after failing to destroy an enemy kite-balloon with bombs, he returned for a fresh supply, went back and brought it down in flames. He has done great execution among enemy aeroplanes. On one occasion he attacked six in one flight, forced down two and drive the others off. This occurred seven miles over the enemy lines.

When the news of the award was confirmed to him by a telegram from Wing HQ he wrote to his father about the receipt of the MC and his life as a Nieuport pilot:

---

19 Ball Archives 28/6/16.

My Nieuport engine has gone poo-poo, so I have not got anything to fly until 2.30 am tomorrow morning. The men will work all night and have a new engine in by 2.0 a.m. in the morning.

The three Nieuport machines stand from 2.30 a.m. until 9.30 at night, so you bet we are getting a rotten time just now. However, things are looking good just now, so we might all help and keep things going at any cost. But it is a long day and I am afraid that if it lasts very long a few of the chaps will be going sick.

You will be pleased to hear that I have now got my Military Cross. I received the wire from Wing yesterday, also congratulations from the Army Commander.

In a few weeks I get four days leave, in order to be decorated by the dear old King. Oh! I am so very pleased, for it has been a rotten job getting it. I cannot say exactly when I shall get the four days, for we have so much work to do just now, that one cannot get off, but I will come first chance I get. I was given the ribbon by the Major today, the cross I shall give to you in order that you may keep it for me. The Wing Wire I sent to Thelma for she will be so very pleased with it and I know you would sooner have the cross than the Wire.

. . . I really love Thelma . . . Well you just give me a test, and see. I love my Tee with all my heart and find such pleasure in having such a first class happiness.

I bet you will have a job in finding any fault in her now for I gave her a good talking to. Now don't forget that I am not exactly an Angel, so don't be too hard on Tee.

I bet you will find both of us both very good from now onwards. Enough about Tee for again I should be loving you.

Well, enough about the MC, for I do not want to bore you, and I must now close for I have heaps to do.[20]

Once again we find Ball mounting a defence of Thelma and his relationship with her. It would be interesting to know the other side of the story and to see what his parents were saying to him.

The end result of six balloons destroyed without incurring the loss of any of the attacking aircraft was a successful outcome for the RFC.

---

20 Ball Archives, date not known.

In addition Trenchard was able to claim his one franc bet from the French.

At the end of the day, when the results were known, Trenchard wrote to his friend Sefton Brancker who was working in London:

> We had our great strafe today. Three Nieuports met their balloons with rockets and brought them down, a fourth missed. . . . One phosphorous bomb hit a balloon as it was being hauled down very quickly . . . There was one hell of an explosion which blew everything into the air . . . Just heard that another has been seen burning.[21]

On 27 June was a reorganisation of the Squadron. All the Scouts, which had been attached to the squadron, were grouped together in one Flight, B Flight. This is what Ball referred to in his letters home as 'The Scout Flight'. Hubbard chose the most experienced single-seat pilots to comprise this flight, Ball himself along with 2nd Lieutenants Anderson and Griffiths and Sergeant Reffell. Of these selected pilots 2nd Lieutenant Anderson was reported by Ball in one of his letters home of the 28 June as having his leg broken in five places.

That same day saw Ball undertaking an early morning patrol in Nieuport A134. The patrol though void of combat success saw him have one of his closest escapes from death.

> On my patrol I saw over the lines a lot of transport etc in a wood. I went over the lines to have a good look, but the old Huns did not like it. They surrounded us with shells from their Archie guns and at last we were hit. One of my cylinders was smashed off, also the machine got a few through it. One only just missed my leg. However, the engine stopped, but I saw what I went to see, and also managed to get my machine far enough over our lines to prevent the old fools from shelling it. Later on I had a new engine in and the machine patched up, and it is now safely in the shed. I am sending half the cylinder to you.[22]

The battle about to be launched had been one of the Allied Offensives agreed upon at the Chantilly conference at the end of November 1915. At that conference Britain, France, Russia and Italy had all agreed to attack somewhere in 1916 and to coordinate their attacks so that the

---

21 Boyle pp182.
22 Ball Archives. 27/6/16.

Germans and Austrians would be unable to move troops from one front to another to bolster the defences where a sector was found to be under pressure. Unfortunately the Germans pre-empted the Allied strategy and launched an attack on the French lines at Verdun in February 1916 with the object of using the minimum amount of force to 'bleed the French white', calculating that the French would make every effort to hold Verdun. The German commander Von Falkenhayn, was right. Although they had no strategic reason to defend Verdun, the French High Command, Government and people were determined not to lose another yard of French soil and threw everything into a stubborn defence. In this struggle the French air and ground forces were reinforced, as were the German and the effect of the concentration of German air strength at Verdun had been felt by the RFC in a lessening of the pressure which it faced on its front.

The French appealed to the British to bring forward the time of their own offensive to relieve the pressure at Verdun. General Haig and his commanders had been struggling to prepare the New Army for the great offensive but with the new Kitchener Divisions the level of expertise was far lower than would have been the case in the old army. When the offensive was launched on the 1 July the battle of Verdun had already being going on for over 140 days and some form of relief was essential.

The RFC formed an integral part of the British preparation and had been identifying the positions of German guns, bringing fire on to them to silence them. Photographic sorties had brought back to the British High Command the knowledge which they needed to see: the layout of the German line and the back areas. The work of the RFC was intense but was now largely carried out with little interference from the German fighter groups thanks to the massing of the German air service at Verdun and the superiority of the Nieuport and DH2 fighters to the opposition. This was only a temporary state of affairs. The Germans had already designed and put into production the fighters which would begin to reverse the situation in a few months. In the meantime, the offensive policy of the RFC could have free rein and British aircraft roamed extensively over the enemy lines, providing the support which the Army required.

As the month of July opened, if the term had been in use at the RFC Headquarters Albert Ball would have been classified as an 'ace', his kite

Balloon on the 25 June having been his fifth victory. Such a term, however, was not acceptable to those in command of the RFC, who did not like to give more publicity to the deeds of the pilots of the RFC than to their comrades fighting on the ground. The RFC was part of the Army and would not be more publicised, yet, than any other corps.

Ball was not the first RFC pilot to achieve that distinction. There were four other RFC pilots who had reached this landmark score before him, Hawker; Wilkinson, Bell and Medlicott and one RNAS pilot, Red Mulock, had also been credited with five victories.

Hawker was the most well known pilot in the RFC. The first man to be awarded the VC for air fighting. An aggressive and charismatic leader he had brought out the first fighter squadron, No.24, equipped with the DH2, and had led them with success to beat back the depredations of the Fokker.

As the air war of the battle of the Somme opened the RFC had about 200 aircraft on the battlefront to face about 130 German aircraft. The Corps reconnaissance and artillery observation machines flew a high number of sorties to report on the progress of the infantry attack and to pinpoint German strong points for bombardment by the British artillery. While the two-seaters were flying the scout pilots were also flying, with the dual purpose of protecting their comrades from the attention of German scouts and to intercept any attempt by the Germans to fly over the British lines.

Albert Ball had a full day's flying. In a letter to his parents he wrote, *Things are on full steam just now, 2.30am to 9.30pm* and that he was 'fagged' with the work which he had put in that day. Despite his sorties over the battlefield he did not have any engagements or victories to report and went to bed that night without adding to his score. With only about a week back in France the increased operational tempo was already beginning to tell on him.

On the 2 July Ball flew as escort in Nieuport A134 to four FE2bs. They crossed the line at 10,000ft and he soon saw a formation of six Roland CIIs coming towards the British lines from the direction of Mercatel. As the two formations approached each other the German formation split up. The British too divided, two of the FEs returning back over the British lines, while the other two, with Ball in his Nieuport went in to the attack. Under fire from one of the FEs one of the Rolands was seen to fall away out of control and to crash near the

Mercatel-Arras Road. Ball meanwhile closed with one of the other Rolands and fired a full drum of Lewis into the side of the fuselage of the German machine and this too was seen to crash near the wreckage of the earlier victim. After this the engagement finished, the Germans disappeared and as the British formation could not be reconstituted Ball continued alone.

Half an hour later while still patrolling at 11,000ft on the German side of the lines he saw an Aviatik two-seater just below him. He dived down to attack from above and the side. His Lewis gun fired only a few rounds before it jammed. Ball swiftly changed the axis of his attack and after rectifying the jam he came up under the belly of the Aviatik and fired the rest of the drum into it using his control stick to spray the fire from end to end of the fuselage, The Aviatik was fatally hit and fell away sideways to crash in a field. This day's fighting represented the first time that Ball had verifiably destroyed two of his opponents. These successes gave Ball his sixth and seventh victories as he wrote to his parents the following day, . . . *I now stand with six machines and one balloon to my credit.* This successful day's fighting brought a telegram of congratulations from Trenchard followed by a visit from both Higgins and Trenchard.

In making this statement regarding his personal score Ball discounted some of the combats in which he had been engaged, but in which he had had not been able to assure himself that the final result had been successful. It became a feature of his later letters home that he kept his parents informed of his 'score' and later compared it with that of his French contemporary Georges Guynemer. Many of the 'aces' did keep their own record of their successes, but often these were at variance with the officially recorded tally. Although Ball had now become an effective 'killer' of his opponents he undoubtedly felt some uneasiness and later grew to hate the business of successful air fighting.

In reply to his father as to whether he thanked God for his success he replied with a simple statement of his faith and the belief that God was looking after him:

> . . . Re saying a few words to God when I am doing my work and when it is done. You ask me if I did when I came back safely. You bet I did! I even do when I am fighting, in fact I put all my trust in God, that is why I feel safe, no matter in what mess I get.[23]

---

23 Ball Archives 6/7/16.

It would have been unthinkable for him to celebrate his individual successes by the making of a silver cup as Von Richthofen did or to decorate his hut with the guns, insignia or serial numbers of his opponents. The mindset of the two men was totally different. Although Ball had volunteered to fight he remained a civilian at heart. Manfred von Richthofen came from a more militiaristic culture, in which service in war was an accepted duty. Ball fought on because his sense of patriotism and duty were still enough to overcome his distaste at the killing which he had to do. Having adopted his methods of attack early in his fighting career he gave no further thought to the matter. Odds meant nothing to him, he fought on in the only way he knew in order to get the job done. He did not make a good patrol leader and would never have been happy as a squadron commander, where he would have been largely stopped from fighting. He was happiest on his own with no one else to limit his freedom of action.

Richthofen had a different attitude. He soon showed a keen sense of being interested in the tactics of air fighting. He saw the 'business' plainly enough of inflicting casualties on the enemy without significant loss to your own side. He recognised the necessity of grouping fighters in 'Staffeln' for their more effective use. His career was based on making the most effective use of his talents and that of his squadron in a situation where the German Air Force was often outnumbered. He understood perfectly, as Lord Nelson did before him that, 'only numbers can annihilate' and the German fighter squadrons, under his leadership and example, were a very successful fighting force. Albert Ball led by example and courage and this was the legacy which he left to the RFC. Richthofen, with equal courage, also left the foundations of fighter tactics which were to stand the test of time.

At this time the achievements of Albert Ball were becoming known in the RFC and the Army as a whole. However, stories had begun to circulate in Britain and France, perhaps by injudicious comments, regarding his letters home. With his essentially retiring nature he did not welcome stories about him in the press:

> Re the newspapers saying anything about me. If they put in any bosh I shall be more than wild. If they just say that I downed five machines and a balloon all well and good, but nothing else. I like doing things but I don't like big songs about them.[24]

24 Ball Archives 10/7/16.

On the 3 July Ball left in Nieuport A134, for a further balloon attack. His ammunition drums were filled with Buckingham ammunition and the Nieuport's struts had been fitted with eight Le Prieur Rockets. Ball left in the afternoon to destroy a kite balloon near Pelves. As he closed on his target the German ground crew began to haul the balloon down. Ball got within 15 yards before he fired his Le Prieur Rockets. At that range a hit with these weapons would have been considered highly possible, but such was the inaccuracy of the rockets that even at this point blank range he missed. He continued, however, to fire his Buckingham ammunition and had the satisfaction of seeing his bullets striking the balloon squarely. The balloon did not ignite but began to deflate and continued to sink towards the ground.

On return to the squadron he did not claim the balloon as destroyed but, that it had been hauled down seemingly uninjured.[25]

Captain Crook, also flying a Nieuport, of No.11 Squadron had successfully carried out an attack on his target, destroying it with his Le Prieur Rockets. Another pilot involved in the attack on the German balloon line, Captain Balcombe-Brown of No.1 Squadron, thought that the balloon he attacked was a decoy around which the Germans had concentrated heavy guns which when they burst created a smoke cloud, surrounding the balloon, and into this cloud the guns fired streams of what the RFC pilots called 'flaming onions'. These were strings of fire balls which ignited the canvas of the attacking aircraft if a hit was secured.

The next day, the 4 July, was a 'washout' quite literally, when heavy rain flooded two of the Squadron's hangars. This was the beginning of a period of unfavourable weather, which, while it did not entirely stop flying, severely restricted it. Ball took the opportunity of this relatively inactive period to work on his Nieuport. He had already decided that his favoured method of fighting was the hidden approach from underneath. He was also confident enough in his ability as a marksman that he would be able to hit his target once he got into this position.

This method of approach meant that at some time when under the belly of his opponent he would have to perform the task of both controlling his aircraft and aiming and firing the gun. He needed to re-rig the Nieuport so that for the period necessary it would be able to fly 'hands off' and thereby give him a chance to use both hands to hold,

---

25 PRO AIR1/ 2011/204/305/23.

aim and fire the Lewis gun. The aircraft was therefore rigged to fly slightly tail heavy and the controls adjusted accordingly. With these modifications carried out he was ready to resume fighting. He had not told any one, not even Major Hubbard, of the modifications which he had made to his machine. It was a sign of his independence, perhaps also a sign of the diffidence in his nature that he regarded such modifications as purely his own affair. In a letter to his parents he called it, *my latest attachment for Nieuports with which which you can make the machine fly more or less itself.*[26]

Any break from flying was welcome to the pilots and observers of the RFC and to Albert Ball, who was feeling the strain of the huge efforts which he had made during this period, it was a respite, which enabled him to stretch his mental and physical resources just a little bit further. On the 5 July he told his father he had made twelve flights from 5 am until flying became impossible, . . . *at last Nature is asking to have its own way. However, I am not done yet, I shall get at them again soon.* The award of the MC was a boost to him but he could not deny the increasing signs of mental and physical exhaustion. The squadron was flying extensively and suffering casualties in the process. Ball was also upset to learn of casualties amongst his former comrades in No.13 Squadron. He told his mother that his old squadron had lost four machines in a week and his own squadron two.[27]

The continual procession of old faces disappearing forever was familiar in all RFC Messes. He kept many of these aspects of his worries out of his letters home, but if he had anyone to whom he could write relatively freely it was Lois (of course it is possible he was also able to do so to Thelma, but his correspondence with her has disappeared). A letter to Lois on the 10 July told her that'three topping chaps' had gone missing on the 6th and that on the 9th, *four of my best pals* had gone[28] and one of the new pilots had gone missing that day after only a short time with the squadron. His father must have written to him under the influence of the'warlike' feeling at home where anti-German feeling became more intense as the war progressed. These ultra virulent feelings were not entirely shared by the men at the front and Ball explained this to his father in another letter of the 10 July:

> You ask me'to let the devils have it' when I fight. Yes, I always let
> them have all I can but really I really don't think them devils. I

26 Ball Archives 6/7/16.
27 Ball Archives 7/7/16.
28 The four members of No.11 Squadron were 2nd Lieutenants Spear and Wedgewood (both KIA) and Floyd (Died of wounds on the 11 July) and MacIntyre (POW).

only scrap because it is my duty, but I do not think anything bad about the Hun. He is just a good chap with very little guts, trying to do his best. Nothing makes me feel more rotten than to see them go down, but you see it is either them or me, so I must do my best to make it a case of them.[29]

James McCudden expressed very similar sentiments in *Five Years in the Royal Flying Corps* though not all British pilots felt the same. Mannock was an example of someone who really hated 'the Hun' and fought them with a burning hatred originating from his own political creed. The reputed remark of Manfred von Richthofen that *Once I have killed an Englishman I am never satisfied until I have killed another*, is in stark contrast in attitudes to the views held by Ball. Both fought because it was their patriotic duty but Ball still remained a civilian at heart and was upset when one of his opponents went to his death.

He had flown that morning and had seen three German two-seaters. The German aircraft were above him and he tried to climb to their altitude. The engine of his Nieuport, despite the attention given to it, was not giving full power and Ball was unable to match the altitude of the German aircraft, not being able, he claimed, to get any closer than 3,000ft below them. He returned to Savy and spent the rest of the time with his mechanics trying to get the rotary engine to run at full power. He hoped, he told his father, that the work would be completed by that evening so that the aircraft would be fit for his early morning patrol.

While Albert Ball was making his contribution to the Battle of the Somme he was fighting a different sort of battle on the home front and the subject was inevitably the relationship with Thelma. On the 10 July he wrote two letters, one to his father and one to his mother which both touched on the subject of Thelma and her acceptance by the Ball family. To his mother he wrote:

I hear you have been to Skeg. Did you go and see Thelma or invite her for tea? I expect not, but if you knew how much I wish you would, perhaps you would do so.

Now promise me one thing. When I get my next leave you will have Thelma staying at our house. You see I always go there and it really is time things were changed. Now do say that you will do

29 Ball Archives 10/7/16.

this for it will make me so happy and contented if you will. And it will be so topping to look forward to it.

Well I know you will agree. I may get four days leave before long so when I send you a letter saying when I shall arrive, you just send a letter off asking Tee over.

I have taken the matter in my own hands and have told her that when I come home to be decorated by the King, she will come up to town with my People and really that will be topping. Now wont it?

Well you will get bored if I say so much about Tee, but I just feel like it this afternoon, for I am a bit poo poo.[30]

On 16 July he was given the task of returning Nieuport A133 to the Aircraft Depot at Candas and collecting another in its place. He returned with Nieuport A117 as its replacement. It was common practice for squadrons to return the aircraft most in need of repair to Depot and collect another in its place. These might very well have been previously issued to another squadron or it might be a delivery fresh from England, or in the case of Nieuports, from the Nieuport factory. A job of this nature would have been a relief to Ball for he knew that he was desperately in need of a rest. The high operational tempo, which he had been operating since the start of the Somme offensive, had taken its toll. He had flown all the designated missions, as well as many others of his own volition. The run of casualties in the squadron had shown what dangers he faced every time he crossed the lines. He knew that he was tired and that he would not be operating at his best in this condition. He believed that if he could have a short break from flying he would be able to recover health and spirits and be his old self again. He never wished to operate at less than his best as this would mean that he was failing in his duty to his country. His father had written to him exhorting him to 'keep his pecker up' and in his reply he assured his father that this he did very easily, but, *I shall be glad when it is over, for at times I feel very whonkey and run down. But . . . if my health holds on tight I shall be OK.*[31]

A few days later he wrote to his father again:

You ask me to come back safely. Oh Yes if God wishes it I shall come back safely. And Oh I do want to. But I want to get a few more scraps yet. For one must stick at it.

30 Ball Archives 10/7/16.
31 Ball Archives 10/7/16.

You say that the Commander ought to recognize my good work in bringing down two Huns in one fight. Well not good work but good luck is what I call it. I think the Commander has tons for me. You know he came down specially to the Aerodrome and congratulated me. And that is a lot for an Army Commander to do. Isn't it?[32]

The letter also included, yet again, the topic of Thelma. Albert Ball's devotion to her at this time seems obvious but he was not able to achieve her acceptance by his family. The occasional crumbs of comfort were thrown his way in the shape of meetings or correspondence. The comments in the letter of 13 July are indicative of the situation which then existed between Albert, Thelma and the Ball family. On this occasion the differences arose from the award of the Military Cross:

Oh so you have been talking to my Thelma have you! Well I am very pleased and I know Tee is too. She says in her letter that you are one of the kindest Fathers she has ever known and you bet I agree.

Now re borrowing Thelma's Wire. You say that you will return when you get my Cross. Well I shall not get my Cross until I come to England to be decorated and as that may be two months I ask you to return the Wire before that.

Please only keep it a week for I do so want Tee to have it. You know Dad I have sent you all the Wires but that one, so you must not be greedy.

I quite understand that you would like it but you will get the Cross, so don't ask for everything. Now do be a dear and send it back in a frame as promised not later than the 24th of this month. Tee thinks you are only keeping it for one or two days and you told her so. Now don't upset the Kid by keeping it will you?

Well now I know you will think me a beast for not giving you everything but Dad I do want to give Tee a real keepsake.

You ask me to let her know how valuable it will be when I get older. You dear old thing. Do you think that it will not be taken care of? Why I bet it will be kept just as it were gold. Tee is mad with joy about it. And I don't mind telling you on the QT I am mad with joy because she is mad with joy.[33]

---

32 Ball Archives 13/7/16.
33 Ball Archives 13/7/16.

On the evening of the 16th he spoke to Major Hubbard and asked if it might be possible to have a few days off from flying. This was not a request that Hubbard could grant of his own responsibility. It would have to be passed up the chain of command, first to Wing for their approval and then to III Brigade Headquarters. This is what Hubbard did but he must have had his doubts as to how the request would be received.. Hubbard, who saw his pilots every day, would have recognised the symptoms of combat stress which Ball was displaying. He was a kind and humane man by nature and would certainly have given the application a favourable comment when he sent it on. The reply came back from Brigadier-General J.F.A. Higgins (nicknamed 'bum & eyeglass' in the RFC) to the effect that if Ball wanted a rest then he could cease to fly scouts and return to flying BE2cs and a posting to No.8 Squadron was arranged. Higgins was not an unpopular figure in the Corps and could not be described in any sense as a martinet. He was, however, a regular Army Officer and would have been shocked and surprised by a request from a junior officer to stop fighting for a while. He was also reflecting the views of General Trenchard, who did not sympathise with pilots who were emotionally and physically tired by a period of operations. He (Trenchard) had reluctantly agreed to a request from Smith-Barry, the Squadron Commander, which was supported by Hugh Dowding, the Wing Commander, to relieve No.60 Squadron temporarily from front line duties but it is evident that he did not agree with the move. Dowding, for his part, was a 'marked man' thereafter. Trenchard recognised the sacrifices made by pilots and observers who had been seriously wounded in the course of their duty but he had more difficulty in recognising that a man could be wounded and ineffective in other ways than the obvious physical wounds of combat.

The posting to No.8 squadron, condemning Ball to fly BE2cs again was a harsh response to the request. There is no doubt that other more imaginative and humane solutions could have been found to the problem which Ball's request presented. A look at his fighting record would have shown that he was not an officer who had ever shirked any duty before and had indeed carried out many operations on his own initiative. It might have been possible to have given Ball a week or so off, to tour the squadrons along the front to explain his methods to other pilots. This would have given Ball the break from operational flying which he was seeking but would have kept him performing a useful task for the benefit of the RFC.

With an order from Headquarters Major Hubbard had no choice but to arrange Albert Ball's transfer from No.11 Squadron to No.8 Squadron and Ball left the Squadron on 17 July. Hubbard sent a note to Major Patrick Playfair, the Commanding Officer of No.8 Squadron outlining Ball's activities while with No.11 Squadron and including the comment 'You will find Ball a good little chap if managed in the right way. He is young, so naturally wants a little more rope than the older pilots'. Hubbard expressed the hope that if, after a few weeks with No.8, Ball felt like returning to No.11 Squadron he would be pleased to have him back.

CHAPTER FIVE

The 'Rest Cure'
Ball with No.8 Squadron

T he day after he arrived in No.8 Squadron at Bellevue Ball told his father about the events which had taken place:

The day before yesterday we had a big day. At night I was feeling very rotten and my nerves were poo-poo. Naturally, I cannot keep on for ever, so at night I went to see the CO and asked him if I could have a short rest, and not fly for a few days. He said he would do his best.

What has taken place has been that I have been sent to No.8 Squadron, back on BE2cs. Oh, I am feeling in the dumps.[1]

The squadron Record Book for No.8 Squadron[2] shows Ball taking part in four bombing missions, four artillery observation missions and one flight which is called a Patrol, the regular activities of the squadron between 24 July and the 12 August. Apart from these missions there was his well known flight behind the German lines at night to drop a spy. Though the records only show Ball's involvement from the 24 July it is known from his own correspondence that from his arrival on the 17 July he flew two operations on the 19 and 21 July.

This latter operation was a bombing raid in which he was a member of a formation of seven BEs led by Captain Parker. The mission was to bomb a railway bridge at Aubigny-au-Bac in order to interrupt the flow of German reinforcements to the front. The BEs were loaded with one 112lb bomb each, the heaviest war load they could carry. Even to carry this amount the Observer had to be left behind, making any defence against attack even more impractical. Ball flew in BE No 1709 and completed the mission successfully. Two German scouts were seen but

---

1 Ball Archives.
2 PRO AIR1/1668/204/109/3.

they made no attempt to interfere with the operation and all the aircraft returned to base.

The following day Ball wrote to his father that he was feeling so much better and that he believed that he would be going back to No.11 Squadron again in a few days.[3] However, this was too optimistic and he continued with his work on BEs.

The separation from his Nieuport and his posting to fly his least favourite aircraft, the BE2c, must have been a severe jolt for Ball. He felt he was being prevented from carrying out his duty in the best way possible, flying Nieuport Scouts. His moods had always tended to vary between the peaks and troughs of great elation and low depressions. In his current situation he must have looked on what had happened to him as an example of what he called 'army law'. However, he soon begin to settle in his new role and by the 20 July he could write to his father that, *all is well again, for I am well on the way to being OK*. He also said that he had managed to get in the flight of Captain Parker who had just returned from leave. Ball regarded this posting as a bonus which would make his time in the squadron more tolerable, though in what connection he knew, or knew of, Parker is not known. He also had an opportunity of discussing his situation direct with General Higgins, for he told his parents that Higgins had been very 'decent' but that instead of the three weeks rest which he had wanted Higgins told him that as he (Ball) had had so much luck recently that he ought not to have asked for a rest!

He had to adapt again to life flying in a Corps squadron. In No.11 Squadron he had gone through an intense period of fighting. He had flown additional patrols as he felt the urge to come to grips with the enemy, in his mind the sole purpose for which he was fighting the war. The routine now was very different. In a BE2c squadron there would be no more lone excursions to hunt out the enemy. He would now fly only when ordered, in a set routine. This lessening in the intensity of the operations which he was called upon to carry out, though each operation would have had some degree of danger, may very well have had a calming effect on his nerves. He was no longer pushing himself to the limit but operating strictly to orders.

---

3 Ball Archives 22/7/116.

He would have been well aware of the shortcomings of the BE2c and the relative defencelessness of the aircraft if attacked.[4]

In addition he now had an Observer and the responsibility of having to fly with someone else in the aircraft was something he did not welcome. The risks, which he was willing to take with his own life, were not possible when he was also responsible for the life of another man. In No.13 Squadron he had had a close relationship with his friend Villiers: they were both of the same stamp and more than willing to engage the enemy whenever they met him. In No.8 Squadron he did not yet have anyone with whom he could enjoy the same close relationship.

There was one activity which the RFC carried out for which the BE2c was particularly suitable. This was the landing of agents behind the German Lines. The work was always carried out by volunteers and, of course, involved flying and navigation by night. Once the front had solidified the best way of getting agents into occupied territory was by secret flights. The first such flights had taken place at about the time of the Battle of Loos and had continued since then.

Such operations were not without danger. Apart from the possibilities of a crash while landing or taking off in the dark, the pilot dropping an agent in enemy territory was liable to be shot as a spy if captured. As there were no parachutes by means of which such passengers could be delivered it necessitated landing with the risk not only of discovery on the ground but of a landing in an unfamiliar field in the dark. The first such flight carried out by the British was when a BE2c of No.6 squadron, flown by Captain T.W. Mulcahy-Morgan, who attempted to land his aircraft in a field which was too small. Although one of the best pilots in the RFC Mulcahy-Morgan was unable to complete the task and smashed his BE on a tree as he attempted to get into the field. Both agent and pilot were injured and taken prisoner by the Germans. Somehow Mulcahy-Morgan escaped the summary execution he might have expected and survived to go into a POW Camp from which he escaped and made a successful run home. Despite this early set back the flights continued, for the need for intelligence was continuous and insatiable. There were always volunteers to fly the planes and equally

---

4 That the BE2c was not entirely defenceless was shown by Lanoe Hawker to Albert Ball. The latter loved to practise his stalking techniques on BE2cs which he met behind the British lines. Diving on a BE2c one day he was amazed to find that the BE was so well handled that he was unable to get into his usual attacking position. Eventually Ball gave up and flew home but he made enquiries as to who the pilot of the BE might have been and was gratified to find that it had been Hawker of whom there was no finer pilot in the RFC. See Barker *The Royal Flying Corps in France*. Mons to the Somme pp151-2.

brave men who undertook the task of the secret agent in enemy territory.[5]

Such a task had now been allotted to No.8 Squadron and Ball had volunteered to undertake it. According to Kiernan[6] the job had been attempted by all of the three flight commanders of the squadron but although the spy was carried over the lines several times, no attempt had been made to land and the pilots returned to base with the mission not accomplished. They took the view that the attempt to put a BE down in the dark in a strange field, carried too high a degree of risk and that while they were willing to attempt it they would do so only under orders. Lieutenant Clarke had also tried on the 19 and 22 July but had been unable to land because of ground mist.

Not only was Ball attracted by the risk involved in this unusual task but he also thought that, if carried out successfully, it would bring his name to the attention of Wing and make his return to No.11 Squadron more certain. He approached Major Playfair with a request to be allowed to attempt the job and was given permission after Playfair had relayed the request to Wing.[7]

On being given the job, Ball was told to practice night flying. He took up BE2c 1709 on the 24 July and flew round in the darkness for some time. He was familiarising himself with how the world looked at night. As it was still the longer summer nights the darkness was not intense, but he stayed up until 9.30 p.m. and found that, by what light was available, he could distinguish different crops in the fields surrounding the airfield. Having landed 1709 he took up another BE later that evening, No. 1752, but engine failure after thirty minutes caused him to land back on the airfield.

In a letter home on the 25 July Ball told them of the task which he had volunteered to undertake:

> I am going back to my old squadron in a few days, but first I have promised to do a job, or at least try to do a job for the squadron. It is a rotten job, and one that has often been tried without success but, if God helps me in his usual way, I shall pull it off. I heard of it and asked for the job. The CO asked the General if I could do it, and at first he said 'No', but yesterday he said I could try, so the first good chance I get the Ball will have another run.

---

5 See Ralph Barker pp128/137 for details of the RFC's involvement in these missions.
6 *Captain Ball VC DSO* by RH Kiernan (John Hamilton 1933)pp67.
7 If the recollections of Frederick Lang, his fitter, are to be relied on, Ball had already landed in German territory while with No.13 Squadron. See *Voices in Flight* p142.

If this is successful I shall run slow for a time, as my nerves are
not quite what they were.[8]

This letter shows that Ball had obviously been given a promise that he
would soon return to his old squadron. There is nothing to indicate,
however, that his return to No.11 Squadron was conditional on his first
carrying out the agent drop. The job was scheduled for the 28 July and
Ball spent the rest of the day preparing. He had been allotted BE 2c 4138
for the task and at 8.15 pm with the agent, named in the Squadron
Records as M. Victor, in the front seat he took off from Belle Vue
Airfield.

At that time of day it was still daylight and as he crossed the lines
he was spotted and attacked by three German scouts. This could have
spelt disaster for the mission but he managed to evade their attack and
continued his flight as the darkness closed in. The lone BE was spotted
by the German anti-aircraft gunners and a barrage of shells was
directed towards him. Finally, Ball was able to identify the area in
which he was to make the drop and began to search for the field he
had been told to look for. Succesful in this, he set the BE down in what
appeared to be a deserted area. He looked at Victor and waited for him
to get out of his cockpit, but the agent refused to budge. This was not
a situation which Ball had contemplated and it first puzzled and then
angered him. Nothing he could do would persuade Victor to disembark
so Ball took off again and made several more landings to try and get
the agent to leave the plane. However, the latter was sufficiently
alarmed for his own safety by the attention that had been directed
towards the BE on its outward flight, let alone the buzzing around of
occupied territory, that he became even more resolute in his refusal to
leave. Finally, Ball had no alternative but to terminate the mission and
return home, landing back at Belle Vue at 9.50pm.

Though the purpose of the mission had not been achieved, General
Higgins appreciated the efforts Ball had made to carry it out and his
courage in volunteering for the trip. He congratulated Ball on his efforts
and more importantly for Ball he promised that he would soon be able
to return to No.11 Squadron. A message also came for Ball from Hugh
Trenchard, thanking him for his efforts. Ball told his parents of the
interview with Higgins and the General's response that he wanted Ball
to do a full month with No.8 Squadron before he was reposted. As he

---

8 Ball Archives 25/7/16.

wrote in his letter . . . *only two more weeks of BE2cs and then I shall go mad dog again.*[9]

On a personal level he still corresponded regularly with his parents about Thelma. He had heard from the latter that she had now received the wire back from Ball's father but with it was a note that it was being returned because his son had asked for it to be done. Thelma generously responded that she was quite willing for Ball's father to keep the wire until the MC was awarded and Ball had to acquiesce in this situation as it made Thelma happy.

Possibly with the spy mission in mind as well as the 'normal' operations he carried out, Ball gave his father instructions as to what he was to do if he was forced down behind the German lines and became a POW. His father was to write a letter to Thelma every week to let her know all the information he had. In addition he was to invite Thelma over to Sedgeley House occasionally.

With the knowledge that his time in No.8 squadron was now coming to a close Ball had something to look forward to, but events were to prove that he would have to wait another two weeks for the much desired event. This did not, however, stop him from taking his full share in the work of the squadron. On the 30 July, in BE2d 5799, he took part in a bombing raid on the rail junction at St. Leger. He was part of a force of seven aircraft contributed by No.8 Squadron to a total force of thirty aircraft. When the formation leader had to drop out with engine trouble Ball assumed the leading position and led the force to successfully complete the mission.

The following day, in the same aircraft, he took part in another bombing mission, on an ammunition dump. These missions were flown without an Observer in order that the maximum load of bombs could be carried. However, on the 1 August he was scheduled for an artillery registration mission. He flew in BE2d 2498 with Lieutenant Hervey as his Observer and carried out a successful shoot for the guns of the 46th Division.

On the 2 August Ball, flying BE 2495, took part in another bombing attack. In the afternoon he test flew BE 6876 with Hervey and later flew it on a bombing raid. On this same day the squadron records mention a test flight carried out by 2nd Lieutenant K.L. Caldwell a young New Zealander who had joined the squadron on the 29 July and was, in course of time, to follow Ball into No.60 Squadron. Caldwell was later

9 Ball Archives 31/7/16.

to be Commanding Officer of No.74 Squadron in 1918. He gained the reputation of being one of the best pilots in the RFC and in one engagement had out flown Werner Voss. If his shooting had been of the standard of such 'aces' as McCudden his victory score could well have been double its accredited twenty-five. Even in No.8 squadron he managed to shoot down a Roland CII in a BE2d as testament to his fighting and aggressive qualities. Caldwell later recorded his memories and thoughts on Ball for Chaz Bowyer:

> Ball was not very long in No.8, but with adjoining tents in the orchard at Bellevue, just across from 8's aerodrome, I did get to know him as much as one could in that short spell. I remember he was pretty upset at being sent over to us to BE2cs from his Nieuport, but we understood that he had become a bit 'difficult' to handle, and his coming to us was in the way of a calming down process at the orders of the Brigade CO General Higgins.
>
> Ball had been doing a lot of flying, many hours a day, and probably badly needed a rest. He would have got this respite with us as our artillery observation role etc on slow old BE2c's would lack much of the excitement he was used to.
>
> The 1916 summer was a lovely, fine, warm one and some of us would gather outside Ball's tent, where he played his gramophone in the long evenings. He was a hero to us, with his successes in many air fights, and he looked the part too; young, alert, ruddy complexion, dark hair and eyes. He was supposed to be a 'loner', but we found him to be friendly. One feels now, looking back, that he would have lacked the balanced capacity for planning or employing strategy in the air, as did Mannock and McCudden to name two who did. I, for one, was not surprised to hear the sad news of his going 'missing' from a No.56 Squadron patrol later. One felt that it could only be a matter of time before he 'bought it', as he was shot about so often.[10]

In the afternoon of the 3 August, Ball went up with Lieutenant Palmer in BE No 1709 on artillery observation. The mission was successfully completed without interference from German aircraft and they returned just after 7pm. On the 6 August he flew with Palmer again on

---

10 Quoted by Bowyer pp86/87.

a similar mission in BE 5738 and, in BE2d 5876, they flew artillery registration missions on the 8 August, taking off for the second mission only forty minutes after landing from the first.

For the rest of his time in No.8 Squadron Ball seems to have flown 5876 including a sortie on the 9 August which was planned as a balloon attack. He had discussed the plan with his flight commander, Captain Parker, suggesting that the two of them could take part in an attack on the German balloon line. Parker received the idea favourably and cleared it with Major Playfair. Ball took Hervey with him on this mission and the result is best described in Hervey's own words:

> We climbed to 4,000ft and hung around until it was time to go. As soon as we poked our nose across No Man's Land the ever watchful anti-aircraft guns started up. I looked across the five miles or so between us and Parker's machine. It was easy to spot. Parker was lower than we were and making for his target, as always, like a bull at a gate. His machine was surrounded by the rather innocent looking white puffs of shrapnel and by the very much more vicious and noisy black bursts of high explosives. Meanwhile the gunners were putting up a spectacular display around our machine. It had been hit a number of times by stray fragments but the damage was superficial.
>
> We saw the balloon starting to descend and soon it was going down at an astonishing rate, swaying drunkenly under the pull of the winch cable. Ball started to dive and the next moments were a confused jumble of sights and sounds. Men running as we fired down on the balloon, machine gunning from emplacements round the winch site, a glimpse of the balloon Observer floating down by parachute, and an exploding shell knocking off a chunk of our port lower wingtip and fracturing a main spar.
>
> Ball was yelling at me to keep my eyes skinned for Huns as I switched the Lewis gun onto the rear mounting, and we started for home. Fortunately the sky was empty of aircraft We crossed low over the German trenches with a final burst of rifle and machine gun fire from the troops who doubtless had been eagerly waiting to join in the fun. As we passed over the lines there was a beautiful silence except for the pleasant sound of our RAF engine pounding away on all cylinders. We landed back at

the aerodrome 55 minutes after take-off, and compared notes with Parker and Erskine (Parker's Observer) while our ground crews crowded round inspecting two rather tatty aircraft.[11]

For this sortie Ball had modified the BE so that Hervey could fire his gun down through the floor of his cockpit as an easier way of being able to sight the balloon, a modification which he was to later fit to his SE5 in No.56 Squadron.

Albert Ball flew his last mission with No.8 squadron on the 12 August, again in BE2d 5876. He was one of a formation of BEs which bombed the village of Beugny. On the return trip he spotted an Albatros two-seater and attacked it. With no observer, and no synchronising gear, this was a feat not easily achieved and he had to operate a Lewis Gun mounted within reach of his cockpit and mounted at an angle to clear the propeller. The Albatros chose not to dispute the matter with Ball and dived steeply away.

That evening he carried out his last duty for the squadron by testing a BE12. The BE 12 was a development of the BE2c but with a more powerful engine and no observer. The original design was not intended as a single seat fighter. Eventually, however, efforts were made to fit a single synchronised Vickers machine gun. The first squadron, No.19, operating BE12s, arrived in France on the 30 July and it did not take long for the deficiencies of the machine to be exposed by operations in France. They were perfectly adequate for Home Defence where no opposition was to be expected but in France they were a failure. Why Ball was asked to test one is not clear for all that needed to be known about the operational capabilities of the type was already known. He was not impressed with the performance and when asked what he thought of it replied tartly, 'Its like all BEs – bloody awful!'. This reflected the fact that having flown the Nieuport with its sharp responses He could not but find the stability and sluggishness of the BE12 unsatisfactory.

On the 13 August he was flight testing some of the Squadron BEs and the following day, his 20th and last birthday, he received a telephone call from Major Hubbard to say that he was to return to No.11 squadron and that a new Nieuport had been allocated for him. He evidently had some previous knowledge of the decision for he had written on the 8th, *I go back to No.11 on the 14th.*[12]

---

11 See Bowyer pp70.
12 Ball Archives 8/8/16.

And on the 13th, *I am going back to my Scout tonight so I shall soon be out again. Oh! Wont it be A1.*[13]

He noted in his letter of the 8th that since he had left No.11 Squadron the Scout Flight had not brought down any more German aircraft. The news was the best birthday present he could have received. and he wrote to his parents showing his delight:

> You bet I shall be able to get my own back now. And wont it be OK to see my garden again? Do you know that if I had not been sent to this Squadron [ie No. 8] I should have been a Flight (commander)by now and three pips? I think it has done me good being here, for I now know artillery work and bombing. All this helps to make a good flying officer.[14]

The reference to the 'three pips' in the letter is to possible promotion to Captain if he had stayed with No.11 Squadron. He had been promoted to full Lieutenant with effect from the 1 August 1916 but in the way of the services had yet to receive permission to wear the badges of this rank. He had to wait for a further 6 weeks before his promotion to Captain was sanctioned.

At about the time his transfer was taking place the first fruits of the newspaper publicity, which had been aired about his deeds, began to appear in the form of letters from family and friends as well as some from young girls. The former letters he sent to Thelma to keep while the latter he just penned a few lines in reply though it is unclear whether he told Thelma about them.

He packed his belongings at Bellevue and made his way to Savy. He found the hut he had built was still habitable and moved in. He had made sure that his garden had been looked after while he was away and he found it was flourishing. He, no doubt, also went to the Hangar to see the new Nieuport, A201, which had been allotted to him. This was a Nieuport 17, the latest development of the Nieuport 16, and was an aircraft which had better handling qualities than that which he had been used to. With this aircraft he could now begin again personal war.

---

13 Ball Archives 13/8/16.
14 Ball Archives 14/8/16.

CHAPTER SIX

The Rising Star
Albert Ball's Combats
August 1916

The period ahead of Albert Ball was to be that of his greatest successes. He became known, not only throughout the RFC, but also to the outside world, first to French and other foreign newspapers and then to the British press. By the time he came home again he was a national hero and feted as such, especially in his home town.

His successful fighting career over these months, using the methods he had developed in his earlier experience, brought him a well deserved reputation for fearlessness, though of course fear was never absent from life in the air. He was only too well aware what the likely outcome was. As he told his parents, any pilot who stuck at air fighting for long was likely to fall victim sooner or later. Mick Mannock was once asked what he intended to do after the war. His reply was that there would be no 'after the war' for a fighter pilot.

Ball easily settled back into his life with No.11 Squadron. He was pleased to find that his hut was still standing and that his garden patch was thriving. He moved back in straight away and told his parents in a letter on the 16 August that he was 'back again in my dear old hut'.

One of the pilots who had joined No.11 squadron during Ball's absence was William Fry. He had been allowed by Major Hubbard to fly single-seaters and after a bad start, crashing a Bristol Scout, he soon became a member of C Flight, the Scout Flight. He was taken round the squadron to meet the other pilots and amongst these was Albert Ball and Fry's impressions are recorded in his autobiography written sixty years later:

It was at this time that I first met Albert Ball who was in the flight. Foot was taking me round and introducing me to the other pilots. Ball was standing outside his canvas living hut near the hangars; around it he had laid out a small flower garden where he spent a lot of his spare time. No one could say he was welcoming or forthcoming, he was briefly polite and then carried on with what he was doing. All the same he was bound to make an impression on anyone. He was short and slight, beautifully proportioned, with black hair, dark eyes and a rosy complexion almost of the kind one would associate with a girl. Withdrawn and not sociable in the Mess he would escape to his hut as soon as he could, where he could be heard sometime practising his violin. He always played his piece in Squadron concerts and even now I can remember that his usual contribution was the old stand-by 'Humoresque'.[1]

In retrospect Fry looked back and gave this verdict on the Albert Ball he knew:

He was a skilled, self-taught fighter well before most of us had gathered much idea what it was all about or had found opportunities open to us of engaging in personal combat in the air when and where we liked . . .

He was intolerant of any interference from senior officers who lacked knowledge of the job . . . His was the only Nieuport in the flight and he was very particular about his Lewis gun and spent hours on the ground-range testing it and lining up the sights. I had then not been long enough in the Squadron to get to know him well, but then no one did and I cannot remember his having any close friends.

Ball was utterly fearless and uncommunicative. Though he was considered somewhat unfriendly, he was never unpopular and did not make unkind remarks to or about anyone. Unexpectedly sensitive, he was nonetheless a self-effacing, skilled and dedicated killer with no other motive than to use his machine and armament to shoot down enemy aeroplanes. There was in his attitude none of that sporting element which to a certain extent formed the basis of many scout pilots' approach to

---

1 Fry p78.

air fighting. Ball never made jokes about it. In the nature of things he was bound to be killed sooner or later as he always looked for and never refused a fight.[2]

Although Ball had probably arrived at the squadron on the 14 August (the squadron records are missing) it is not certain when he flew his first patrol in his new Nieuport. The letter of the 16 August, quoted above, records that, flying Nieuport A 201, he had a combat with five German 2-seaters escorted by a Roland 2-seater. The Roland is credited to him as definitely forced to land and two other German aircraft made to dive away. In his usual manner Ball had spotted the Germans before they had seen him. He dived and fired a full drum into the Roland but this was not effective and the Roland pilot turned out of the path of Ball and then came round to attack him. The Nieuport out manoeuvred the German two-seater; Ball secured his favourite firing position and fired another drum at only 20 yards range. This was enough to send the Roland down with a wounded or dead Observer to crash land near St. Leger. Having disposed of the escort Ball attacked the reconnaissance machines and fired his remaining ammunition at them. Two of the German machines dived away from the formation but still under control. Ball was now out of ammunition and returned home.

Albert Ball had easily slipped back into his old routine at No.11 squadron. He lived in his hut on the aerodrome so as to be close to his machine and able to fly whenever he got the opportunity. He did not live in the Mess or eat there and asked his parents to send him tinned meats so he could eat in his hut thereby maintaining a permanent state of readiness. As usual in his off-duty time he tended his garden which offered great comfort and interest to him. He was therefore to a large extent cut off from the companionship of his fellow officers. He did not indulge in the boisterous antics of the other members of the Officers Mess and seems to have rarely indulged in alcohol. He had dedicated his life to fighting and allowed nothing to distract him. In this he was happy with his own company and although friendly to others he did not need company to support him. He had his family and his belief in God to get him through and throughout his career he leant heavily on these.

On 20 August Ball was told by Major Hubbard that he was to occupy the position of temporary flight commander while the permanent

2 Fry pp78/79.

occupant was on leave. This did not mean promotion for him, he remained a Lieutenant, but he had been told that he had been recommended for promotion. He wrote to his mother on this day:

> So sorry that I have been such an age without writing you a line, but work has been on all sides, so it had to come first.
>
> I am acting Flight Commander just now, so have many little jobs to do . . .
>
> Re addressing my letters. Lt & MC. I have been recommended for a second pip, but it is not through yet. Re the MC (M.C. is not put at the end of my name) only MC is, if you manage to get it.
>
> Hut and garden are very topping just now. I am writing the letter in my Hut with the door wide open. It is OK.
>
> I think all the Scouts are going to No. 60 Squadron before long, if this is so I shall go with them. But they may come here, so I shall only change my Squadron not my hut.
>
> Well Tee is going on OK and so am I, in fact all is OK.
>
> PS Am just off up after a Hun.[3]

There was no success for Ball in the sortie which he mentions at the end of his letter. The letter also gives the first news that a move to No.60 squadron by all the Scouts attached to No.11 Squadron was to be made.

The following day was one of intense activity for Ball. He flew eight sorties, which included the voluntary ones, undertaken in order to seek out German aircraft. All this effort was unproductive, however, and the day passed without a decisive combat.

In his Nieuport 17 A201 he took off early on the 22nd and went up over the lines seeking his prey. Again his run of bad luck continued until 7pm that evening when he was escorting a formation of FE2bs of the squadron. The formation crossed the lines at 5,000ft and soon met up with a German formation of fifteen machines both Rolands and LVGs. The RFC Communiqué reporting this engagement indicates that this formation was engaged by the FEs only ('assisted by one Nieuport'). One machine was sent down out of control by the FE of 2nd Lt Morris and Lt Rees which was later seen crashed. Three others were driven down by the rest of the formation. The communiqué also

---

3 Ball Archives 20/8/1916.

mentions that Ball himself engaged three separate formations of
German aircraft in his defence of the FE formation. His first
engagement was with seven Rolands south of Bapaume. Ball dived on
the formation and, getting to the east of them, attacked the rear
machine, into which he emptied 1½ drums of Lewis. At the sound of
the first shots the formation scattered, but Ball stuck with his target
firing continuously. The German Observer returned the fire as Ball
turned to change the empty first drum. With drum fitted Ball came in
and closed to 15 yards and under the effect of his fire the Roland began
to sideslip falling vertically before again turning on its side and in that
position hitting the ground west of Bapaume.

After this combat Ball turned away to rejoin the FEs but saw five
more Roland two-seaters coming from the south-west at 7,000ft. Ball
was slightly below this level and climbed up under the rear of the
German formation. As was now becoming his style of attack, he
secured a firing position under the rear Roland and fired a full drum
into the area of the pilot's cockpit and engine at what he estimated as
10 yards range. The German pilot did not react to this attack, possibly
due to his being wounded, and Ball had time to change the drum and
fire another full drum into the fuselage of the Roland. The Roland
turned in a wing down attitude and then began to fall emitting smoke
and flames from the fuselage.

Ball then came under attack from three of the other Rolands, who
engaged him with both their front and rear guns. He closed with the
nearest German and fired his last drum of Lewis into it from only 20ft.
The effect was immediate and the Roland fell out of control, with the
Observer mortally wounded, to crash on the roof of a house. The
remaining Germans pressed their attacks on Ball and drove him down
to 2,000ft before he was able to shake them off and head for the British
lines. He was now very low on fuel as well as ammunition and he
landed at Bellevue to replenish both.

With both fuel and ammunition replaced Ball took off again to
rejoin the FEs but once again ran into a formation of three Rolands
over Vaux. He attacked all three of the formation in turn without
success, but the attack was enough to cause the Germans to dive away
and head east back to their own lines.[4]

By now low on petrol, again out of ammunition, and with his
aircraft having suffered damage, Ball was unable to make it back to his

4 See Cole pp229/231 for RFC Communiqués.

own aerodrome and force landed at Senlis. He was emotionally and physically exhausted and after getting a message through to No.11 Squadron to send a repair party he settled down to sleep beside his Nieuport. The repair party from No.11 Squadron arrived during the night and carried out the necessary repairs to enable Ball to fly the machine home the following morning.

In his letter to his parents describing this action, in which he misdates to the 22 August, he listed the damage to his Nieuport as *My windscreen hit in four places, mirror broken, the spar of the left plane broken . . .* , but he considered it, *good sport and good luck.*[5]

He sent the windscreen home and asked his parents to make sure that both Thelma and Cyril got to see it.

The mirror mentioned was a personal modification which he had had fitted to the centre section cut-out within easy view of the cockpit. It was a motor car mirror and it gave him a little extra visibility in the vital rear direction to warn him if any enemy was trying to get behind him. It became a standard fitting on later fighters on both sides and in the 1939-1945 War.

With this final combat, so typical of his aggressive attitude, Ball's career in No.11 squadron came to an end. The rumours which had been circulating, of a move to No.60 squadron, were true. Ball flew over to No.60 Squadron on the 23 August and spent the rest of that day and the 24th settling in and getting his machine ready. He had a short unsuccessful flight on that day chasing one German two-seater which he failed to catch. He also met General Higgins who congratulated him on his fighting record and said that he was having a board put up in the trenches with Ball's name on it to 'frighten the Huns!' As Ball told his parents, *So much for the G. I am now in his good books again.*[6]

Ball's new squadron had first been deployed on the Western Front on the 16 June 1916 equipped with an assortment of Morane aircraft: four Morane Bullets comprised A Flight; four Morane Parasols B Flight and four Morane Biplanes C Flight. The Parasols of B Flight had been replaced by further Bullets before the deployment in France.[7]

The squadron had been withdrawn from the fighting three weeks earlier at the request of Smith-Barry the Commanding Officer. It had suffered a period of high casualties and morale was low. It was re-formed as a single-seater scout squadron, equipped with Nieuports

---

5 Ball Archives 26/8/1916.
6 Ditto.
7 See *60 Squadron – A Detailed History* by Joe Warne. Cross & Cockade Great Britain Journal. Vol.11 No.1 pp 29/30.

and Ball was to take his Nieuport A201 and join the squadron when it returned to operations. Before leaving for No.60 Squadron, Ball persuaded his friend Captain Foot to give an exhibition of aerobatics to No.11 Squadron. Foot was to follow him to No.60 Squadron as a casualty replacement within a month.

Their new squadron was based at Izel-le-Hameau between St. Pol and Arras, moving there on the 23 August. The airfield was a large area with three squadrons operating from it. On landing Ball reported to Robert Smith-Barry, an original member of the RFC and one whose name would be forever associated with the method of flying training which he later created at Gosport.

Smith-Barry knew of Ball by reputation, and the reports which had been written on him by Major Hubbard. He recognised, in what he saw of Ball, and what he had read, that Ball was an individualist, with his own way of fighting which was beginning to show results. If he was to get the most out of Ball it would not be as part of a flight or as a flight commander. Ball had to be allowed to operate in his own way and on this basis Smith-Barry gave him virtually a free hand to continue fighting the way he liked best. Within a day, Smith-Barry had informed Ball that he was being promoted to captain and would be a flight commander. Ball told his parents that Thelma liked the ranks of both 2nd Lieutenant and Captain but not Lieutenant!

With his personal Nieuport A201, Ball soon settled at his new squadron. He was given two airmen to look after his Nieuport. One was Corporal Walter Bourne an experienced man, who was to be responsible for the mechanical side while the rigger was Corporal J.R. Henderson. As we have already seen from the reminiscences of William Fry, Ball liked to look after the alignment of his gun himself.

Soon after his posting to No.60 Squadron Ball was presented with a red spinner to fit on his Nieuport. It was the work of air mechanic Charles Simpkins and seems to have been an old Morane spinner which Simpkins had adapted. Ball was delighted with it and fitted it to all his Nieuports from then on. The spinner became known to the Germans and, according to Stanley Vincent,[8] one of the No.60 Squadron pilots, who flew Ball's Nieuport when the latter was on leave, found that the Germans dived away as soon as the red nosed Nieuport appeared.[9]

8 later Air Vice Marshal Stanley Vincent.
9 *Flying Fever* by S.F. Vincent (London 1972) pp30/31.

Vincent's impression of Ball was of a man dedicated to duty and of outstanding courage. In one of their conversations Ball told Vincent that once, when he had run out of ammunition, he made his escape by opting to fly very close underneath a two seater which was heading in the general direction of the lines. He chose this position because he was so close that the plane that was sheltering him could not bank away from the fear of collision and the rest could not fire at him for fear of hitting their companion! This incident is not reported in any of the existing combat reports. Because of Ball's decision to live 'on the job' he had a solitary existence away from the companionship of his colleagues. According to Vincent this isolation earned him the nickname of 'the lonely pillock' a (rude) alternative to his surname.[10]

On the 25 August Ball opened his score with his new squadron. He took off on his morning patrol and at 10,000ft over Bapaume saw two Rolands, which he describes in his report as 'one old type and one new type.'[11]

This is assumed to be a reference to the original CII and the CIIa. The CIIa had minor structural differences, which would not have been obvious to Ball, but it had been fitted with a forward firing machine gun, the lack of which had been a complaint of the operational crews flying the first version.

As soon as Ball saw the two Rolands he closed with them and secured his firing position underneath the nearest machine, noting that it had a 3-ply fuselage. He fired one drum at 20 yards range and then turned away to change drums. Once this was accomplished he bore in again and fired half of another drum. The Roland immediately began to dive and forced landed in a cornfield. Ball had followed it down to 3,000ft, but there was no return fire from the Observer. The second of the Rolands also dived away, the Observer firing at Ball from the rear cockpit.

Having seen his opponent crash, Ball climbed to regain his height. It was not long before he saw another Roland at about 7,000ft and immediately chased it. However, he was unable to get close enough to engage and he broke off the pursuit and returned home.

Although no combat report exists, in a letter home of the 25 August he states that he had been in three fights, with a result of two machines brought down and one crashed.[12]

---

10 ditto pp31.
11 NA AIR1/1225/204/5/2634.
12 Ball Archives 25/8/16.

The 26th and 27th provided no success for Ball. Flying was restricted for most of the day by the weather and it was not until evening that limited operations could begin. Ball had been up, despite the weather, flying well behind the German lines but had seen nothing and returned home with no success to report.

The 28th, however, was a day of success, starting in the morning when on an Offensive Patrol. Ball saw two Rolands south-east of Bapaume and dived to secure his firing position. Still unseen by his opponents, he came up under his selected target and fired a drum into it at 20 yards range. Ball then changed drums and again fired into the underneath of the Roland. The pilot, Leutnant Joachim von Arnim, had been killed by Ball's fire and the Roland began to fall steeply. The Observer, who had a set of duplicate controls, wrestled to control the machine, and succeeded in crash landing near Transloy. Arnim was flying his fourth patrol of the day and had earlier scored his first victory. He was a talented pilot and had been selected by Boelcke to join the newly forming *Jagdstaffel 2,* whose pilots would include Manfred von Richthofen, and the flight on which Ball had intercepted him had been his last for his old unit, *Fliegerabteilung 207, Kampstaffel 3.*[13]

Ball next saw another two-seater over Bapaume. Still having ammunition left he pursued for a short distance but, mindful of his low fuel state, he gave up the chase and returned to base.

That evening was a period of intense activity for Ball in A201. He was the escort for a formation of BEs and FEs which were on a bombing mission to strike the ammunition dump at Loupart Wood. Ball took off at about 6.30pm and crossed the lines in advance of the bombing formation at 10,000ft. He spotted a mixed formation of Rolands and LVGs about 3,000ft below him and dived to attack. He came up under the nearest machine and emptied the contents of one drum in short bursts alongside the underside of its belly. The German dived out of the formation and force landed (Ball called it 'uncrashed') in a field near Grevillers. He then attacked a Roland over the Cambrai-Bapaume Road. Firing from underneath he used up one drum at his opponent and forced it to land near Beugny but without visible damage.

Following this engagement Ball started to climb back to the bombing formation but at 9,000ft he saw a formation made up of two Rolands and two LVGs. The Germans were east of Bapaume and about

13 Bowyer pp78.

2,000ft below him. He dived, firing as he went passing through the middle of the German aircraft as they broke formation. He came up under the nearest one firing a drum into the underneath of the fuselage. The German machine fell away from the formation and Ball followed it down, closing to 20 yards, still firing. The Roland continued its nosedive until it struck the ground east of Ayette.

The final combat of the evening saw Ball attack a mixed formation of Rolands, LVGs and Albatros. He climbed above them and dived into the middle of the formation, which split up as he passed through. He secured his firing position under the nearest machine and fired one drum. The German machine dived away and Ball followed, but he found that the ammunition drum was jammed. With his gun now inoperative Ball broke away and returned home.

The 29th was a day of unfavourable weather with high winds, strong enough to blow down a Bessoneau Hangar at No.21 Squadron, wrecking all the machines inside. The 30th was yet another day of bad weather with continuous rain, which put a stop to all flying. The rest was no doubt welcome to Ball and to others. He took the chance to reply to some of the letters he had waiting. It seems that he had been asked by Major Smith-Barry to compile a list of his fighting successes. Writing to Lois he gave the following details of his fighting career to date:

84 Combats
11 Hun Machines and one balloon brought down and seen to crash.
5 Hun Machines brought down but not seen to crash.
12 forced down and damaged.

As he told Lois: *So it is not so bad, and I have done my best.*[14] Ball was obviously aware of the situation of the other Allied pilots for he told Lois that he had more Huns to his credit than any other British or French pilot. This information obviously got into the press and was the start of his period of fame. It was the French press that first brought his deeds to the notice of the wider world. The description of his deeds in one French paper is obviously based on the information which Ball had put down for Hubbard and which Hubbard had presumably sent on to Wing:

14 Ball Archives 30/8/16.

A young British airman has a record which surpasses even that of Maxine Lenoir[15] who has received the Legion of Honour....he is Lieutenant Albert Ball, the son of a former Mayor of Nottingham. He has taken part in 84 fights, and has brought down 22 enemy aeroplanes . . . [16]

Other French papers lauded the deeds, real or imaginary, of Ball. Their readers were regaled with tales of Ball having been attacked by four enemy machines at night and having brought them all down! *Le Miroir* proclaimed that French pilots received publicity and the designation as 'ace' after five victories but Ball 'had accounted for more than twenty before he knew the honours of popularity.'[17]

The publicity spread from the French press to the British press and the RFC could no longer wrap their fighter pilots in the cloak of anonymity. Perhaps they, and the Government, were glad to give the British public a 'hero' to offset the lengthening casualties of the Somme which were appearing daily in British newspapers. The exploits, or in some cases, the imagined exploits of Albert Ball, gave the war a more personal, even knightly, aspect which contrasted to the grim slaughter on the ground. Six months later, after Ball was dead, some suspect that there was a similar campaign to build up the character and achievements of Billy Bishop with, it was suggested, the motive of keeping Canada happy and in the war after the losses in the Arras offensive.

For Ball, the publicity was unwelcome, whether from British or French sources, and he was to find when he came home on leave that his fame did not allow him to walk the streets of his home town without being hailed and greeted by enthusiastic citizens. It was leave Ball wanted, a rest from operations, and Smith-Barry gave him hope that it would not be long in coming:

The Major had a long talk with me today. He is very pleased and says I may have leave, next but one. Also I shall be coming home for a long rest soon, and I really think I shall get it. Oh won't it be A1? I do so want to leave all this beastly killing for a time. Well, I expect to be in my dear old hut before long, for I think we are going to the old aerodrome.[18]

15 Adjutant Maxine Lenoir. Born 1888. Killed in Action 25/10/16. Credited with a final total of eleven victories and had been awarded the *Medaille Militaire* and the *Legion d'Honneur*. He had eight recorded victories by the end of August 1916 when Ball was compiling his record.
16 Quoted in Briscoe and Stannard p188.
17 Briscoe & Stannard p189.
18 Ball Archives 29/8/16.

This letter shows that he was now beginning to feel revulsion at the thought that the success he had achieved was based on the personal killing of his opponents. It was not the anonymous killing that went on in the trenches or the death dealt by the gunners in the artillery batteries behind the lines. Ball could, in many cases, see his opponents and sometimes see the effect of his fire. He might be able to summarise his record as machines brought down but he was increasingly aware that machines meant men. With his deep Christian belief and non-military background the job he was doing, which he still believed necessary to win the war, became increasingly distasteful to him. In contrast to such feelings he still felt it necessary to keep account of his 'score' and to compare it with his rivals, particularly George Guynemer. Although he wanted to be able to stop flying such was his sense of duty that, when he was offered the chance to work in the aviation industry rather than go back to France, he chose to go back to France with No.56 Squadron and his eventual death.

Even with the promise of a period of leave, which Smith-Barry had given him, Ball did not give up his lone patrolling. On the 31 August, flying A201, he took off at 6.30pm with the intention to attack a German airfield. He climbed to 11,000ft and patrolled along the Bapaume-Cambrai Road, which gave him the chance to watch a German airfield near Cambrai. His patience was rewarded when he saw a formation of twelve Rolands circling over their own airfield. He dived to 7,000ft into the middle of the formation and caused them to scatter in all directions. Slipping under the nearest machine he fired one drum into the pilot's seat area and the machine went down to crash near Cambrai. Ball was now in the middle of the formation and the remaining Germans were bent on revenge. He was the target of fire from several directions and he flung his Nieuport around, firing as opportunity offered. He forced one more Roland to drop out of the formation out of control, which crash-landed SE of Bapaume. His luck could not last, however, and eventually the fire from the remaining Rolands brought his engine to a halt by severing the ignition leads.

Ball was now in a tricky situation, out of power and still behind the German lines. Some of his opponents had now given up the fight and gone back to land but, of the others, one which came close was subject to a full clip of bullets from his pistol. In the end the Germans gave up the pursuit and he was able to get back over the British lines and crash

Albert, sister Lois & Cyril
c 1913.

Albert Ball and his brother
Cyril at Trent College.

Ball in his home-made
punt. He poled this craft
from Trent College to
Sedgeley House along
the Trent and
Nottingham Canal.

Ball in his OTC uniform at Trent College in 1913.

An informal studio photo of Albert and Thelma taken in about 1913.

Nieuport 16 A126 Flown by Ball with 11 Squadron.

Ball with the Caudron trainer. The picture used by Ball for his RAeC Ticket (No 1898) which was awarded on 15 October 1915, said to be taken on the day he passed his test.

Ball on Campion Motor Cycle. Taken after his transfer to the NMDCC in 1915.

Ball with his parents at Sedgeley House on 5 October 1916.

13 Squadron Officers on 17 March 1916. Extreme left is Wolff Joel, one of Ball's Observers; Ball is second left. 6th left is Lt. Medhurst (later ACM).

Ball and his family outside Buckingham Palace for the investiture of the DSO on 18 November 1916.

Presentation of a silver rose bowl by the citizens of Lenton to Ball on 19 December 1916.

Sketch of Ball's Nieuport 17 with spinner. By Roderic Hill (later ACM Sir Roderic Hill).

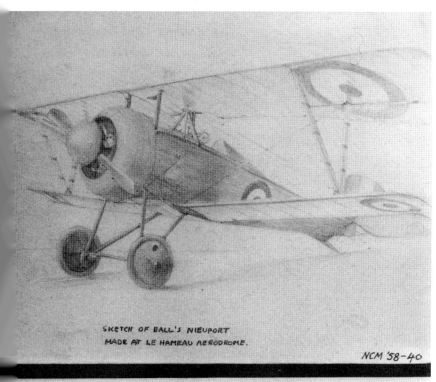

SKETCH OF BALL'S NIEUPORT
MADE AT LE HAMEAU AERODROME.

NCM '58-40

CAPTAIN BALL'S NIEUPORT SCOUT 'PLANE

Drawn on the back of an R.F.C. record card by R.M.Hill, 2/Lt. 12th Northumberland Fusiliers (afterwards Air Chief Marshall Sir Roderick Hill) at Le Hameau aerodrome in 1916.

Studio Portrait of Ball in 1916.

Ball with the propeller and red
spinner from his Nieuport 5173
in the garden at Sedgeley House.
Believed taken in October 1916.

Pilots of 56 Squadron at
London Colney.

Lt. W.B. Melville.

Ball in his SE5 A4850 at London
Colney on 7 April 1917.

Lt. K.J. Knaggs.

Ball in the Oldsmobile.

Ball poses outside Sedgeley House after the Freedom Ceremony on 19th February 1917.

Ball being awarded the Freedom of Nottingham in February 1917.

Captain E.L. Foot.

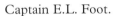

Ball in front of one of his Nieuport 16s of 60 Squadron in Savy, September 1916.

Lt. L.M.Barlow.

Ball (in slippers);
unknown; Cyril.

Ball in his SE5 A4850 at
London Colney.

A family group. Rear:
Alderman Ball and Albert.
Front: Mother, Lois and 'Goffe'.

Close-up of Ball
taken from the photo
of the group of 56
Squadron pilots.

Ball's SE5 No. A4850 at
London Colney in
March/April 1917. Ball was
killed in this aircraft.

L to R. Villiers, Cook (Wireless Officer) and Ball September 1916.

Lois having collected Ball from the station brings him back to Sedgeley House in October 1916. Ball was on his last leave from France. Car believed to be an Oldsmobile.

Albert Ball taking delivery of a new Morgan 3-wheele

BE2c No. 4136. Flown by Ball while with 8 Squadron.

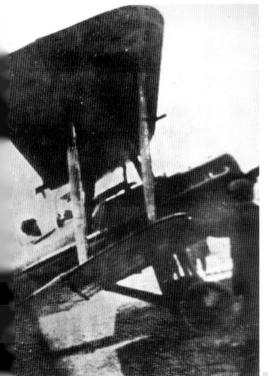

Thought to be the last picture taken of Ball on the evening of 6 May 1917. Seated in his SE5 A4850. Note long SPAD type exhausts and Vickers Gun mounted above the fuselage. Believed taken at a RNAS airfield.

56 Squadron SE5 No. A4863 at London Colney. 7/4/1917. Prior to going to France.

2/Lt. R.C. Musters. Musters was to be KIA on the same patrol as Ball.

Lt. A.P.F. Rhys-Davids.

Ball during the last to take off from London Colney.

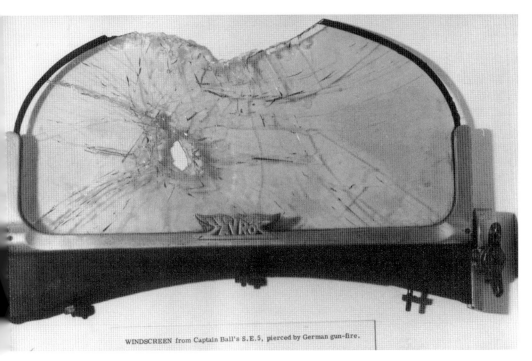

WINDSCREEN from Captain Ball's S.E.5, pierced by German gun-fire.

The damaged "Avro" windscreen of Ball's SE5 pierced by German gun fire. It is held by Nottingham Castle Museum.

Lois laying a wreath at the opening of the Ball Memorial.

Ball's Grave at Annouellin.

land near Colincamps, It was now nearly 8.30pm and Ball was unable to get back to the squadron that night. The intensity of the combat had drained him of mental and physical energy and he slept by his Nieuport.

Ball got back to the squadron the following morning to receive the news that he had been awarded the Distinguished Service Order (DSO) for his action of 22 August. He also came back to the squadron packing up to move from Izel-Le-Hameau to Savy Aubigny; a move that would reunite him with his hut and garden. Only one thing could have made him more happy, a period of leave, and a warrant for this was handed to him by Smith-Barry that night. The leave was effective from the following day and would give him 10 days at home. About this time his ground crew made the red spinner for him to fix to the front of his Nieuport.

While Albert Ball was happily settling in at Savy and anticipating his home leave, a new arrival to the Western Front was settling in across the lines. Manfred von Richthofen arrived on his posting to *Jasta 2* on the 1 September. He had been asked by Boelcke to join, as the great German 'ace' sought pilots to form his new *Jasta* and to handle the new fighters which were being produced and were on the eve of deployment. If Ball had stayed longer he might have met *Jasta 2* in combat and history might have been different. The first of the new German fighters had been engaged by a patrol of No.24 Squadron on the 31 August. Captain Andrews and Lieutenant Glew in their DH2s met three EA which they described as '. . . a new type, extremely fast and climbing quickly. They were biplanes, with a streamlined propeller boss, apparently single-seater, but firing both in front and over the tail from what appeared to be a rear mounting on the left-hand side. The tailplane was very large and rounded'.[19]

The new machines were the Albatros D1 of *Jasta 1* and soon demonstrated their superiority to the DH2 after this initial combat.

CHAPTER SEVEN

The Consummate Fighter Pilot Combats

September–October 1916

A lbert Ball had been eagerly anticipating his period of leave. He looked forward to a time of relaxation, indulging in all the pursuits, particularly fishing, that he enjoyed. He would be looking forward to the chance to spend some time with Thelma and as we have seen he had told his parents that when he next came on leave he would collect her on his way to Nottingham.

While he may well have been looking forward to the period at home as a time to rest and 'recharge his batteries' he found the reality of his fame presented him with a problem. His winning a DSO and an MC had been eagerly reported in the local press and his photograph in these papers made sure that he could not walk around the city without being recognised. People stopped to talk to him in the street and young girls were eager to make the acquaintance of the local hero. He was in demand to attend social gatherings and his attendance in support of meetings to promote War Bonds and to keep up support for the war. He declined as many of these as he could in order to be more with his family and Thelma. His attraction to young girls must have been a source of worry to Thelma but at this time Albert Ball was totally in love with her and while flattered by female attention was not likely to succumb to any other approaches. The period at home passed soon enough and once again he found himself in the painful position of saying goodbye to his family and Thelma. He knew that Smith-Barry had promised him that very soon he would be getting a home posting and he would have this to look forward to. It is natural that some thoughts of his not lasting long enough to see this day arrive must have gone through his mind. He had already lightly touched on the possible fate awaiting him in some of his letters home and his recent combat experiences, particularly when his engine had been shattered by machine-gun fire, had shown just how precarious was his hold on life. His mode of fighting did not allow for caution or restraint. It relied on luck and skill and, in the situation which was now developing in France, those qualities might not be enough.

He wrote to his mother at the end of his leave from the Charing Cross Hotel while he waited for the train to Dover.

> Really, dear, my leave has been so very happy. It is hard to leave such dear people, but you are brave as well as dear, and it makes it less hard. It is an honour to be able to fight and do one's best for such a country and such dear people . . . Mother, I shall fight for you and come home for you, and God always looks after me and makes me strong. May he look after you also.[1]

Ever since the appearance of the Fokker Monoplane in 1915 the struggle for aerial supremacy had begun. The Allies had finally been able to produce aircraft superior to the Fokker with the introduction into service of the Nieuport Bebe (Type 11) and the DH2, while the FE2b and later the Sopwith 1½ Strutter had reinforced the Allied supremacy.

This supremacy, once achieved, gave the British in particular a dominance in the air which they exploited during the battle of the Somme, to the great benefit of the ground forces. The Trenchard doctrine was to give full support to the ground forces and to resist attempts by the Germans to operate over the British lines.

In the early summer of 1916 Germans recognised that the superiority that they had once enjoyed was gone and that their ground forces were being damaged by the activities of the British artillery observation and reconnaissance aircraft. They had already begun to work on replacement aircraft which would eventually enable them to dominate the skies again over the Western Front. There had been earlier attempts to replace the Fokker monoplane with the Fokker DI and DII Biplanes. However, their performance was very little advanced on the previous Fokker EIII and EIV and they were not a success. They were tested by Oswald Boelcke to see whether they were suitable for

---

1 Ball Archives 11/9/1916.

production for the new fighter *Jagdstaffeln* which were bring formed. Boelcke did not report favourably on them and they were turned down for large production orders. The Fokker DIII which followed was an improvement and had twin Spandau guns and the 160hp Oberursel rotary, and the DIV with the 160hp Mercedes also had a useful performance, but they were both overshadowed by the appearance from the Albatros works of an advanced single-seater, the DI, produced in August 1916. With twin machine-guns and a top speed of 110 mph it outclassed its domestic rivals as well as its allied opponents. The twin gun format was to remain the standard layout for such aircraft until the emergence of the new monoplane fighters in the mid 1930s. The DH2 could only achieve 92 mph, the Nieuport Bebe 97 mph, and both aircraft were fitted with only one gun.

The Albatros D series of scouts employed wooden fuselage construction and attention to aerodynamic detail which gave the company a series of attractive, clean-line aircraft. The power of the Mercedes engine gave it the ability to carry the extra machine-gun giving it greater fire power than its adversaries. Although there were both British and French aircraft which would match the performance of the new Albatros, such as the Nieuport 17 and the Sopwith Pup and, even more so, the powerful new Spad, they did not carry the second gun to give that extra destructive power.

There is certainly a case to be made that, throughout the period of the war, the German aircraft industry was far more forward thinking than the Allies. The Germans were first to introduce into service a working synchronising gear for machine-guns, the first with multi-gun fighters; far more adventurous with regard to aircraft construction with the extensive use of wooden monococque fuselages and metal construction.

Contemporary with the Albatros DI was the Halberstadt Scout. The Halberstadt DII was powered by the 120 hp Mercedes but was far inferior in performance to the Albatros. The Halberstadts were not produced in quantity and, with the exception of the DV, their performance was poor.

Drawing strongly on their experience with the CII, the Roland Company also produced a fighter, the DI. The DI was tested in July 1916 and bore the trademark of attention to aerodynamic detail that the CII had done. The view from the cockpit was poor however, due to the wing being mounted directly on the fuselage. These defects were remedied in the DII and DIII which went into limited service. They, like many of their contemporaries, were outclassed by the Albatros, particularly the Albatros DIII which was the most famous and successful of the line of Albatros Scouts.

It was the Albatros DI and DII which were to provide the opposition to the RFC on the Western Front in late 1916. The Germans decided, like the British, to group their fighters in dedicated units and they had formed several *Jagdstaffeln* to operate the new fighters. In the late Autumn of 1916, *Jasta 1* was commanded by *Hauptman* Martin Zander; *Jasta 2* by Oswald Boelcke; *Jasta 3* by Lt. Ewald Von Mellinthin; *Jasta 4* by Oblt. Hans Joachim Buddecke; *Jasta 5* by Oblt. Hans Berr; *Jasta 6* by Lt. Otto Bernert; the name of the CO of *Jasta 7* at this time does not seem to have survived. The initial equipment was a mixture of Fokkers, Halberstadts and Albatros but as the latter became more available from production so the other types were returned to training schools. Significantly they were reinforcing the Somme front from forces previously deployed at Verdun, as had happened with their ground forces.

Boelcke secured the first victory for his *Jasta* on the 2 September flying a Fokker DIII, but the first *Staffel* patrol was not made until the 17 September when six Albatros operated together. On that day von Richthofen had opened his score by shooting down an FE2b of No.11 Squadron over Villers-Pluich.

However, on the 15 September Boelcke had shown the potential of the new machines when, in a long combat over Havrincourt Wood, he shot down Captain G. L. Cruickshank who was flying a Sopwith 1½ Strutter of No.70 Squadron. The loss of Cruickshank, one of the early pioneers of the RFC was an indication that even with an accomplished pilot, as Cruickshank was, one of the best of the current Allied aircraft could not cope with a well handled Albatros. This was the new situation into which Albert Ball would find himself on his return. In the Nieuport 17 he did, however, have a machine which was capable of holding its own with the new German Scouts.

On his return from leave Ball was told that he was now A Flight Commander but he did not immediately get the promotion. This vacancy was caused by the death of Captain Goodrich. Goodrich and another officer, Lieutenant Parker, were due to leave for Home

Establishment and planned a party to celebrate the event. Goodrich climbed into his Morane and took off to say farewell to friends in No.3 Squadron, where he had served previously. His Morane Bullet A166, stalled during his initial climb and he was killed in the resulting crash.[2]

The first success for Ball, after his return from leave, came on a balloon attack on the 15 September. The third phase of the battle of the Somme was scheduled to start that day and orders had been given for German balloons to be shot down. Trenchard was visiting No.60 squadron and he asked for three volunteers to shoot down three Observation Balloons which could possibly observe the tanks that were being introduced as they advanced to the line prior to the attack.

Ball had Nieuport A200 on this occasion and took off from Savy with 2nd Lt Walters at about 7.30am. Both Nieuports were armed with Le Prieur Rockets. On reaching the German balloon line they found that the balloons were not yet up. Looking for other targets Ball sighted a Roland Scout NE of Bapaume. He dived at the Roland and fired his rockets which missed their target, but in the meantime Ball had closed to 50 yards and fired one drum at the Roland which went down and crashed E of Beugny. Second Lieutenant Walters also achieved success, but with his rockets. He had attacked the LVG two-seater which the Roland had been escorting. One of his rockets entered the fuselage and the machine burst into flames and crashed. There was also success against the balloons. One was destroyed by 2nd Lieutenant Gilchrist near Bapaume and Captain Summers, who failed to return from the operation, was credited with another which was seen to go down.

In Nieuport A212, when on an offensive patrol in the region of Bapaume, that afternoon, Ball saw an Albatros two-seater going south at 7,000ft. He secured his underneath firing position and emptied one drum into it but, in trying to change the drum, by sliding the gun down the Foster mount, he was hit on the head by the gun. The Albatros had dived away after his first attack and in the confusion Ball was unable to follow.

In his last mission for the day Ball took off at about 6.30 pm with his machine once again fitted with rockets. Again he was diverted before he reached his intended target when he saw a formation of five Roland two-seaters NE of Bertincourt. He dived on the formation and fired his rockets to break them up. As the Germans scattered he attacked the

---

2 Warne: *Cross & Cockade GB* Vol.11 No.1 p34.

nearest, firing one drum into it at 20 yards. The Roland fell away and Ball saw it crash.

In these combats he had used three different Nieuports. At this time he took over the recently delivered Nieuport A213 as his personal aircraft and had it fitted out to his personal requirements, including the red spinner. It was this Nieuport which he continued to use for the rest of his time in No.60 Squadron.

The day's fighting had cost the Squadron Captain Summers, the B Flight Commander. He had been shot down during the balloon attack and was first reported missing but later his death was confirmed. His replacement arrived the following day, Captain E.L. Foot a friend of Ball from No.11 squadron. Ball must have been glad of the friendly face for he had not really 'socialised' with his fellow officers in the squadron.

The day on which these combats took place, 15 September, was also the opening of the battle of Flers, with tanks used in attack for the first time, and there was considerable aerial activity in support of this operation. This was the reason for Ball's aircraft being equipped with rockets, for along with other No. 60 Squadron pilots he was designated for attacks on the German balloon line. About this time Ball learned that he had been awarded a Bar to his recently announced DSO. This was awarded for his actions of the 28 and 31 August and both awards were published in the *London Gazette* of the 26 September. Ball wrote to his father enclosing the wire which notified him of the award of the Bar to his DSO commenting, *I have now got as far as I can get at my age so I am satisfied and I know you will be.*[3] At this time he was still feeling the beneficial effects of the leave from which he had just returned. In particular he seems to have had a happy time in his meetings with Thelma or at least he told his father so, but within a couple of months his relationship with Thelma seems to have broken down, though no reason can be found for this in the surviving correspondence.[4]

According to Kiernan[5], who must have had the information from Smith-Barry, the latter always regretted that he did not strive harder for Ball to be awarded the VC that year (1916). The fact that Kiernan uses the term 'strive harder' implies that Smith-Barry had in fact put forward the recommendation to higher authority and that it seems to have been refused on the grounds that the exploits of Ball were all done on his lone hunting over the German lines, possibly implying a lack of

3 Ball Archives 15/9/1916.
4 According to Thelma's daughter it was Thelma who initiated the break.
5 Kiernan p87.

verification. Such standards did not apply the following year when Billy Bishop was awarded the VC for his attack on a German aerodrome, in which his report was the only evidence as the attack was a solo effort. Ball also heard that he had been awarded the Russian Order of St. George 4th Class. He was presented with this decoration on the 24 September.

The 18 September is recorded as having heavy rain all day, but despite this Ball and Foot were detailed by Smith-Barry to carry out a bluff attack on a line of German balloons near Bapaume. The two Nieuports took off under orders to patrol in the area but not to attack, except in exceptional circumstances. The two pilots reached the area only to find that most of the balloons had been hauled down except for three, which presented tempting targets. Mindful of their orders these remaining balloons were not attacked and the two pilots returned home. Smith-Barry was reprimanded for this patrol, being accused of trespassing on another squadron's area of responsibility. All this activity had been carried out by Ball when he had not been feeling well for a couple of days.

On 19 September the weather started fine but deteriorated after 3pm. Despite this Ball took off in Nieuport A213 for an evening patrol. He saw an Albatros two-seater below him dived from 7,000ft to 2,000ft and closed to 50 yds. He fired one drum from that range and the Albatros dived towards St. Leger. Ball changed drums and closed again, this time to 25 yards and fired the second drum. Under this attack the two-seater steepened its dive and force landed in a field east of St. Leger. In his report Ball did not claim this machine as 'out of control' but said that it seemed to be 'all right'. This day saw another loss for No.60 Squadron when Captain H.C. Tower was reported missing. His death was later confirmed. He had been flying as one of the escort to a formation of FEs. The formation, and its escort, were attacked by Boelcke and his pilots of *Jasta 1*. It was Boelcke himself who attacked Tower and after a short combat, in which Boelcke said that one of his guns had jammed, he shot the Morane down in flames to fall in a wood near Grevillers. Tower, at the age of 30, was relatively old for a scout pilot and had been in the RFC from August 1914.

The 21 September proved to be a successful day for Ball. On A213, fitted with Le Prieur Rockets he met six Roland single seaters at 2,000ft near Bapaume. He dived on the formation and fired his rockets, not with much hope of securing a hit but as a shock weapon to startle the German pilots and break up the formation. This effect was achieved and he dived under the nearest Roland, secured his firing position and emptied one drum into the German scout, which dropped sharply away from the formation and made an emergency landing. Hardly waiting to watch the fate of his first opponent Ball attacked a second Roland and emptied two drums into it from his underneath position. The German went out of control and crashed near the first. Following the destruction of this Roland, Ball was chased back to the lines by the remainder of the formation. During his escape Ball turned occasionally to engage his pursuers and eventually got across the British lines and landed at Savy at 4.30pm.

After his Nieuport had been refuelled and rearmed, Ball took off again at 5.15pm and re-crossed the German lines. He patrolled for a while at 7,000ft but on seeing two Roland CII two seaters at 4,000ft he dived to engage. He opened fire at a range of 30 yards and continued firing until he broke away close to the German's tail. He was joined in this combat by a British pusher scout, though he does not identify it as a DH2 or an FE8. The two Rolands broke off the combat and dived away to safety and Ball climbed again to continue his patrol. A few minutes later he saw the same machines returning to their interrupted task and he dived to attack. Under his fire the Roland began to spin down to earth and Ball turned to attack the other two-seater. The German had, however, dived away and after some ineffectual firing Ball broke off the pursuit to look for the wreckage of his first victim. He found it scattered across a field and fired two drums into it '..to make certain of the passengers' as he stated in his combat report.

This was an unusual action for Ball and perhaps indicates the strain which he was feeling after an intense period of combat. As will have been seen from his earlier correspondence, he felt no hatred for the Germans but he accepted that he had to fight and kill them as his country's enemies.

He had been pursuing his usual practice of flying at every opportunity and this was bound to induce a state of nervous strain in Ball, which Ball himself recognised. He approached Smith-Barry at this time and told him that he was in need of a rest. Like Major Hubbard earlier in the year, Smith-Barry was sympathetic to the request and he asked Ball how he knew that he had reached this state. Ball replied that he knew his nerves were going because he was taking unnecessary and foolish chances in his fighting. This was enough for Smith-Barry who knew enough of the fighting qualities of Ball to know that such a request would not have been made lightly and set about getting Ball the period of rest which he so badly needed.

The 22 September proved to be another day of intense fighting for Ball. His first flight of the day was in Nieuport A213 when he took off at 11.30 am as escort for a small bombing formation. Flying at 7,000ft he saw two Roland CIIs over Bapaume. He dived to attack and was joined in his dive by an FE2b. Ball outpaced his companion, secured his usual firing position and fired two drums into the underside of the Roland, which immediately started to descend and eventually landed south-east of Bapaume. The other Roland abandoned its mission and dived east.

In the afternoon Ball was airborne again. He took off, again in A213, and patrolled for an hour in the area of the Bapaume-Cambrai road. Suddenly, he spotted a German scout emerging from the clouds below. In his combat report Ball describes this scout as a Roland, but Bowyer correctly records it, from recorded German losses, as a Fokker DIII. This type would not have been unknown to Ball and was considerably more angular in appearance than the Roland Scout which he recorded, but whichever it was the pilot was completely unaware of Ball's presence and Ball was able to get into his usual firing position and fired one drum of Buckingham ammunition into the area of the cockpit. The Fokker went down in '. . . a half nose dive, half side slip' and eventually crashed east of Bapaume, the pilot being killed.

With his patrol time coming to an end Ball had just one more encounter when he met two Roland two-seaters. He attacked the nearest firing a drum as he approached, then getting underneath to fire again, but the German crew forestalled him and dived steeply away. Ball was unable to match their speed, abandoned the pursuit and returned home.

The following day Ball made several abortive trips over the lines looking for trouble, but luck was not with him. It was not until his last flight of the day that he found a German formation which he could attack. Flying Nieuport A213 he attacked a formation of four Roland CIIs coming from the direction of Cambrai. This time the Nieuport was fitted with some of the new double size Lewis ammunition drums.

These gave a total of ninety-seven rounds instead of the usual drum of forty-seven rounds. As he approached Ball fired a short burst from about 30 yards which had the desired effect of causing the German formation to split up. Following his usual tactics he attacked the nearest Roland but with apparently no effect. In his combat report Ball states that following this first ineffective attack he attacked another EA and fired a drum of 1 in 3 Buckingham ammunition which briefly set his opponent on fire. The EA then fell away and crashed near Mory.

This seems to indicate that he had destroyed one of the Rolands, but in effect, after his first ineffective attack on the Roland, he ran into a formation of Albatros two-seaters. He fired a general burst in the direction of the Albatros formation and then went to change the drum on the Lewis. The additional weight of the double size drum caused Ball to mishandle the drum which fell from his hand into the cockpit where it jammed his rudder control wires. This mishap put the Nieuport temporarily out of control and he veered crazily through the Albatros formation where he was the subject of concentrated fire from several German observers. In this situation he was frantically trying to pick up the fallen drum and regain full control of his aircraft. Finally achieving this he regained control of the Nieuport and saw that he was flying alongside one of the Albatros whose Observer was firing at him. Having fixed a new drum on his Lewis he side slipped under his opponent and fired a drum from only 15 yards range. This caused the Albatros to burn briefly and then to fall away and crash. Ball had by now finished all his ammunition and turned for the lines pursued by the rest of the German formation. Ball's retreat was punctuated by his occasionally turning to face his pursuers and pretending to put his aircraft into a position to attack which had the effect of discouraging his pursuers. In this manner he got over the lines but was unable to make Savy and he landed at Bailleulmont for the night (it was by then nearly 7pm) and returned to base on the morning of the 24th. His mechanics counted thirteen bullet holes in his fuselage, some close to the cockpit area.

He wrote to his father on the 24th in response to the telegram he had received from him following the award of the bar to his DSO. In a long 'newsy' letter he covered several topics:

Am simply mad with delight. Have just received your Wire and also many other wires & letters. . .

Tee has sent me 12 pages of just what I like. Oh! I am a lucky boy & so very happy & thankful.

Well I am now a Flight Commander & my letters should be addressed to Captain Ball DSO, A Flight Commander, No.60 Squadron, RFC, BEF.

This is all the address I meant to get before I finished and now I have got it, and I don't care how soon the War ends. But I hope it wont be too long. My Flight is one to be proud of. Two of my pilots got the MC yesterday and all of them have got either two or three Huns each, but one, and he has only just started.

Last night I went up for a bit of sport, on a patrol, to try a new gun. I met four Huns and succeeded in fighting them and brought one down in flames. I was forced down in the end myself for my ammunition was out but they only got ten hits on my machine.

I stopped the night at another Squadron and flew back this morning. It was very nice and they gave me a topping time.

I have enclosed the ribbon of the Order of St. George. Thought you might like it.[6]

His Nieuport was ready for action soon but it was not until the 25th September that Ball had his next combat. He took A213 up at about noon on what his combat report records as a Balloon Patrol. While flying at 7,000 ft over Bucquoy he saw a German two-seater which he identified as an Albatros Type A, but is presumed to be an Albatros CIII. The Albatros crew must have seen Ball almost at the same time as he saw them, for although he dived to get his usual underneath position he was foiled in this attempt by skilful piloting on the part of the German. Then began a battle of manoeuvring which, according to Ball's combat report, lasted for thirty minutes. This is an incredibly long time for an aerial combat and what is unusual is that no other aircraft, British or German, attempted to interfere. Indeed, Ball makes no mention of the sighting of any machine during the time he was engaged with the Albatros.

The two machines circled each other, firing snap shots as opportunity offered. Ball thought his fire was having no effect, but in fact at some time his fire killed the observer, Leutenant Hoffman and wounded the pilot, flieger Tewes. Ball expended 300 rounds of Lewis

6 Ball Archives 24/9/1916.

gun ammunition which was all he had and he had to break off the combat. For a while the two machines flew alongside each other, according to Ball, smiling and waving, before he went back to Savy. The German pilot may well have waved, despite his wounds, and it also possible that he knew that he was up against a top British pilot. By this time the Nieuport with the red spinner was known as a formidable opponent amongst German aircrew. Although he did not claim the victory, in fact the Albatros, from *Fliegerabteilung* A237, later crashed with a dead observer and a seriously wounded pilot. In his report on this combat, Ball signs himself for the first time as 'Captain' the rank to which he had recently been promoted. This promotion he told his parents was the height of his ambition.

In a final patrol for that day Ball took off again in A213. He climbed to 11,000 ft and patrolled NE of Bapaume. where he saw a formation of two Roland and two Albatros two seaters flying together. He attacked the nearest by diving and securing his underneath position and emptied a drum into it. He saw the observer collapse in the rear cockpit and the machine start to go down. Ball considered the German machine to be still under control and did not make any claim for a victory.

Ball was now avidly looking forward to coming home. Smith-Barry had told him that he would be going home soon on a posting to Home Establishment. He told his mother that he would join a 'Zepp Squadron' when he got back! He received regular news from home about the progress of Cyril through his training and promised to visit his brother's squadron and 'put him right' when he got back.

On the 28th Ball took of in A213 at 5.45pm on a personal 'Balloon Busting' mission to attack the German balloon line SE of Haplincourt. He had loaded his drums with Buckingham incendiary ammunition and had the double sized drums fitted. The objective of the mission was not particularly to destroy the balloon, for squadrons were under orders not to carry out such attacks on an ad hoc basis, but only in response to a specific requirement. He was hoping that his attack on the balloons would bring up some of the defending aircraft, which were the real object of his mission. This stratagem was successful and as he started to attack the balloons he spotted three Albatros two-seaters coming up towards him. Ball immediately broke off his attack on the balloons and went for the nearest two-seater. He fired a complete double drum into this aircraft from 15 yards range and was rewarded by seeing the German aircraft spinning out control to crash near Haplincourt. The remaining two German aircraft did not bother him and he had no ammunition left to attack them so he returned to Savy.

Landing at just before 6pm Ball refuelled and re-armed A213 and took off again at 6.10pm in the company of Captain Foot who was flying a Spad newly allotted to the squadron for tests. The two flew in company into the evening sky and found that the air was full of aircraft of both sides. They selected a formation of five Rolands and dived to attack. The Spad was a strong aircraft and could be dived steeply and Foot was the first to fire. His opponent dived, seemingly out of control, but Foot was unable to concentrate on its fate as he was attacked by another Roland. Ball, however, was able to confirm that it crashed N of Avesnes les Bapaumes. His own opponent also went down but he thought that it was still under control.

Ball had become separated from Foot during the combat and, in his usual solitary state, he climbed to 7,000 ft to continue his patrol. He saw yet another formation of Rolands and attacked the nearest from underneath. A full drum fired into the fuselage was enough to force the German pilot to go down and land his machine. Ball turned for home but saw a German machine attacking a British aeroplane and with his remaining ammunition he forced it to give up its attack.

That evening he penned another letter to his father reassuring him that he would return home safely and continued:

> My Flight is going OK and another chap has been put in for the MC. Oh! It is a topping Flight.
>
> You ask what I would like in honour of the latest (word missing ? decoration). You are really a dear to wish to buy me anything. Well I would like anything that would be useful to me when I get older.[7]

The 29th September was unfit for flying with low clouds and rain throughout the day. Such days were welcome to all pilots, even one as aggressive as Albert Ball. Nerves were given a chance to ease off and for ground crew to get working to clear any back log which might have accumulated.

---

7 Ball Archives 28/9/1916.

In a letter written that day Ball touched on many things; his appreciation of the 'new machine' which he was to fly in a few days. He commented that 'it was much faster than the one I have now and I think will be good for the job.' He flew no other aircraft than Nieuports while with No. 60 Squadron and was already flying the Nieuport 17, the latest type in service, so it is difficult to know to what type he was referring. It is possible that he was being given a chance to fly an advanced production model of the Nieuport 23, in effect a more powerful Nieuport 17 fitted with 120 hp Le Rhone. The first examples of this aircraft were not issued to the RFC, for squadron service, until May 1917. Ball hoped, however, that as he would be home in a few more days that he would do no more fighting. He included in this letter some thoughts on the job he had to do. With his own love for his family he thought of the effect which his success in shooting down German aircraft and thereby killing some of the occupants, must have on the families:

> I feel so sorry for the chaps I have killed. Just imagine what their poor people must feel like. I must have sent at least 40 chaps to their deaths. However, it must be done or they would kill me, would they not?[8]

The last day of the month saw an intensive day of flying with Ball airborne at every opportunity. His Nieuport A213 was having an engine change and for his first two operations he flew A201. The first duty was to escort a force of eleven BEs to bomb the German aerodrome at Lagnicourt. This airfield was the home of *Jagdstaffel* 2 as well as other units. There was a strong escort, six Nieuport and two Moranes from No. 60 Squadron and a force of FE2b's from No. 11 Squadron. Take off time for 60 Squadron was just before 11 am. The whole force assembled at 7,000 ft before crossing the lines and setting course for Lagnicourt.

Progress to the target was largely uneventful until they were close to Lagnicourt. Ball noticed two Albatros two-seaters some 5,000 ft below him. The convention of the escort staying with their charges did not resonate with Ball's independent spirit and although the Albatros' could have been no threat to the formation he dived to attack. The first of the machines he attacked evaded his attempt to get underneath and

8 Ball Archives 29/9/1916.

dived east. Pulling up he saw another two-seater just above him and fired just a few rounds before his opponent burst into flames and began to go down. As the machine fell Ball saw the German observer abandon his cockpit and jump to his death, as many other airman were to do, rather than be burnt to death. Such an event always made an impression on all those who witnessed it and all could appreciate the choice which had to be made, for fire in the air was the greatest and most feared threat which the aircrew of both sides faced. This success on the part of Ball was witnessed by two fellow members of No. 60 Squadron, Lieutenants Bell-Irving and Walters. Ball also acknowledged in his combat report that an FE from the formation also fired at the Albatros and the success was shared between Ball and the FE crew.

On return from this operation Ball was relaxing at Savy outside his hut when he saw white British AA bursts to the north of the aerodrome, being directed against a German two-seater. His Nieuport was ready for immediate operation and Ball took off in A201 in pursuit of the German reconnaissance machine. He followed the German machine, an Albatros CIII, and managed to get within 30 yards. From here he fired a drum into the fuselage but his aim was not accurate enough to bring it down and the German dived steeply away towards his own lines. Ball followed the two-seater but found that he was being left behind by its speed and he gave up the pursuit and returned to Savy.

Just before 7pm Ball was airborne again in the newly repaired A213. He climbed to a height of 12,000 ft and proceeded to patrol the line Bapaume-Graincourt-Cambrai and seeing anti-aircraft fire he flew in that direction and saw a formation of eight Roland CIIs in formation over Bapaume. As he closed, the German formation turned towards Cambrai. Ball attacked the nearest one, which he drove out of the formation. Ball recorded it as out of control, but he did not have time to watch its fate as he was attacked by another Roland. Finding his gun jammed he dived for the British lines and outdistanced his pursuers. Rectifying his gun jamb Ball climbed to 14,000 ft and resumed his patrol. Seeing the same formation of Rolands Ball set off in pursuit. Again, he selected the nearest one and fired a drum into it plus a further drum as it began to drop to earth. He was now out of ammunition and evading the attack of the second German he made for home.

The next day was to prove to be the last day on which Ball flew with No. 60 Squadron and it proved to be a busy one. In the morning he took off to look for German machines reported to be on the British side of the lines. Flying his old favourite, A213, he searched the area in which the intruders had been reported, but finding nothing he crossed the lines and made for the German aerodrome at Lagnicourt, the home of *Jasgdstaffel* 2. He was trailing his coat hoping that someone would come up and attack him. He was successful in this and three single seaters were soon to be seen climbing towards him. In his report Ball identifies them as Roland scouts but the Roland D type did not enter operational service until early 1917. As the field he was flying over was the home of *Jasgdstaffel* 2 the opponents were probably either the new Albatros scouts or Fokker DIIIs. As the Germans came up he dived to attack them. Fastening on the nearest and diving underneath he fired half a drum into it. Under this attack his opponent dived and made a hurried force landing, while the remaining two scouts made off east. Ball climbed back to his patrol height and continued to look for possible prey. His first chance came in the form of an Albatros two-seater, painted all over brown, which he saw 4,000 ft below him. He fired a full drum of Buckingham bullets into the two-seater and noted that the bullets were entering the fuselage. The German Observer fired back, using what Ball described as 'explosive bullets' but he was untouched by this return fire. The two-seater went down and force landed near Hamlincourt. On his way back to the lines Ball met yet another Albatros, this one painted all white. Ball came up under its tail and fired, but after only fifty rounds the Lewis gun jammed but this was enough for the Albatros which also landed near Hamlincourt. In his report of these combats Ball wondered whether the fields around Hamlincourt might contain a German airfield as he had noted several other German aircraft land there.

With his fuel running low, and the Lewis gun jammed, Ball now had no option but to set course for Savy. On landing he was met by Major Smith-Barry who told him that he was soon to be sent home, news which Ball would have greeted with joy. He was first to have a spell of leave and then to take up a posting in Home Establishment. At last he was to get the rest he needed, but this time he could not simply get on with his leave. He was now a celebrated pilot, the leading fighting pilot in the RFC, and his superiors wished to see him and to congratulate him on his outstanding record.

On 3 October Ball met the Army Commander, Brigadier General Higgins, and then his Wing Commander, Lt. Colonel Playfair, his former commander in No. 8 Squadron. Both men were profusive in their thanks for his outstanding record. This showering of compliments was probably as equally unnerving to Ball as the return fire from his opponents!

If the weather had been favourable Ball might have flown over the lines again, but the RFC Communiqué describes the weather from 2 October to 6 October as 'unfavourable for aerial operations' with strong westerly and south westerly winds and, on most days, continual heavy rain. Such weather would have given Ball no excuse to follow his strong sense of duty and continue with his operational flights.

On the evening of the 3rd he was guest of honour at a celebratory dinner in the Mess. The attendees included his fellow pilots from No. 60 Squadron and other crews from neighbouring squadrons. His fellow pilots may have regarded him as 'out of the ordinary' for his reclusive life style, but they knew and appreciated his sheer courage and professionalism. They had respect and admiration for a unique individual who had inspired the whole of the RFC with his fighting spirit. Ball was overwhelmed by this display on the part of his fellow officers, but he was never a 'party animal' and was glad to get away early before the evening became too riotous.

The following day he tidied up the loose ends of his life in No. 60 Squadron. He said personal farewells to Smith-Barry, whom he had come to appreciate and admire, and to his close friend in the squadron, Leslie Foot. He handed his record player and records over to his ground crew in appreciation of their efforts and then left the squadron on his journey home.

-oOo-

As will be seen from Ball's patrol on 28 September, apart from the Nieuports with which the squadron had been equipped, No.60 was also given the task of testing the first of the new Spad Scouts, the SVII, (given serial Number A253) to be issued to the RFC. The machine was given to Captain Foot who had made the first flight in it on 22 September.

The prototype Spad had made its first flight in April 1916 and was immediately a subject of interest to the RFC. It was powered by the new 150hp Hispano Suiza engine, designed by Marc Birkigt, and fitted with a single synchronised Vickers machine-gun. The British observers reported favourably to Trenchard and within a few days of the first flight the latter had written to the French asking for a total of three SPADs for trial by the RFC. It was the first of these that was delivered to No. 60 Squadron on the 20 September and given to Captain Foot.

On his first patrol, Foot engaged a formation of three Roland two-seaters over Bapaume. In the course of this combat his gun jammed and he had to break off. Having cleared the jam he later attacked three Albatros but again the gun failed and he had to return home. Both the engine and the synchronising gear had been designed by Birkigt and would take some getting used to. On 28 September, Foot was again over the lines and attacked four Albatros two-seaters over Bapaume and forced his opponent to dive away. He was immediately attacked by another Albatros so could not keep sight of his previous opponent. However, Ball was able to confirm that the German machine had crashed near Avesnes.[9]

Foot had the use of this Spad for a period of four weeks before it was returned to Candas after which he reverted to the Nieuport.

---

9 PRO AIR1/225/205/5/2634. Foot combat reports dated 22/9/1916 and 28/9/1916.

CHAPTER EIGHT

Leave and Home Establishment

On 5 October Ball arrived at Nottingham station to be met by Lois in the family Humber car and driven to Sedgley House. Unlike his previous leave, this time he arrived in Nottingham with his name already known, not only locally but to the world. The local press became aware of his return and a crowd of reporters and photographers were waiting outside his parents' house.

Ball's return had also been reported in the national as well as the local press. His parents' home was bombarded with congratulatory telephone calls and messages in the days following his arrival. On the afternoon of his return a photographic session had been arranged by his parents. A local man, Charles Shaw, came round along with his two sons who had pressed their father to be able to meet Ball. Shaw spent some time taking photographs of Ball and his family and these were soon circulated world wide, where Ball and his achievements were of interest to the Allied nations. To complete a memorable day for Shaw's two sons the boys were photographed in the garden of Sedgley House with Ball. The only person who seemed to be missing from the occasion was Thelma.

During his last leave when he was able to relax and do more or less what he wanted and not be driven by any desire other than to spend time with his family, this time he had two other imperatives. One was the question of the specification for the new scout which he wanted to see Austin's construct for him. It is not known when exactly he first went to see the firm but by the end of October he was close to bringing the matter to the position in which it was likely to become a practicable proposition, and to have both the War Office and Austin's talking to each other. The full story of the process of bringing the Austin-Ball to the position where the order was placed for two prototypes is given in Appendix 2. There is no doubt that Ball felt a sense of urgency about the matter and may even have hoped that an example would be available for him before his time at home was finished.

The second matter, which bore heavily on him, was his fame. He was by now a 'hero figure' to the Allied nations and the world. His name was now known more widely than any other pilot in the RFC or RNAS, and within Nottingham he was a subject of constant attention by both the public and the city authorities.

The *Nottingham Evening News* had a reporter interview him at Sedgeley House on the day of his return. This interview was published in the issue of the 9 October. The following extracts give some idea of the sort of publicity to which he was now subject:

> Captain and Flight Commander Albert Ball DSO MC, the distinguished young Nottingham airman who is home on a few days leave, had some remarkable aerial adventures to relate to a *Nottingham Evening News* representative who sought him out at his father's (Alderman A. Ball's) house in The Park on the evening of his return.
>
> He is barely twenty years old, this short but sturdily built young airman who in four months has fought over a hundred air fights and brought down some thirty Hun machines. As I entered the hall at his home he was bending lovingly, almost reverently, over an aeroplane propeller, which, he told me afterwards, was a magnificent specimen of French manufacture in this direction and was worth £60. On a sofa near by stood the aluminium bonnet, circular in form. Apart from the Royal Flying Corps badge on his tunic, and a deep rooted love of adventure in his heart, those two adjuncts of aviation were all that the young airman would have for 14 days to remind him of the gloriously venturesome life he had just left behind him.
>
> He told me that as he had had some leave only a few weeks before, he would just as soon have kept going at the front. The fact is that he loves the aviation game for its own sake. It appeals to his sense of sportsmanship, and through all the destruction that he has wrought he still honours above all the foe who puts up a good fight.[1]

1 *Nottingham Evening News* archive 9 October 1916.

The tone of this interview was what was expected of a 'national hero' at the time. As with other servicemen home on leave from the front he could not tell it as it really was. Air combat *had* been regarded by Ball as a 'sport' when he first came to the front but by now, he had seen too many of his friends and comrades shot down, and some of his opponents despatched in flames to hold to that view. Nevertheless it was a view widely held by the general public, who looked on air fighting as an equivalent of the chivalry of the medieval joust. But Ball had developed his own tactics, which meant that his opponent was shot down from beneath and behind and not from a chivalric form of single combat.

Ball gave his view that the German pilots were inferior to the British and seldom crossed the British lines and, when encountered, would not stop to fight. He found that flying alone encouraged the Germans to challenge him and hence his chance to destroy them. This view of German flyers was not uncommon, at least in public pronouncements, but someone with Ball's experience of fighting on the Western Front could not seriously subscribe to the theory that there was something inherently inferior about German flying men.

Later in the interview he referred to a combat he had had on 25 September when he had engaged an Aviatik above Bucquoy. This had been an indecisive combat and eventually Ball ran out of ammunition. In speaking to the reporter Ball said that they had both exhausted their ammunition and for a few moments flew alongside each other smiling and waving. 'We had both fought to win', Ball said, 'and honours were even'. Ball was certain that the German would have been sorry to have shot him (Ball) down as he would have been to have shot the German down, perhaps an echo of a sporting instinct. In fact, German records show that the Observer had been killed by Ball's fire and the pilot seriously wounded. This was the reality of the war in the air. One may wish to practice chivalrous combat but such precepts were more often than not doomed by the necessity to kill and not be killed. As the numbers of aircraft engaged in combats became larger as 1916 progressed into 1917 there became less room for the 'sporting joust'.

The Reporter says that Ball mentioned an occasion, which had been publicised in a recent French Communiqué, where he opposed twelve German machines. Ball described the fight in graphic terms, 'I went at them and tackled the nearest machine. Having brought it down, I turned to the others and smashed two more.' By this time he was out of ammunition and returned to a British aerodrome for more and then returned to the attack and 'smashed' one more. This is probably a reference to the engagement of the 31 August when he attacked a formation of twelve Roland two-seaters over Cambrai. In this engagement he shot one down which he saw crash and one which went down under control and landed. He did exhaust his ammunition and after an engine failure had to force land at Colincamps. His report does not mention his returning to the attack with new supplies of ammunition.

The interview with the local reporter was probably the idea of his father, who was, naturally enough, proud of his son. Cyril Ball said later in life that while his father loved the public attention which his brother attracted, Albert himself hated it and would as soon not have taken part in it. He had hoped for a quiet period away from the stress of operational flying, just to relax with his family and indulge his love of fishing and gardening. His hope was in vain, the Ball house was deluged in telephone calls and letters as well as personal callers. He had two weeks leave before he would commence his UK posting. This time was precious for him and he wanted to be with his family. Such occasions as the luncheon he had in Nottingham City Hall with the Mayor and Aldermen was a trial to him. He did not enjoy public speaking and it probably gave him more trouble to reply to the Mayor with a few simple words, than flying in France!

To maintain his privacy and to protect himself from being accosted by well wishers Ball took to wearing a service raincoat when out and about in the town. His photograph had, however, been published in the press, and recognition was sometimes inevitable. One day he went to his old engineering firm in Castle Boulevarde, and on others he went on trips to the families of local airmen and officers who he had known in France and was able to talk to them about their loved ones safety.

From his correspondence with his father it seems that the two of them were going to start some form of motor dealership. On the day following his arrival in Nottingham he was in London and he scribbled his father a quick note from the Hotel Victoria:

Re cars. We will take over the 12 two-seaters and three Trucks on the terms you have stated. I have got mine at £200.

> Five of the two-seaters will be ready this weekend. The remainder I am having finished in blue.[2]

Not much can be found out about this deal. It is possible that the cars concerned were Morgan sports cars but no proof can be found of this being the case. There is a picture of Albert Ball sitting in a 'Grand Prix' model which dates from this time. The picture was taken at the premises of the Colmore Depot, a famous car dealership, based in Colmore Row, Birmingham. The car apparently has a unique feature in the shape of the tail, which was not general for this type at the time. It is not possible, however, to definitely identify it as the car referred to in his letter.[3]

Later that day he sent a further note to his father:

> Since then (his previous note of the afternoon) I have had a word with Mr White about the Cars. Well now perhaps it will be better for you to come over and see White, you only showed Mr White the paper you drew up. I have not signed any papers. So you come over and see what you think.
>
> The car that I have got is good. If we take up the matter you only pay £200, if you don't think you wish to take it up we will have to draw up another plan.
>
> As I stated in my other letter we can get five of the cars on Wednesday next and the others will come along as soon as they are ready.
>
> Now if you think fit we will not settle on the matter for a few days.
>
> You come over and see White and in the meantime I will run my car and see what people think of it, if it pleases them we can take the matter up . . . They will be finished in about six weeks. This is OK for we shall not have a lot on our hands at the same time.
>
> If possible it will be wise for you to come over and see Mr White.[4]

There is no indication in the correspondence as to who Mr White is. It transpires from Albert Ball's letters from No.56 Squadron that White had paid him a retainer of £2,000.[5]

---

2 Ball Archives 6/10/1916.

3 I am indebted to Mr J. Alderson and Gregory Houston Bowden for the details on Morgans and the connections with Ball.

4 Ball Archives 6/10/1916.

5 Equivalent to about £86,000 in current values.

He was worried that White might start agitating for him to be withdrawn from service and returned home sooner than was expected to be the case. He told his father to tell White that if he did that he would repay all the £2,000 and not do a thing for him. If Ball was afraid that White might have influence to affect the decisions of the War Office, in which case he must have been a person of some consequence or knew people who had that sort of influence. In Kiernan[6] there is mention of a group of businessmen, connected with the aircraft industry, offering Ball a retainer of £1,000 on condition that he withdrew from active service with the RFC. Ball declined this offer so long as there was fighting to be done in France. The money seems to have been paid, however, and is said to have remained untouched in his bank account when he was killed. I have found no trace of this transaction in his existing correspondence, only the offer of £2,000 mentioned above. So there remains two mysteries finally to be reconciled as to Albert Ball's intentions during his final leave. All this took place while he was fully engaged in the advancement of the Austin Ball scout with the War Office and Austin's. It shows just how active Ball liked to be and that his mind was always seeking new areas of interest and advancement.

When his two weeks leave was up, Ball was posted to Orfordness for duty with No.34 (Reserve) Squadron as a fighting instructor. As the foremost fighting pilot of the RFC, Ball would have seemed to be ideally suited to the post. If he undertook much fighting instruction in this post is difficult to establish, but generally his duties seem to have been on a much lower more relaxed level consisting of short flights in Bristol scouts and the Avro 504.

The day after his arrival, the 19 October, he was invited down to London to have breakfast with the Minister for Munitions, Lloyd George and his daughter Megan. Lloyd George was an expansive man who liked good conversation and he may have charmed Ball into being more talkative. Certainly Lloyd George would have been interested in Ball's opinions on the war in the air and the capabilities of the various machines in service. However, the only comment which Ball made to his family about the affair was that, 'It was very nice'.

While he was in London on this day he also called in at the War Office and he told his father that he had been given instructions that on no account was he to go for a Zeppelin even if it passed over his

---

6 Kiernan p119.

head. He was told that he was being given an instructional post to teach other people to fight. His first assignment was to give a lecture at Oxford where he would be staying a few days, accommodated at Christ Church College.

It must have been while he was stationed at Orfordness that he made a flight in the Nottingham area, a flight which ended unfortunately for him. A gamekeeper and his son were walking in some woods on Lord Middleton's Estate. Their peace was disturbed by the sound of an aircraft going overhead. As the two watched the plane descended sharply towards the ground across the other side of a ploughed field. They raced over to the site of the crash to find the pilot standing by the side of the wreckage. The father recognised the pilot immediately as he had had dealings with the Ball family and had often taken game round to the Ball household. He shouted across to the pilot 'Is that you young Mr Albert?' To which Ball answered in the affirmative. On being asked if he was alright he answered sharply that he was. The father asked if he might keep a piece of the wreckage as a memento, to which Ball replied, 'you can have the whole bloody lot!' The gamekeeper contented himself to a broken part of the propeller blade.

Within three weeks Ball had left Orfordness and reported to the RFC School of Gunnery in Kent on the 7 November. Although he was undoubtedly in need of a rest from the demanding schedule of operational flying, the idea was always in his mind to return to the front. If he had had postings to appointments which were more to his taste, and to which he could have made a genuine contribution, this feeling may have been suppressed for a little while longer. The fact remains, however, that he was a fighting pilot, pure and simple, he was not a regular soldier. He had volunteered in the enthusiasm of 1914 to fight for his country and the transfer to the RFC had been merely to speed his movement to the front. Ball had made up his mind that he wished to return to the front. He told his Mother on the 14 November:

> ... I have offered to go out again and have another smack. I don't offer because I want to go, but because every boy who has loving people and a good home should go out and stand up for it. You think I have done enough but oh no, there is not or at least should not be such a thought in such a War as this.

Don't think me unfair in wishing to go again, for I don't do it because I wish to.

I must tell you that I love Dollie and shall find it so hard to go but you will all back me up, and I will try again to help my Country and bring credit to my dear Mother.

It will take a short time to arrange things, but Lord Derby is going to see to everything. I expect it may even be (within) a month.[7]

This letter shows that Ball still retained that patriotism which had taken him into the War in the first place. It was not the heady spirit of 1914 but the determination to see through the long grind, which the defeat of Germany would take. He felt that all should make the effort and sacrifice that was needed by the country. He still believed in the cause for which the War was being fought, but idealism no longer came into it. Ball wanted to fly and fight again as he believed that he was good at it and that this was the best way to help the country win through.

Interestingly, a new name appears in the letter to show a change in the love interest in Ball's life. Thelma seems to have been given up, with no explanation that I can see, and she appears only once more in the correspondence between Ball and his family. It would be interesting to know what was the cause of the break with Thelma when only a few weeks earlier he told his father that he and Thelma 'were a couple of the happiest Nippers ever'. According to Thelma's daughter it was because Thelma had met someone else but again, Ball does not mention it, which you would have thought he would have done. There is no indication as to when and where he met Dollie or even her surname. She was not to be long in his affections for, in early 1917, after joining No.56 squadron, he met Flora Young who proved to be the true love of his life. As for Thelma, records show that she married in 1921 and died on the 31 August 1986 in Melton Mowbray Leicestershire.

At Hythe Ball was given instruction on the Lewis and Vickers machine guns with a view to his being made an instructor. This was another post in which he felt bored and resentful. Although his interest in getting the Austin-Ball project moving was taking up a lot of his time, he began to press those in authority in the RFC to let him return to the front.

7 Ball Archives 14/11/1916.

The changes in air fighting tactics, which had begun to appear in the autumn of 1916, were still evolving and marking down the role of the lone fighter such as Ball. Even if the top brass of the RFC recognised that Albert Ball was purely a lone fighter and could never be happy or as effective as leader of a fighting patrol, which is doubtful, they would find it difficult to resist his pressure for a return to the fighting. To retain Ball in the UK, in effect to preserve his life for the benefit of the RFC, would require more imagination than they had shown in the postings they had arranged for him. It is possible that he might have been tempted by, say, an appointment as a liaison officer with Austin's, a post in which he could put all his enthusiasm for his projected fighter into effect. In such a post he would have the job satisfaction that he was being usefully employed in getting what he considered a superior fighting aircraft completed and into production.

Ball realised what pain it would cause his mother if he returned to France. He was not quite honest in telling her that he did not want to go, but he was doing it out of duty to his family and his country. However, his first application to go back was refused and his commanding officer advised him to make the best of his present situation. On arriving at Hythe his new commanding officer told him that he was, 'to learn all about guns' and then he was to teach other officers how to use those guns. Ball commented to his father that he would 'pass away' if he didn't get a different job soon. He felt unappreciated and that his talents going to waste, 'I cannot think why they are such fools!'[8]

As another step to getting back to flying he asked to be posted to a position involving some form of flying training rather than weapon training, which he found so irksome. All attempts to put his case for a return to France seemed to meet a blank wall; the reply of the War Office was always on the lines that they knew what was best for him and that when his services were again required in France he would be sent there. Ball had initiated an approach to General Sir David Henderson[9], via a friend of his father, a Mr Duckham, who worked in the Ministry of Munitions.

Among those Ball approached for assistance to get back to France was his local member of parliament, a Mr Richardson. He asked his father to send on to Richardson a note in which he made his feelings plain:

8 Ball Archives 16/11/1916.
9 Sir David Henderson (1862-1921), Director General of Military Aeronautics 1915-1917. First Commander of the RFC in the field.

I am at this school of Gunnery now and my orders are 'To learn about all the guns' and in a few weeks I shall be put on a job instructing others. May I see you on Monday?

I simply must get out again or at least get a job instructing on machines so that I can help OK. Please let me know what you think.[10]

While devoting time to his family, his service life and his efforts to get back to France, he also devoted attention to the Austin-Ball. He believed, perhaps rightly, that the project would never move forward unless he pushed it. There was probably not another officer, either before or since, who could do what Ball could and did do. From pursuing minor technical points, to confronting Brancker and Henderson face to face, to force the pace of getting the contract signed. It is these efforts on the part of Ball which led Austin's to believe that a quantity production order was to be placed when in fact only an order for two prototypes was intended. On the 21 November we find him writing from London that he will send some plans up to his father so he can give them to Austins. A few days later on finding that Austins had done very little about obtaining a 200hp Hispano Suiza engine he spent three hours at the War Office and arranged everything.

In the middle of these efforts Ball and his family went to Buckingham Palace on the 18 November to collect his DSO and two bars. The second bar to his DSO was to be officially notified in the *London Gazette* on the 24 November, but Ball had been notified before the official announcement making him the first officer to be awarded three DSOs. Ball was accompanied to Buckingham Palace by his parents, Lois and Cyril. The photograph of the group outside the Palace excludes Cyril, who was presumably taking the photograph, but it does show a third female figure as well as his Mother and Lois. It is likely that this is Dollie, for he appears to have wished her to be there.

Less than a week after his investiture at Buckingham Palace he was invited down to Farnborough to test the SE5 Scout. This machine had been designed by the Royal Aircraft Factory to make use of the promising new 150hp Hispano Suiza engine. The design for the SE5 had been undertaken by Henry Folland and John Kenworthy, though it is almost certain that Frank Goodden, the Factory's chief test pilot also had a hand in the design. The originally intended armament was

---

10 Ball Archives 16/11/1916.

to be a single Lewis gun firing through a hollow airscrew shaft. To make the arrangement practical the engine was to be a modified version having a geared drive to the airscrew to raise this to the level of the gun barrel. It is a coincidence that both the SE5 and the Austin-Ball had this feature and perhaps reflects the desire to do away with the, sometimes, unreliable interrupter gears. It was not possible for Ball to have influenced the SE5, for this design had been started in the summer of 1916, well before he had given any thought to the proposed layout of the new fighter he was proposing. The prototype, however, had a direct drive Hispano and had an intended armament of a synchronised Vickers gun. Production models were later fitted with the overwing mounted Lewis Gun, the idea for which might very well have come from Ball. It would certainly have been desirable to have a two gun armament, for pilots at the front flying the Sopwith Pup found themselves at a disadvantage against the twin-gun mountings of the German scouts, though not all pilots liked the arrangement of a Lewis gun on the top wing.

Ball flew the SE5 for a short ten minute flight on 23 November, the aircraft having been flown for the first time by Goodden the previous day. Being used to the more agile and lighter Nieuport he was, apparently, not favourably impressed with the new scout. His comments on the aircraft do not seem to have survived but are reckoned to have been unfavourable to the SE5.

Whatever his comments, and he was the first regular service pilot to have flown the type, they were not to have any effect on the decision regarding the future production of the SE5. The machine was one of the new aircraft which represented the future for the RFC and which were desperately needed in the face of German air superiority. On the very day that Ball flew the SE5 the RFC lost Lanoe Hawker to von Richthofen, to underline the fact that the old designs had had their day.

A month after Ball had flown the SE5, two more service pilots tried it. One was Lieutenant Selous of No. 19 squadron, where he had been flying Spads, and the other was Roderic Hill, a companion of Ball in No.60 squadron. They were both experienced pilots and Hill in particular was to be an excellent test pilot later on in his career. They flew the second prototype, A4562, which had been flown to St. Omer by Goodden on 24 December. With their combined experience of the latest French designs it would be possible to make a comparison with the SE and the French designs.

The comments of Selous were laudatory of the SE5:

> The range of speed is astonishing. I should put it at from 40 mph to 125 mph.
>
> It appears easier to fly (than the SPAD) and strong. In my opinion this is the best single seater I have seen.
>
> Lighter in the elevator than the SPAD but harder to keep in a steep dive.
>
> View is better in all directions than the SPAD.
>
> SE has a greater speed range than the SPAD.
>
> Is stable but can be manoeuvred as well as the SPAD. The SE can be landed much slower than a SPAD and has a flatter glide.[11]

The comments of Roderic Hill were equally complimentary to the SE and he compared the performance with that of the 110hp Nieuport and the 150hp SPAD:

> Speed near the ground is superior to the Nieuport and equal to the SPAD. Range of speed is greater.
>
> Climb near the ground of all three is equal. At 10,000ft the Nieuport falls off but the SPAD and the SE are assumed equal as they have the same engine and a similar wing section. The Nieuport ceiling is 17,000 and the SPAD 20,000 with the SE expected to be the same.
>
> The SE5 has, in my opinion, certain advantages over both the Nieuport and the SPAD. Its speed is good; it involves little strain on the pilot; it lands as slowly as a Nieuport and slower than the SPAD. Its gun mountings are superior. Its disadvantage with respect to the Nieuport is that it cannot be manoeuvred with quite the same rapidity, although at high altitudes swift manoeuvres should be possible with a much smaller loss of height.[12]

These reports must have been encouraging to those concerned with the development of the SE5 and those who had to take the responsibility of ordering new aircraft for the RFC. For some reason the SE5 remained an aircraft viewed with deep suspicion by members of the Air Board. In France, when it arrived with No.56 squadron, Trenchard reported to the Air Board that he was disappointed with the

---

11 NA AIR1/1077/204/5/1674 Reports & Correspondence on SE5 Aeroplanes.
12 ditto.

SEs that had been issued to the squadron. He did not like the gravity tank on the top wing surface, nor what he called 'the conservatory' for the pilot and the 35lb of armour plating which had been fitted. All these things, he said, reduced its performance, but they were being put right by the squadron in the field and the Aircraft Depot. At this same meeting Sir William Weir commented that the 'design of the SE5 had not worked out well'. General Pitcher agreed and that the sooner it was replaced by the 200 hp Spad the better and he had sent to Paris for the drawings of the 200hp Spad. He had to concede, however, that his Department still thought the SE5 a good machine. General Henderson shared the general dislike of the SE5. Weir mentioned that he had a directive to order 200 more SE5s from Vickers and suggested that if the drawings for the Spad were complete Vickers could build those. The meeting agreed to suspend the order for more SE5s for the moment.[13]

These doubts at higher levels about the SE5 did not affect the position that the machine had to be ordered in quantity. There was enough that was encouraging about the performance of the machine to give it its proper place as one of the mainstays of the future equipment of the RFC scout squadrons. There was one final tragic incident in the tale of the development of the SE5. The second prototype, A4562, which had been tested in France was flown back to Farnborough by Goodden on 26 January. Two days later on a cold Sunday morning he took off in A4562 for a short flight. Ten minutes later, as he was approaching Farnborough, the aircraft broke up in the air and Goodden was killed in the subsequent crash, a great loss to British aviation and Farnborough in particular. A painstaking investigation established that the failure had been caused by a weakness in the lower wing and this fault was rectified in the production machines.

The SE5 and the 5a went on to become one of the best fighters of the war. Even Ball was to become reconciled to it as he realised its advantages over the Nieuport. Though the probable cause of his death was an endemic fault in the carburation system of the Hispano engine which caused his engine to fail at the critical moment.

While Ball continued his efforts to get back to France the honours still continued to fall on him. Shortly after his trip to Buckingham Palace, Nottingham City Council passed a resolution to make him an

---

13 NA AIR6/7. Meeting of the Air Board 13 April 1917.

Honorary Freeman of the City. Then on 19 December, in the Albert Hall in Nottingham, he was guest of honour at a ceremony, a tribute from the citizens of Lenton, his home area. He was presented with an illuminated address and a silver rose bowl suitably inscribed.

At about this time Albert Ball met James McCudden in London and the two talked of air fighting techniques. McCudden was impressed by Ball's method of attack on two-seaters by approaching from underneath[14]. Later when McCudden had taken part in the interception of a Gotha bomber he had tried this tactic but on the larger opponent it was not a success. Ball noticed McCudden's Croix de Guerre and remarked that he would like to have a French medal![15]

McCudden was impressed with the spirit of Ball and he recognised the great example which Ball had set for the RFC.

On 2 January yet another instructional post came up for Ball when he was posted to the 7th Wing at Kings Lynn in Norfolk. On 4 January his name was in the *London Gazette* for a 'Mentioned in Despatches'. At the same time Ball was at Kings Lynn, his brother Cyril was also there undergoing training, and the two brothers were able to fly together. Ball was anxious about the possibilities for Cyril when he went to France and wanted to get him to a Spad squadron. He believed the Spad to be the only Allied scout, in British service, which would give his brother a chance against the German scouts. He considered the SE5 to be a flop and inferior to both the Nieuport and his own machine, on which he pinned his ultimate hopes, was progressing slowly.

On 18 January Ball wrote to Brigadier Charlton with another request to be sent to France. Charlton,[16] who was Director of Air Organisation, wrote back a sympathetic letter on 24 January. He recognised Ball's sincere motives for wishing to be sent back to the Front, and promised that as soon as it was considered necessary he should go. He finished with the hopeful expression 'I have my eye on you, and shall not forget you'.

All the avenues that Ball tried to obtain his return to France had failed, so as a last resort he approached Lord Northcliffe, the press baron and a man of great influence. He was promised that Northcliffe would raise his case with the Government and also push the case for

14 Cole, *McCudden VC* p89.
15 Kiernan p116.
16 Brigadier General Lionel Edwyn Oswald Charlton(1879-1958). Served in the Boer War and was seriously wounded at Spion Kop. Joined the RFC April 1914 and served on the Western Front with Nos 3 & 8 Squadrons. He tried to prevent under trained pilots from being sent out to the front. He was successful in stopping three such pilots from being sent but his orders were immediately countermanded by Trenchard. He clashed again with Trenchard over the policy of bombing Iraqi villages and resigned from his position as CSO in Iraq.

the Austin-Ball. On 8 February Ball told his mother that he was seeing Lord Northcliffe that afternoon and hoped the intervention of the press baron would be successful, for he didn't like Cyril, who was now in France, being out on his own. A couple of days later he was confident enough to tell his mother that 'Lord Northcliffe is getting me out'.

Whether it was the influence of Lord Northcliffe or not, he was informed on 17 February that he would be joining No.56 (Training Squadron) based at London Colney. The Squadron was working up to go to France and it was the intention to equip it with the new SE5. Prior to this last posting he was given a short spell of leave, which he spent in Nottingham. During this period he had to undergo the ceremony enrolling him as a Freeman of the City. He was presented with an illuminated scroll and a silver casket with a replica of his Nieuport mounted on the top. In the week following this ceremony Ball reported to London Colney.

Writing to his mother on the morning of 25 February he told her that he was joining No.56 squadron at London Colney and would not be able to get home. He said that he was sorry that he was not going out at once but he would ensure that everything was, 'OK and ready for France'.

CHAPTER NINE

With No.56 Squadron
February to March 1917

The new Squadron, which Ball joined in February 1917, had been long in gestation. In April 1916 the War Office had approved the formation of new squadrons during 1916, one of which was listed as '56 Squadron – Scouts'. The system allowed for the creation of these new squadrons by the formation of a nucleus flight. Each of these flights was attached to a parent squadron and for No.56 Squadron the nucleus flight was attached to No.28 Squadron stationed at Fort Grange, Gosport. No pilots or aeroplanes were posted to these flights, they consisted solely of maintenance personnel and the first airmen posted to the nucleus flight arrived on 8 June 1916. They were three 2nd Class Air Mechanics.[1] The squadron seems to have been made into an official identity on 23 June, with the first commanding officer being Major Ernest Leslie Gossage.[2]

London Colney aerodrome was situated on the road running from the village of Shenley near to St. Albans. No.56 Squadron arrived there on 14 July to find the proposed flying field covered in corn. Some permanent buildings had already been erected which were to contain the administrative and work areas of the squadron. Tents were erected for the airmen's accommodation.

As the summer and autumn of 1916 changed to winter, commanding officers came and went. Gossage was succeeded by Major A. A. Thompson, then Major R. M. Vaughan and in December 1916 command passed to Major H. D. Harvey-Kelly, who for many years was credited with being the first pilot of the RFC to land in France in 1914. Harvey-Kelly then left to command No.19 Squadron in which post he lost his life in combat with the von Richthofen's *Jasta* in April 1917. The command of the squadron was temporarily held by Captain

---

1 See Alex Revell's excellent work *High in the Empty Blue* pp 1-4 for details of the Squadron prior to Ball's arrival.
2 Later Air Marshal Sir Ernest Gossage (1891-1949) Joined RFC 1915. Flew with No.6 Squadron and Commanded No.8 Squadron.

Clive Gallop until Major Richard Blomfield[3] was appointed on 6 February 1917. With the appointment of Blomfield things began to move, the final shape of the squadron began to form and Blomfield is credited with securing the appointment of Albert Ball as a flight commander when he knew that Ball was agitating for a return to the fighting. The wish of Blomfield was to make No.56 Squadron the best squadron in the RFC and the appointment of Ball was a building block in this process. The worth of Blomfield to the squadron at this time was noted by 2nd Lt T. B. Marson:

> He was . . . an excellent organiser, full of energy and initiative. It was under Major Blomfield's auspices that No.56 Squadron completed its formation and went to France, and to his powers of organisation and hard work were due a great proportion of the success which it gained overseas . . . He determined to spare no efforts to make the success unmistakeable, and to this end, which was attained, he devoted all his energies.[4]

The other two Flight Commanders were Captain Ian Henderson, son of Sir David Henderson, and Captain Ernest Foot, a companion of Ball in No.60 Squadron and probably included by Blomfield on the recommendation of Ball. All the Flight Commanders chosen were experienced pilots, veterans of previous service in France and all were above average pilots. Only Ball had a public reputation, but Foot was credited with five victories from his service with Nos 11 and 60 Squadrons, while Henderson had three from his service with No.19 Squadron, which score included two gained on the unlikely BE12. It is not perfectly clear, as no official record seem to have survived as to the allocation of the flight commanders, we know (from his own letters) that Ball was to be in command of A Flight. It is a reasonable assumption that Henderson was to have B Flight and Foot C Flight.

When Henderson was unable to proceed Crowe replaced him as B Flight Commander. Despite a short illness, Crowe took over B Flight again when he eventually went back to France and Meintjes, who had come in to replace Foot, had command of C Flight.[5]

Henderson was not, however, able to go to France with the Unit in April, having broken his nose and he was posted away while this injury

---

3 Richard G. Blomfield. Seconded to the RFC in 1915. After leaving No.56 Squadron he went with the British Mission to the USA and was awarded the DSO. He remained in the RAF after the War with the rank of Wing Commander. He was Director of Recruiting from 1922-1924 and retired from the RAF in 1924.

4 Marson, *Scarlet and Khaki* (London 1930)p135

5 Letter from Alex Revell to the author 19/8/2008.

was cured. He did return to the squadron later, and served as B Flight Commander until the arrival of McCudden. He was to lose his life in a flying accident on 21 June 1918.

Henderson's immediate replacement was Captain Cyril Marconi Crowe (known as 'Billy'). Crowe had served in France with both Nos 8 and 16 Squadrons but had no experience with single-seaters, all his experience being with the BE. He too was not to make it to France with the initial detachment, being taken ill with measles and was consequently temporarily invalided out of the squadron. His replacement, again possibly with Ball's influence to the fore, was Captain Henry Meintjes, a South African, who had been with Ball in No.60 Squadron, and by this time had been credited with four victories. Meintjes had been sent home for a rest but with a recommendation from the commander of No.60 Squadron that he was possessed, 'of all the qualities a scout pilot and patrol leader should have', and would make an ideal flight commander.

While the question as to who should fill the posts of flight commanders was, after some disruption, settled, the question of filling the rest of the flying posts was equally important. Although Blomfield wanted to make the squadron the best in the RFC he could never have a free hand to pick and chose amongst the best pilots in the RFC. He would have to take his choice from amongst those available in Home Establishment postings, especially the Training Squadrons. Like Boelcke before him, Ball was sent to 'talent spot' suitable pilots from the mass of those available, and both Barlow and Maxwell were amongst those chosen by Ball[6].

Among those joining the squadron was Cecil Lewis. He had served with No.3 Squadron during the Somme battles, flying the difficult Morane Parasols and for his work had been awarded the MC. He was even younger than Ball and had joined the squadron just before his 19th birthday. Lewis had a long and varied life before dying at the advanced age of 98, the last survivor of the original No.56 Squadron. As an experienced officer Lewis recognised the strength given to the squadron by its flight commanders, but more importantly he was impressed by the character of Major Blomfield:

> Major Blomfield . . . was determined to allow nothing to come
> between him and making his the crack fighting squadron in the

---

6 See Revell, *High in the Empty Blue* p5.

RFC. His geniality did not prevent him being very sharp eyed and nimble-witted. Efficiency was his watchword.

In appearance he was shortish and slightly built. He wore leggings, and invariably carried a short leather covered cane, with which he directed everything, reminding one irresistibly of a dapper little ringmaster. Tremendously energetic and keen he was always to be seen hurrying here and there giving close personal supervision to every detail of the squadron's work – activity and organisation personified. He had all his pilots out for a run before breakfast, kept them busy round the sheds all day, and turned them loose in town at night. They had to be tip-top aviators and bring down Huns. Nothing else mattered.[7]

The attachment of pilots to the squadron continued in February and March. Apart from the flight commanders, Lewis was one of the few to have had any previous flying experience at the front. Some had had front line experience in the army before transferring to the RFC, but even those came to the squadron from the flying training schools. Ball was said to have spotted the potential of Maxwell and Barlow, and if that is the case his judgement was more than justified. The appointment of Chaworth-Musters may also have been due to Ball as they were a prominent Nottingham family and Ball may have used his influence to get the posting to No.56 Squadron.

Among those joining in March was Arthur Percival Foley Rhys Davids. He had been recruited by Foot and recounted the event in a letter to his mother:

Just a line to say I have got a job on the new scouts at London Colney near St. Albans . . . Isn't it splendid? Muspratt and two others have got it. I was playing billiards with Muspratt this morning . . . When Captain Foot came in. He is second only to Ball as a fighting expert and **both** are to be flight commanders in the new squadron. Well he is a temporary fighting instructor here and he came up to me and said 'Would you like to fly SE5s (ie Scout Experimental, 5th type). So of course I said that I would love to. Then he said that we would go along to London Colney as soon as the machines arrived there and we would go out at

---

7 Lewis, *Sagitarrius Rising* (Greenhill Books London 2006) pp 163/164.

the end of this month, (he was writing on 7 March) which probably means the first week in April. Gee! Aint I bucked.[8]

Rhys Davids had a brief hiatus when counter orders arrived posting him to the newly forming No.66 Squadron but eventually things sorted themselves out and he was destined for No.56 Squadron. Foot also chose Keith Muspratt who was a close friend of Rhys Davids. Two other pilots from Upavon, Barlow and Maxwell, were, as already mentioned, also chosen for the squadron, apparently on the recommendation of Ball.

On arrival at London Rhys Davids met, and gave his impression of, Albert Ball, calling him the 'great Ball'. Rhys Davids described Ball as 'quite dark and very small and very unassuming and quiet'. The following day he described Ball as 'A funny little dark fellow: very homely and absolutely no 'side' – with **rows** of medals'.

Rhys Davids was academically brilliant with a first class mind, but was also a first class snob, believing that his education made him so much better than most of his companions, and that few were worth making friends with. One of the few who did get close to him was Cecil Lewis and they had long philosophical discussions together. Although his attitude to others later mellowed, and his achievements as an air fighter justified his selection for the squadron, he probably found it difficult later on in the year to come under the command of James McCudden, an ex-ranker, with a limited education, but supreme talent as an air fighter.

As will be seen from the Appendix, most of the pilots who flew to France with the squadron had arrived by the time the first SE5 was flown in by Ball on 15 March. Only Leach arrived the day after and Cecil Lewis four days after that.

Perhaps the most important member of the squadron at this time, after Major Blomfield, was the engineering officer. The man appointed to this post was Lieutenant H.N. Charles and he had been in post since December. The possibility of trouble with the SE5 had been foreseen by Trenchard and he had asked John Salmond to keep a look out for a good candidate to fill the post. Charles had been responsible at one time for the maintenance of Salmond's own aircraft and Salmond recommended him to Trenchard for the post with No.56 Squadron, a recommendation which was more than justified by the excellent work

8 Revell, *Brief Glory* pp80/81.

which Charles put in over the next few months getting the SE5 suitable for service.[9]

Without the work of Charles the squadron would not have had the serviceability levels and success rate which it did. Charles held an honours degree in engineering from London University and Ball with his engineering background would have appreciated his work. Rhys Davids with his classical education did not, and described him as 'a common place young man'.

Albert Ball wrote home on 14 March, an interesting letter in which Thelma is mentioned for the last time in his correspondence. Whatever the state of relations with Thelma at that time they seem to have been on friendly terms and not to have any ill feeling towards each other. His father seems to have asked Ball to get back some decoration from Thelma, which Ball had allowed her to keep. It is not clear which decoration this was, but it was probably the Russian Order of St. George. His father was jealously possessive of any honours which were awarded to his son. He made it clear that he wanted this medal back to be retained by the family. Ball really did not relish the task:

Well now about the award from Thelma.

I don't want to do it and I don't think you are a sport to ask me.

I told her that I wanted it to go to a wedding. Now she will send it if I promise to send it back again. How can I promise? If I do and don't keep my word, I shall be considered a cad. However, I will do it for you, but please understand that I do not like taking it.

Well now I am on Cyril's trail and hope to get him into my Squadron. I am giving my word that he could fly SE5s and the CO is going to write to Leobury for me and see what he can do. I bet I shall manage it when I get out.

Villiers will arrive in the morning and I do hope he will work hard and be a credit to my Flight for he is to be my right hand man.

All the chaps in my flight are young boys, so they should do well.[10]

Villiers, his old Observer in No.13 Squadron, did arrive with the

---

9 Revell, *High in the Empty Blue* p7.
10 Ball Archives 14/3/1917.

squadron, but did not make it out to France. He had gone home for pilot training while serving with No.13 Squadron and it is possible that when the final selection came to be made of the pilots to go to France he was considered lacking in the skills to handle the SE5. Cyril never did arrive in No.56 Squadron. He completed his pilot training later in the year and was posted to No.60 Squadron in December 1917. On a patrol on 5 February 1918 his SE5a was hit by anti-aircraft fire and his engine was disabled. Gliding towards the British lines he was attacked by Albatros Scouts from *Jasta 26* and forced to land behind the German lines. He was to spend the rest of the war as a POW. He died in 1958.

On 15 March, Ball and Foot went to Farnborough to collect the first SE5s. They were said to have engaged in a private race to be the first to land an SE at London Colney. Ball was the winner of this race when Foot was forced to land near Hendon with engine trouble. When he arrived back at London Colney and flew the machine round the field the watchers were not impressed. Lieutenant Charles remembers:

> . . . when he started flying the thing around London Colney, before landing, everybody simply couldn't believe it – that this was the new SE5 fighter? The thing looked hopeless! It was obviously slow and Ball obviously didn't want to do any aerobatics on it. When it landed it was boiling. The paint was all stuck to the outside of the cylinder block. The very first thing we did was to take the radiator off and wash it out backwards with a mixture of weak washing soda and water and fit it with a wire mesh filter bag in the header tank, so that if any more paint came out of the water jacket it wouldn't block the radiator, washed out the water jacket and put the whole thing back. From then on the engine ran without boiling, so that was stage one. Then, one by one, we went through the other rather obvious faults. The aim of all our efforts simply became to get the aeroplanes to fly to France with their Lewis guns, engines and controls working and leave the Vickers and the interrupter gear until France.[11]

The SE5 in question, A4850[12], was to become Ball's own aircraft and the one in which he was to be killed. Another SE5 came in from Farnborough (A4848) that same day flown by Foot, and Lieutenant Kay collected four more, A4853; A4862; A4866; and A4863 during the next

---

11 Revel *High in the Enpty* Blue p9.
12 Bowyer (p112) says that A4850 arrived in a crate where it was adopted by Ball as his personal aircraft. I have preferred to follow Revell that Ball flew back in this machine.

couple of weeks. The problems with the SE5 were immediately apparent to the pilots of the squadron, though Rhys Davids assured his sister that they looked 'A1', and they were also a revelation to Hubert Charles, who, as engineering officer, was faced with the job of getting them ready for France. One thing with which all the pilots expressed dissatisfaction was the large enclosing windscreen round the cockpit. Only Albert Ball seems to have had this construction removed immediately and replaced with a simpler Avro type windshield. The other pilots seem to have waited until they got to France before this modification was made. Also unusual was the high seating position which exposed the pilots upper body well clear of the cockpit. At least Ball and Hoidge altered this seating position on their machines before the squadron left London Colney, as contemporary photographs show.

Most important of all was the appalling state of the synchronising gear for the single Vickers gun. The problems with this were so many, mainly due to poor manufacturing standards, that they were unable to be rectified before the squadron went to France. Once in France the gear was worked on and modified until all the troubles were cured and pilots could rely on the gear not to let them down.

Ball made considerable changes to his SE5. The performance of the machine he had flown from Farnborough had confirmed his already bad opinion of the type. He wanted to save weight with a view to improving performance. Recognising the considerable problems which existed with the installation of the Vickers and the synchronising gear, he had this gun and gear taken off his plane. In the space vacated by the synchronising mechanism he replaced the existing fuel tank by a slightly larger one. In addition he added an extra Lewis gun to fire downwards through the floor of the cockpit. These two additions must have more than compensated for the lost weight of the missing Vickers and its associated gear. What Ball's thinking was when he asked for the fitting of a downward firing Lewis is difficult to imagine. Such guns were specified later in the war for types dedicated to trench strafing, but for a pilot like Ball, whose fighting method relied solely on surprise and shock, it is difficult to see how a mounting of this type could have been useful to him. Over the period from 15 March to 2 April Ball had the windscreen changed; the seating position altered to give him a lower position in the aircraft, the centre section altered to have an enlarged cut-out to give better upwards vision and also incorporating a revised gravity tank. He also added a small headrest behind the cockpit, had 'Bristol' type wheels fitted and the tailplane controls altered. He seems to have been the only pilot to go to such an extensive list of changes. Most of these alterations would later be fitted to other squadron machines, but this was after they arrived in France. Ball told his father of his opinion of the SE5 and the work he was doing:

> The SE5 has turned out a dud. Its speed is only about Nieuport speed and it is not so fast in getting up. It is a great shame for everyone thinks they are so good and expect such a lot from them.
>
> Well I am making the best of a bad job. If Austin's will not buck up and finish a machine for me I shall have to out on the SE5 and do my best.
>
> I am getting one ready. I am taking one gun off in order to lose weight, also I am lowering the windscreen in order to take off head resistance. A great many things I am taking off in the hopes that I shall get a little better control and speed. But it is a rotten machine and if the Austin's machine is not finished I am afraid that things will not go very OK.[13]

As departure for France approached his thoughts turned more to the job ahead. As the letter quoted above shows, he was well aware that the German air services had now regained aerial supremacy and that conditions were much more difficult than they had been before. There seems to have been an understanding, whether official or unofficial, that he would serve only a month in France and then return home. I have not been able to find any definite proof that he had such an assurance from the War Office but he seems to have been aware of it and in the same letter quoted above he mentioned the matter to his father in the context of his business deals:

> Now re coming home in a month.
>
> Well, White must keep shut up until I give the word or he will spoil everything. If I get my own machine I will come in a month but if I have to work on SE5s the job I am out to do will take longer, so I may be two months. In any case White must not start asking for me to come home until I am ready or I shall return his £1,000 and shall refuse to do anything. It will help the firm if I stay out a little longer and this War is at no end yet.[14]

---

13 Ball Archives 23/3/1917.
14 Ibid.

This is an interesting letter for the questions it raises. There is still the question as to who is Mr. White. This letter seems to show that White had influence, or access to people who had influence, which might get Ball recalled from the front. What did Ball mean when he said that White would 'spoil everything'. We know, from previous correspondence, that the agreement between Mr White and the Ball family was in relation to a motor agency. So what was there to spoil? Then there is the phrase 'the job I am out to do'. It is known that Ball kept a keen eye on the victory score of the French Ace Guynemer. It is possible that he wanted to beat Guynemer to be the first Allied pilot to score fifty victories before he went home.

At London Colney Ball's personal life took another twist when he met his final, and probably deepest love, Flora Young. At that time Ball seems to have parted from Thelma and no other girl seems to have occupied his attention. He had a lot on his mind with the preparation of his aircraft for his eventual posting back to the front, the problems arising from the production of the Austin Ball, as well as the duties concerned with the management of 'A' Flight. He was therefore not much concerned with his own personal affairs in the matter of female attachments. However, for all his preoccupation, he did meet, and was immediately taken by an attractive young woman he met on the airfield at London Colney. Mr Piper, a family friend, who lived in the area decided to renew his acquaintance with Ball. The Piper family had had Albert Ball billeted on them in the early days of his service career. Mr Piper either could not, or chose not to, drive and asked Flora Young to take him over to the airfield. Flora was living in St. Albans and working in agriculture as part of the war effort. When the car drew up two officers approached and began to talk to Mr Piper. One of them was the Canadian J. O. Leach and the other was Albert Ball. Flora had heard of Ball but had never seen him and her first sight was of a short, dark haired man in a scruffy and stained uniform and dirty boots. If she had any doubt that the man she was looking at was Ball these were soon settled when she was formally introduced to him by Mr. Piper.

The two young people were much of an age[15]. Flora was about a year younger than Ball and the attraction, at least as far as Ball was concerned, was instant. Ball asked Flora whether she would like a flight and on her accepting the offer she was dressed in a flying coat

---

15 Flora was born on 12 September 1897, the daughter of architect William Young and his wife Flora in St. Albans. Following the death of Ball she married Charles Thornhill in St. Georges Church, Hanover Square, London in 1925. She died in April 1985.

borrowed from Leach. An Avro 504K was available and Flora was installed in the rear seat. Ball took her for a short trip round the aerodrome and the surrounding area. After landing they talked together for a while but without either of them speaking of their personal feelings. After Flora had left he was unable to get her out of his mind and that night he wrote her a short note, 'Just cannot sleep without first sending you a line to thank you for the topping day I have had with you. I am simply full of joy to have met you . . .'. This seems to have been a much deeper and more mature feeling on his part than he had felt before. There was no doubt that that he had been in love with Thelma, but his feelings for Flora seem to have been more intense. He met her again the following day and in writing to her nicknamed her 'Bobs' though the reason for the nickname is not known!

Whether he told anybody of his feelings or not it must have soon become plain, for he followed Flora to wherever she might happen to be working. Word of the affair reached the London *Evening Standard* who ran the story under the headline 'A Modern Romeo' His fellow officers, even if they had not already guessed, light heartedly ribbed him about it! He was perhaps the happiest he had ever been and the growing love between himself and Flora gave him every reason to look forward to the future, for he had found the girl he wanted to marry.

That future was in the hands of fate. On 29 March Major Blomfield received orders that the squadron was to prepare for immediate departure to France. The schedule laid down by the War Office called for the transport to leave on 3 April, personnel on 5 April and machines to be flown off on 7 April. All those officers on leave were immediately recalled by Major Blomfield. The squadron now had its full establishment of SE5s and these had been made as fit as possible for the trip to France.

CHAPTER TEN

Back to France
April 1917

The last few days before the squadron was to leave for France were a busy time for everyone. Stores had to be checked and packed and aircraft made ready for their departure. All those officers who were flying across had packed their personal kit for onward transmission to France. Only the very basics were left for them to live on prior to their departure.

A party of men, together with Captain Meintjes, Lt. Kay and the Squadron Recording Officer, 2nd Lt. T.B. Marson left on 5 April. This party took with them a selection of general and aircraft stores. Their destination was to be the aerodrome of Vert Galant in Northern France. This movement seems to have been arranged as an emergency action when the Admiralty informed the War Office that due to the moonlight nights they were not willing to ship the squadron's heavy transport from Southampton until 11 April,

The following day, Good Friday, 6 April, snow fell, a light scattering which features so prominently on the photographs taken of Ball in A4850 on that day. That evening a combined celebration dinner and farewell party was held at an hotel in Radlett. It was a restrained affair, all the pilots, according to Cecil Lewis, being determined to go to bed sober and early. That night the mechanics worked late, making the last minute adjustments to the machines.

It is known that Albert Ball was at the party. As a senior flight commander he was expected to be, but he left early as he had decided to spend his last hours at home with Flora. He had had a small brooch made for her in the form of the RFC wings in silver and decorated with diamonds. He presented this gift to her as she was driving him back to the airfield that evening. That he presented it to her at this time rather than earlier in the evening seems to show that he had to screw his courage up for the occasion, perhaps not being sure of its reception. Flora was delighted with the gift and the surprise of receiving it at such a time almost caused her to crash the car.

Given Ball's strong religious beliefs the Easter period was important to him. He attended the local church on the evening of 5 April going in civilian clothes to preserve his anonymity. The rest of the evening he spent at home with Flora.

On 6 April, after leaving the party to be with Flora he told her that he wanted to marry her when he returned from his period in France, and in token of his feelings he presented her with his small gold identity bracelet from his wrist. Flora gave him a small book of Robert Louis Stevenson's prayers and when he asked her to sing to him (she had had operatic training) she sang *Thank God for a Garden*. Perhaps for the first time in his life Ball now had a love as strong as that he felt for his family. Now, after his time in France, he could look forward to a golden future with the girl he loved.

The squadron was to fly off the following morning but fate had one more surprise in store. Captain Foot who was to have led the flight to France had been involved in a car accident on 6 April and was too seriously injured in the crash to be considered for service in France.[1] In his place Cecil Lewis would lead the squadron to Vert Galant.

For the flight across the Channel each pilot had been issued with a life jacket for use in the event that a forced landing might have to be made in the Channel. These jackets are shown in the photographs of the various pilots taken that day, but it is uncertain whether all, or any, of the pilots actually wore them for the flight. They would have made the cockpit conditions more cramped than they already were. No pictures seem to exist of the arrival of the squadron in France, so there is no proof one way or the other if the jackets were worn.

A number of civilians came down to see the squadron off. Ball had asked Flora not to attend, but her 17 year old brother Bill did attend, along with her father. Also present were members of the de la Rue family who owned the land on which the airfield stood, and two young girls who had been celebrating with the officers the night before in Radlett. Before Ball had got into his machine he scribbled a pencil note to Flora giving the time and date *7th April 1917. 8.30* there are two

---

1 In fact Foot did not fly on operations again in France. He was to be killed in a crash in 1923.

versions as to what the note said, *Goodbye Bobs. Albert*[2] and *God Bless you dear*.[3] The note was handed to Bill to deliver to Flora.

All engines were started and at 11.50am with the SEs all ready to go Major Blomfield gave the signal for the take-off. One by one they taxied and turned into the wind, then Lewis (in A4853) opened up the engine and began his take-off, followed by Ball (A4850); Barlow (A4858); Knight (A4855); Melville (A4852); Hoidge (A4862); Rhys Davids (A4847); Leach (A4856); Lehman (A4861); Chaworth-Musters (A4860); Maxwell (A4863); Knaggs (A4854) and finally Major Blomfield (A4866). The squadron circled the field once then turned east to begin the flight to France. They were not to fly directly across London, but travelled north of the capital and followed the route: Chingford; Romford; Gravesend and Maidstone before crossing the coast at Folkestone.

The squadron crossed the Channel to Calais then went on to St. Omer, the headquarters of the RFC, where they landed and had lunch in the town. After lunch they made the short further flight to Vert Galant. They were to operate from this farm situated some 6 miles south of Doullens and adjacent to the Amiens-Doullen road. The field had been an RFC operating base since the early days of the war and they would be sharing with No.66 Squadron operating Pups and No.19 Squadron operating Spads. The field to the west of the road was to be used by No.66 Squadron while that to the east would be shared by Nos 19 and 56 Squadrons. The squadron was still disorganised, as the heavy transport under the command of Lt Charles was not due to arrive until 18 April. Temporary transport had been arranged by Headquarters RFC until the arrival of the squadron's own transport. This arrived at Rouen on the early morning of 17 April and was unloaded and formed into a convoy. It crawled across France stopping on the way at Neufchatel for the night and arrived at Vert Galant on the evening of the 18th.

The day following their arrival saw the visit of General Trenchard who was on a round of visiting the fighting squadrons. He arrived in an RE8 with his assistant Maurice Baring in a BE2c and spoke to the commanding officers and pilots of the squadrons. The presence of Trenchard spurred Ball to push his request for the use of a Nieuport as well as the SE5. He followed the departing visitors to Le Hameau aerodrome and again pressed his case on Trenchard.

---

2 Revell *High in the Empty Blue* p14.
3 Bowyer p117 and Kiernan p125.

This request was to be the start of an intense period of pressure by both Ball and his father to get him the Nieuport Scout so that he could do what he called 'his job'. So poor was his opinion of the SE5 that he told his father that Cyril should try to go out on Spads and promised his father that he would arrange this! At this time he seems to have had the impression that his personal intervention could open all doors, as witness his efforts to push the Austin-Ball forward, and that bureaucratic obstacles could be overcome. He certainly made use of the fame he had earned in making this rather presumptious demand to higher authorities.

He wrote to his father on 11 April:

> I have got a job for you and if you will, I should like you to take it up at once. They have put me on this SE5 and simply will not let me get back on a Nieuport.
>
> Now I must get back and as soon as possible or I shall never be able to do my job.
>
> I must either fly a Nieuport or a SPAD and then I can get along with the job. Just put it in the right hands and all will be OK.
>
> Well things are going and I think we shall be at work on Monday. Our kit has not arrived yet but it may do so in the morning.[4]

Matters were amicably settled on 13 April when he and Blomfield went to tea with Trenchard. According to Maurice Baring,[5] Trenchard 'was delighted with Ball and is giving him two machines: the SE5 for his ordinary work and the Nieuport for his individual enterprises'. The Nieuport allotted to Ball was a Nieuport 23, serial number B1522. Ball and Meintjes went to Candas that evening and Meintjes flew back the new Nieuport and Ball collected his SE5, A4850, which had now been standardised in line with the other machines of the squadron.

The Squadron suffered its first casualty on 9 April when Lt. Bailey, a new pilot who had been posted in the previous day crashed on taking his first flight on an SE5. Bailey was badly enough injured in the crash to be taken to hospital and the machine, A4854, was wrecked. The cause of the crash is not known but was probably due to pilot error.

The squadron was not due to fly any offensive sorties for the next

---

4 Ball Archives 11/4/1917.
5 Baring, *Flying Corps Headquarters 1914-1918* (London Buchan and Enright 1985) p214.

few days. Time was allotted to make the machines ready for war. In this period Ball made his usual arrangements to provide his own sleeping accommodation. This time he did opt to share with Gerald Maxwell and they constructed a hut together. Major Blomfield, now that he was in France, gave orders to set to work to modify the SEs generally on the lines of Ball's machine, except that the Vickers gun was retained and a downward firing Lewis gun was not fitted. This was in accordance with a directive from HQ RFC dated 8 April[6] which listed the alterations as windscreens to be changed, armoured seat to be taken out and a board fitted across, and to improve the Lewis gun mounting and fit longer Spad type exhausts. The squadron commander was to ensure that all machines were the same. It also stated that the modification of Ball's machine to fit the downward firing Lewis was not approved. That Headquarters had noticed the attention Ball was paying to his machine was obvious from two communications dated 10 April 1917. The first was to the 9th Wing under which No.56 Squadron operated, as to why Ball had flown his aircraft to No.2 Aircraft Depot at Candas on the 9th. The other was to Candas, to say that A4850 was to be standardised in line with the other machines in the squadron. This included replacing the Vickers gun which Ball had had removed. In order to retain the larger fuel tank in A4850, which Ball had had fitted in place of the Vickers, the gun was mounted above the fuselage, a fixing which is clearly demonstrated in the last ever photograph taken of Ball on the evening of 6 May.

Major Blomfield replied to the enquiry from 9th Wing on 12 April:

Captain Ball asked if he might fly his machine over to No.2 AD to show the Aeroplane Repair Section exactly how far he wanted the Gun Mounting on the top plane lengthened. I accordingly gave this officer permission to do so.

I regret I made an error in allowing this machine to go away from the aerodrome, and will be careful to see in future that an occurrence of this sort will not happen again.

For your information I am sending Captain Ball to collect this machine from 2 AD today.[7]

Trenchard had also written to London about the modifications to Ball's machine. noting that it had arrived in France with the condenser and the gravity tank in the centre section of the top plane. This work was

6 NA AIR1/1077/204/5/1764.
7 Ibid.

understood to have been done by the Training Brigade in England and the RFC in France would like to see the drawings for this modification as they were working on a similar system for the other squadron machines.

The SE5 had created the same feeling of disappointment in France that it had engendered at all levels in Britain. As seen earlier Trenchard had complained that the machine, which he was being asked to accept for squadron service, was a vastly different machine from that which had been demonstrated to the RFC in France a few months earlier. Its performance had been degraded by the extra weight (including 35lb of armour) that it was now carrying, but he had been assured by General Pitcher at the War Office that these matters were being taken care of.

With most of the pilots of the squadron being new to combat flying, fighting techniques had to be practised in order that they would have a better chance of survival when they did eventually meet the enemy. It was also necessary to fly familiarisation flights in order that the pilots could make themselves thoroughly familiar with the local geography, a vital knowledge if they were trying to break off from a dog fight and make their way home.

With a Nieuport now for his personal use, Ball went up on the morning of 14 April and flew for nearly two hours. It seems likely that he had some rigging alterations done to get the machine as he liked it to maximise the possibilities of his utilising his favourite firing position from underneath. He flew it again for just over an hour in the evening. Although there is no confirmation in the squadron records Ball told Flora that he had had 'my first two fights this morning'. In the first he had forced his opponent to dive away before he had the chance to fire. In the second he fired a few rounds before this opponent also broke off and dived for home.

Over this period the remainder of the squadron personnel were gradually coming in and the unit was soon up to full strength. A period of intensive work had brought the squadron machines up to standard and all the pilots were now looking to the time they would be able to fly their first patrol. Ball wrote to his mother on 18 April that *all my machines and officers are at last ready for War and we hope to have a smack in a day or so,* and that he was just about ready to *start the great game again.*[8]

In this same letter he said that he had given his machine a red cowl though whether he is referring to the Nieuport or the SE5 is unclear

---

8 Ball Archives 18/4/1917.

but it was probably the latter, as this would be the aircraft he would be using on his missions as flight commander and red was the recognition colour of A Flight. Writing to Flora he said that he was feeling *so very happy and OK* and he had moved all his flight into one big hut.

It seems from a letter to Flora that Ball took an opportunity of a 'test' flight with his Nieuport to seek out German aircraft over the lines. He is said to have encountered two Albatros scouts, which he engaged briefly without success. He did not make out an official report of the flight or the encounter with the two German scouts.

After what had been a final day of testing for the rest of the squadron, the first offensive patrol was to be flown on 22 April and the operational life of No.56 Squadron had begun. Whether lots were drawn, or whether it had been decided that the flights would go off in alphabetical order is not certain, but Ball and A Flight took off first at 10.18am under orders that they were not to cross the front line. The flight consisted of Ball (A4850); Knaggs (A4854); Maxwell (A4863); Barlow (A4858); Kay (A4866) and Chaworth-Musters (A4860). Having achieved a height of between 11,000 and 13,000ft they patrolled just behind the British lines. The formation did not remain complete for long for Maxwell dropped out with engine trouble even before the flight had reached its patrol area.

This loss of strength from the patrol represented a problem for the squadron just as important as their combating the Richthofen Circus. They had to achieve mechanical reliability with the Hispano Suiza engines and reliability with the Vickers gun synchronising gear and eliminate trouble with the Lewis gun feed. Gun jams were endemic in all squadrons on both sides and had to be lived with. Even so careful a pilot as McCudden, who took a great deal of time with his guns and ammunition, suffered jams. The problem would never be completely cleared so that all guns worked satisfactorily all the time. The engines were a different matter and they were the responsibility of Lieutenant Charles (as were the guns) whose job it was to clear 'the bugs' from the engine and give the squadron pilots a machine they could rely on.

The patrol continued and at 11,000ft between Lievin and Croiselles Ball saw an Albatros two-seater over Adinfer Wood to the east and slightly higher. He fired the red light signal and led his patrol towards the two-seater. The German crew saw the danger and dived eastwards.

Ball led the pursuit and got within 150 yards and fired three drums of Lewis at the Albatros. No visible effect was seen and the patrol gave up the pursuit as the German crossed into his own lines. There was no further action during the patrol and they returned to Vert Galant at midday. To lead a patrol was a relatively new experience for Ball for although he had been nominated a Flight Commander in No.60 Squadron he had not, as far as the records show, led any patrols. Flying solo there would have been no red light signal to alert the patrol of the presence of a German aircraft. He would have dived in to attack and occupied his usual position underneath his opponent. It is more than likely that the German would have had no warning of the attack and been in serious danger. The safety of patrolling in numbers was partially offset, for Ball, by the decreased opportunity for surprise attacks.

The second patrol of the day took off at 4pm lead by Meintjes and including Melville, Lehman, Hoidge, and Leach. Crowe and Knight also flew as members of this patrol. They flew on the same path as the morning patrol but saw nothing and returned to Vert Galant.

The 23rd saw the first patrol of the day take off at 6am led by Crowe. The flight consisted of six SEs, Crowe, Barlow, Kay, Knaggs, Maxwell and Knight. Once again Maxwell had to drop out with engine trouble and once again the patrol returned without seeing any sign of German aircraft. Also taking off at 6am was Ball in his Nieuport. Although the SEs had an instruction not to cross the lines, no such restriction applied to the Nieuport. Ball made for the Douai-Cambrai area and at 6.45am spotted two Albatros two-seaters, which he describes as *painted a mixture of colours*, at 8,000ft over Cambrai. Ball dived, firing his Lewis. One of the two-seaters dived steeply away, but the rearmost was caught by Ball and he secured his favourite underneath position and fired half a drum. The aircraft fell away and he followed it down to see it crash upside down. He remarked in his report that *no one got out*.

A short while later, he saw another two-seater Albatros, south east of Arras, and attacked. He attempted to get underneath, but overshot and exposed his aircraft to a retaliatory burst from the two-seater. The fire hit his top wing and caused some damage to the wing spars. Having beaten off the initial attack the German aircraft dived for cloud cover and Ball, seeing the damage to his aircraft, broke off the engagement and returned home. The repairs to the Nieuport were enough to put it out of action for several days and he had to use the still unfavoured SE.

Ball took off later in the morning in his SE5 on another solo mission. At 12,000ft he saw a white Albatros two-seater. He dived underneath it and fired five rounds before his Lewis gun jammed. The Albatros dived away and Ball broke off the combat to correct his gun jam. Not being able to rectify this in the air he landed at No.60 Squadron airfield to have it corrected. This work completed he took off again and climbed in the direction of Cambrai. He saw a formation of five Albatros scouts painted pale green and he set off in pursuit. As he closed, he fired 150 rounds from his Vickers into the nearest Albatros. The Albatros immediately dropped away and burst into flames before reaching the ground. The four remaining scouts fired a few rounds at Ball as he made his escape, but he had the advantage in speed and they gave up the pursuit.

Ball continued to patrol at 12,000ft north of Cambrai and saw an all white two-seater Albatros. He dived to attack, then quickly switched to his favourite underneath position and fired half a drum of Lewis ammunition into it. The Albatros went down, with Ball following, and he saw it land. This last combat finished the day's fighting for him and on returning to Vert Galant he had been airborne for three and a quarter hours, in excess of the usual SE duration time and testimony to the extra fuel tankage which he had installed in his machine. He made a final balloon sortie that evening, accompanied by Knight and Leach, but nothing came of the mission and the three machines returned after half an hour.

Writing to his family that night he said that he felt 'fagged' and continued, *We did our first two real jobs today and I got two Huns ...* [9]

He also wrote to Flora:

Have got my first two Huns down today. I had three fights and managed to bring one down crashed in a road. This I did with my Nieuport. After coming down I had to have new planes, for the Hun had got about 15 shots through my spars. Well next I went up in my SE5 and had a poo-poo time. Five shots in my right strut, four in the planes, and two just behind my head. This was done by five Albatros scouts, but I got one of them and set it on fire at 14,000ft. Poor old chap inside. I should simply hate

9 Ball Archives 23/4/1917.

to be set on fire. The General rang me up and congratulated me, also the CO of our Wing. I am keeping the strut and shall give it to you when I come home.[10]

It is not known whether this strut ever reached Flora or his family but it is not listed among the surviving relics of Ball given by Chaz Bowyer.

The following day, in an evening patrol with Melville, Ball saw an Albatros two-seater south of Douai. In his report he described this machine as 'very fast' and it outdistanced them as it dived away. Both Ball and Melville fired at it with their Vickers guns, but Ball suffered a jam after firing fifty rounds. Melville's gun continued to work and he continued to fire as the Albatros gained on them.

That evening he wrote to Flora about the fight and how the squadron was doing:

> The squadron now has five huns. One was got by Lieutenant Barlow of B Flight. The other four have been got by my Flight, A. Lieutenant Maxwell got one this morning and Lieutenant Knaggs this afternoon, and I got the other two yesterday. Not bad is it? I am so pleased my flight is top.[11]

The 25 April was a wasted day as far as flying was concerned. Low clouds prevailed and the spring weather still continued bitterly cold. Ball was not one to be idle and he devoted this time to starting work on a garden alongside his hut and to supplement this he started on the construction of a greenhouse. In addition he began planning, and gathering the material for a hot-water system for his hut, which was to include an overhead shower.

After the enforced rest of 25 April the next day did not look much more promising and it was not until the evening that the next patrols took off. With his Nieuport still under repair, Ball used A4850, leading Lehmann, Melville and Barlow. Disregarding the now accepted practice that safety and efficiency lay in numbers, the patrol split up. Ball went to his favoured hunting ground to the west of Douai and Barlow also went off on his own. Melville and Lehmann went on together, but saw no sign of the enemy and returned to Vert Galant with nothing to report. This incident shows more than anything else the deficiencies of Ball as a patrol leader. He might talk fondly and proudly of 'his flight' but he felt uncomfortable when flying with

10 Quoted by Bowyer p124.
11 Ibid p125.

responsibility for other people. There is no doubt that with his operational experience and the ability he had developed to see the enemy before he was himself seen would have been a great asset to a patrol. It would be unthinkable for any patrol led by McCudden or Mannock, or any experienced patrol leader, to have allowed one of their patrols to split up with everybody 'doing their own thing'. In Ball the habits, which he had learned in 1916, and which had been so successful, did not die away as he faced the new conditions of the spring of 1917. He remained a lone air fighter. Happiest on his own he relied on the old remedies of surprise and daring to see him through. On 26 April these were almost not enough and he was lucky to survive. His combat report describes what must have been some of the most dangerous moments in his career so far.

He climbed to 13,000ft and flew in the direction of Cambrai, now his favourite hunting ground. He saw a formation of FE2bs coming from Cambrai and at the same time noticed German aircraft taking off from an airfield near Cambrai with the intention, he assumed, of attacking the British formation. Ball retained his height and watched as the German scouts, which he could now identify as Albatros, climb up to attack the FEs.

When the German machines had got to about 6,000ft Ball dived to attack the nearest. This Albatros he noted was painted white. He fired a complete drum of Lewis and 20 rounds of Vickers at 20 yards range and the Albatros went down under his fire to crash near Cambrai. Having completed his surprise attack, Ball turned to head back over the British lines but found that the remaining five Albatros had got to the west of him and there was no way through. He attempted to break through this barrier to safety and made for the Germans firing his Vickers, but they refused to give way and he had to turn south-east. He continued in this direction having to turn sharply from time to time to avoid the fire of the enemy pilots who were making every effort to bring him down. Flying south-east, with the Germans in pursuit, he must have been glad to see that the speed of the SE5 enabled him to gain on his opponents. He noticed that one of the pursuing Albatros pilots had got some way in advance of his companions and Ball swiftly turned and headed for the leading Albatros firing both guns. He exhausted the remaining Vickers ammunition in doing this, but his attack was effective and his opponent was fatally hit, burst into flames and dropped to earth. These moments of conflict enabled the other Albatros to get up with him and he had another moment of extreme danger as he manoeuvred his SE5 to avoid the fire being directed at him. He emptied his last two drums of Lewis into a scout which he described as having 'a very long tail and sharp nose'. This opponent dived away from his fire and Ball was able to break away again to the south-east. With no more ammunition left he had no other hope than to rely on the speed of the SE5. Eventually, with dusk falling the Albatros broke off the pursuit and he was able to get back across the lines and landed back at Vert Galant at 8.30 pm.

Ball's SE had serious damage to the centre section and the right-hand lower wing. New sections had to be fitted by his ground crew overnight, as well as patching the bullet holes in the fuselage. If Ball thought about these moments of extreme danger against the Albatros formation, as he surely must have done, then he would have seen that the SE5 had demonstrated its advantages to him. Its superior speed, its two-gun armament and its strength had all helped to get him through. According to Kiernan[12] this was the moment he became reconciled to the SE5 and that he told Trenchard that he now preferred the SE5.

The following day, both the SE5 and the Nieuport were ready for him. In the morning conditions were not good enough to fly over the lines so he tested both of his machines. In the afternoon the conditions improved a little and he took off on a lone patrol in his Nieuport, but saw no hostile aircraft and returned to base. In the early evening he went out again, this time in his SE, but again there were no hostile machines to be seen and he returned without having seen any German aircraft all day. This enforced lay off must have been good for Ball, following his fight on 26th and perhaps gave him time to reflect on his return home. He wrote a letter to Flora that evening:

> I have now got another two Huns, making four this time, and my total is now 34. Only three more to get before I am top of England and France again. In order to whack the German man I have got to get about ten more to get. If it is God's will that I should do it then I will come home.[13]

The 'German man' is assumed to be Boelcke and his competition from France to be Georges Guynemer. Again Ball talks about coming home

12 Kiernan p142.
13 Bowyer p127.

leading to the assumption that the authorities had promised him, or his family, that he would only do a short period in France. No proof of such a promise made to him has been found, but Ball seems to have been fully aware of it and relied on it as something he could look forward to. According to Bowyer[14], the reference to a month in France for Ball was founded on a verbal undertaking by Trenchard, that he would only serve with No.56 Squadron for the first month of their operations, so that his experience would help the operationally inexperienced pilots by example. Trenchard is said to have been reluctant to have accepted him at all, recognising the value of Ball as a living symbol of the spirit of the RFC and fearing that his loss in action was likely, given his style of fighting. He gave in to the pressure of the various people working on Ball's behalf to get him back to the fighting, and the one month period was probably a compromise. This would all hang together very nicely, but for the last letter, which he wrote to Lois on 6 May. In it he spoke of lots being drawn for leave and that he had come last.[15]

This was on the day before his month with the squadron would be up so, if the undertaking given by Trenchard is true, why was he telling Lois that he had lost out in the draw for leave? In the same letter he speaks of being four in front of Guynemer, even more reason for him to accept that one of his reputed 'markers' for his length of service had been met.

The 28 April was a better day and aircraft took off to resume patrols. Crowe, Leach and Kay took off at 9.45am but saw nothing. A further patrol in the early afternoon also saw no enemy activity, but at 4.50pm Ball led some of A Flight (Knight, Knaggs and Maxwell) and patrolled along the line Lens, Le Forest, Fontaine, Moreuil. This took them over the Bapaume-Cambrai road, an area familiar to Ball from the previous year. A formation of three Albatros two-seaters was sighted at about 8,000ft. Ball fired a red light and approached through cloud cover to within 150 yards of the German formation. Ball fired first, but after a few rounds his guns jammed and he banked away to clear the stoppage. His opponent took the opportunity to dive away for safety. Having re-formed his flight and rectified his gun jam, Ball led it into a new attack and fired a long burst at one of the other two-seaters. This one began to go down, but Ball noted that it was under control and he did not follow it down. He turned his attention to the remaining two-seater and this one he sent down to crash near Fontaine.

---

14 Bowyer p129.
15 Briscoe & Stannard p268.

After this combat the various members of the flight failed to reconnect with each other. Ball retained his height and remained in the area until he saw another two-seater emerging from the clouds. He dived after this Albatros but was unable to catch it as it put its nose down when it saw him approaching. Having chased it for so long, Ball was unaware of the amount of height which he had lost until he became the subject of heavy anti-aircraft fire and he realised that he was down to 500ft. Probably the German crew had deliberately led him over this particular hot spot. At that range the ground fire was that much more dangerous and almost immediately Ball was in trouble. His controls were shot away and his aircraft fell away in to a spin with very little height to rectify it. He regained control, however, and discovered that only his left elevator was working and when this was inspected back on the ground only one wire was intact. In this condition, with very little control he had to get himself out of the danger zone and back across the British lines. This he managed to do but chose not to land at the first available spot across the lines but to make it back to Vert Galant.

At Vert Galant, squadron members were anxiously looking for the missing members of Ball's flight. Knight and Knaggs had already returned, but Ball and Maxwell were missing when the sound of an aircraft engine was heard. An SE5 was seen approaching very low and as it approached the airfield it was identified as Ball's. Cecil Lewis was one of those watching the scene:

> . . . we saw him coming in rather clumsily to land. He was not a stunt pilot, but flew very safely and accurately, so that, watching him, we could not understand his awkward floating landing. But when he taxied up to the sheds we saw his elevators were flapping loose – controls had been completely shot away! He had flown back from the lines and made his landing entirely by winding his adjustable tail up and down! It was incredible he had not crashed. His oil tank had been riddled, and his face and the whole nose of the machine were running with black castor oil.[16]

As soon as his machine had come to a stop Ball, in a furious temper, got out and cleaned himself up with a piece of rag. He then ran to the shed and ordered his Nieuport out and made ready. He took off

16 Lewis pp173/174.

looking for some Germans to revenge himself and it was nearly two hours before he returned, not having seen anything to attack. It is a point to debate as to whether Major Blomfield, who was in the crowd watching for the return of Ball, should have ordered him not to fly. Ball was not in the mood to take a rational decision and it is likely that he would have taken unnecessary risks had been able to find a German aircraft.

The missing Maxwell was also another success for the German anti-aircraft fire. Unlike Ball he had been at the respectable height of 10,000ft when he was hit by an accurate burst of shell fire. His engine seized and his machine was forced to come down and hit the ground at Combles. The machine was completely wrecked and for a short distance Maxwell tobogganed across the ground in the shell of the fuselage. He survived unhurt, a tribute to the strength of the SE5.

The damage suffered by Ball's SE A4850 was considerable and more than could be repaired on station. It was therefore dismantled and sent to the depot at Candas for the extensive repairs to be done. For his evening patrol Ball was temporarily given A4858, a machine previously flown by Barlow. He went up in the evening of 29 April accompanied by Knaggs and Knight. At 13,000ft over Bapaume he saw British anti-aircraft fire over Adinfer Wood. Ball went in that direction and intercepted a German formation north of Lens. Selecting his opponent Ball fired 1½ drums of Lewis gun ammunition before the gun jammed. He switched to the Vickers but this managed only two rounds before that too jammed. The German went down under control after this attack. Ball broke away and fired a green light to indicate to the others that they should continue the attack. Knaggs and Knight had, however, lost contact and were pursuing a pair of two-seaters north of Lens rather than the falling Albatros scout. Neither was successful in destroying either of the prey they were chasing and Knight was able to catch up with Ball again. As he was unable to fix either jam, Ball decided to return to Vert Galant where he landed at 6.30pm followed down by Knight. Knaggs returned at 7.30pm.

The following day Ball did little flying apart from a test flight in his Nieuport. However, on this day the squadron suffered its first fatality when 2nd Lieutenant Kay was lost on a morning patrol. Crowe, Leach and Kay had taken off just after 8am to patrol the area from Vitry to Villers. Crowe led the formation to attack a force of German scouts which were trying to intercept a formation of FE2ds. Crowe became engaged in a dog fight with an experienced opponent in which he suffered gun jams. He cleared these and eventually managed to shoot his opponent down. Leach and Kay also found the enemy pilots to be experienced opponents and Leach, after shaking off his opponent, saw Kay under attack. The Albatros pilot hit Kay's machine with explosive bullets. Kay went into a downward spiral and shook off his first opponent, but was immediately attacked by another. Leach fastened on the tail of this Albatros and fired a long burst into it. He overshot turned away and saw both Kay and the Albatros both still going down until they hit the ground and erupted in flames.

When Crowe eventually returned to Vert Galant with the news of the loss of Kay a deep gloom was cast over the squadron. Kay had been developing into a competent air fighter and was popular in the squadron making his loss all the more keenly felt. Thus April ended on a gloomy note. Ball did no more operational flying that day, but he did bring in another SE5 to the squadron, A8898, which existing photos show to still have the large windscreen. It is said[17] that he flew a patrol in this aircraft that evening, but this is not the case. The patrol in question was flown on the evening of 1 May as shown by the combat report.

---

17 See Bowyer pp129/130.

CHAPTER ELEVEN

The Final Days
1 to 7 May 1917

T he end of April 1917 saw the end of a month in which the British air services had suffered the highest casualties of the war. The reasons for this are well enough known, the Germans had the superior aircraft in their fighting squadrons which reaffirmed the superiority they had won in the last three months of 1916. In addition, there is no doubt that the German application of fighting tactics was superior to those of the British air service. The grouping of several *Staffeln* together and using them where they were needed had proved itself successful. There is also no doubt that individually the average German fighter pilot was more skilful than his British opponent. Given these advantages it is not surprising that the Germans were overwhelmingly successful in the April fighting.

Trenchard's aggressive response to this situation, a German superiority which he had foreseen and warned about, was not to vary his offensive tactics. His view was that the RFC (and by implication the RNAS units attached to it) were there to serve the army. The army was engaged in the Arras offensive and therefore needed all the various facets of air support. The fact that this involved flying obsolescent aircraft over the German lines, and meeting the Germans on their side of the lines and thereby involving heavy casualties did not deter Trenchard. The losses to the RFC were considered a price worth paying for the advantages gained for the army. The acceptance of such losses for a worthwhile operational gain was a valid argument. The losses in the sky could be offset by the increased efficiency of the British artillery by the support of the RFC and the consequent increased loss to the German Army.

For Albert Ball personally it meant that he was facing air fighting of an intensity that he had never experienced before. Not only was he now finding the German fighting units operated in larger numbers than in 1916, they were now armed with two machine guns, doubling the amount of bullets which could be fired at him. He would find that the German scout pilots were confident in their superiority and less likely to break up formation when he carried out one of his surprise attacks. This may have given him pause for thought, but it did not cause him to alter his tactics. The lone sortie with the surprise attack remained the basis of his fighting technique. The additional dangers he faced did not deter him; he remained the same uncomplicated fighter he had always been. The enemy was there to be fought and he fought them in the way he always had. The fact that he came back on occasions with serious damage to his machine must have been warning signs to him that things had changed since he was last at the front. He did not change. He led by example and he was a splendid example to the RFC. He did not leave a doctrine of air tactics as did Boelcke and Richthofen but he left in the memory of everyone he met an indelible impression of sheer courage. No one could imitate his tactics though some tried. McCudden was also, when occasion demanded, a superb lone fighter, but he would never do what Ball did regularly, attack regardless of odds.

May opened with fine weather and it looked as if Spring was now to arrive after weeks of cold and depressing weather. Patrols were able to take off as normal and the turn of Ball and A Flight came late in the day. He took off about 6pm leading Knight and Lehmann to patrol the line Arras-Aubigny-St Hilaire-Bantouzille taken by the earlier patrols. He was flying SE5, number A8898, which he had collected earlier in the day from Candas. His own machine had not yet been repaired and his mechanics had worked all day to get the new SE into the same operational state as the rest of the squadron. Flying at 15,000ft Ball saw six Albatros two-seaters near Marquion and led the SEs into the attack. Ball fired at the nearest which dived away from his attack and he was attacked by one of the others. He easily out manoeuvred the Albatros, fired a burst of fifty rounds from his Vickers, and the Albatros went down to crash.

He re-formed the patrol and shortly they saw another formation of two-seaters. Again, Ball selected his target and attacked, but again the German dived away from him and he attacked another. He drove this one down but did not see it crash and as fuel was running low returned to Vert Galant. Knight had been separated and made his way home independently, though he did not reach Vert Galant, landing at Louvencourt and returning to Vert Galant the next day.

On 2 May Ball flew two patrols. In the early afternoon he flew A8898 with Knight and Lehmann to patrol the Cambrai-Douai area. Lehmann had to force land with engine trouble; Knight landed with him, took off later to continue his patrol but was unable to find Ball. The latter had an unsuccessful patrol troubled by continual gun jams and eventually returned to Vert Galant.

In the evening he flew A4855, an aircraft allotted to Knight, in company with Knaggs. It was an evening patrol and Ball expected activity in the area of Douai. At 7.30pm he saw a formation of four all red Albatros scouts coming south from Douai and heading towards the trenches. Without looking to see whether the formation might be a decoy, a basic rule of air fighting, he dived at the nearest Albatros, but four more German aircraft, which had been waiting at a higher level, dived on his tail. Ball turned his SE5 into a steep bank and pulled down his Lewis gun. The nearest Albatros of the attacking formation had opened fire at him but Ball's sudden manoeuvre made him overshoot and Ball fired fifty rounds of Vickers into him, then fastened onto its tail and continued to fire at it until it went into the ground near Vitry. Ball then climbed back up to regain his height and joined a general fight which was going on between about twenty Albatros and varying types of British aircraft Bristol fighters of No.48 squadron, Sopwith Pups of No.66 squadron and some FE2ds of No.20 Squadron. The German aircraft finding themselves outnumbered and out manoeuvred, retreated towards Douai and the dog fight ended. Ball then went south and attacked a white Albatros two-seater. He fired his Vickers and a full drum of Lewis into it closing to 25 yards. The Albatros started to go down with the crew mortally wounded, but Ball was unable to see it crash as his fuel was running low and it was getting dark. The Albatros continued down until it crashed behind the British lines, the crew taken out and put in a field hospital, but both died of their wounds.

Leaving the scene of the engagement, Ball turned for home to be joined by Knaggs and the two flew home together. Darkness was falling as the two SEs reached Vert Galant and landed at 8.30pm.

He described the days fighting in a letter to his family:

My total up to last night was 38. I got two last night. Oh! It was a topping fight. About twenty of the Huns and fifteen of ours.

Well now I will tell you why I don't get a chance to write. First of all, a few days ago, all my controls were shot away on my SE5 'But I got the Hun that did it'. That machine had to go to the doctors and is still there but it will be finished soon. Secondly I got a new SE5 but it is now out of order and I am at the doctors with it. It is all trouble and is so getting on my mind, am feeling very old just now.[1]

That night, No.56 Squadron gave a concert. While the squadron was forming in the UK Major Blomfield had made a point of collecting together groundcrew who were accomplished musicians, with the view of forming a squadron orchestra. He had apparently toured round with a lorry full of men who were not musicians and when he came across one who was he arranged a swap with an equivalent rank of a non-musician from his own resources. By this means he soon assembled a respectable band, which he calculated would help improve the morale of the squadron. What this 'horse trading' did to the feelings of the men who were posted out of the squadron in this way can only be imagined. The concert given on the evening of 2 May included performances from this orchestra as well as turns from suitable talented officers and men.

General Trenchard was invited to attend. Which he was glad to do and took the opportunity to talk to Ball. It did not take long for him to realise that Ball was suffering from combat fatigue and was seriously stressed and overwrought. He offered Ball a two week break in England as a means of giving him the rest which he so badly needed. Ball declined the offer. His dedication to duty and his determination to make himself the top scoring Allied pilot, were overriding and he could not accept the offer. This gesture shows great understanding on the part of Trenchard. He had not wanted the return of Ball at all, but had been forced into accepting him because of the high profile campaign which Ball and his supporters had fought. Trenchard had reluctantly agreed, with a caveat, that Ball would only serve one month with No.56 Squadron, to impart his experience to the relatively inexperienced pilots of the squadron. Again, this mention of a month in France comes up as a verbal agreement by Trenchard. If this was the case why did he

1 Ball Archives 3/5/1917.

offer Ball a period of leave when his 'time' was almost up? Why did he not, as Officer Commanding the RFC in the field give Ball a direct order to go home? Ball would have been furious, but he could not have refused to obey a direct order. Until more evidence comes up this matter of the promise to Ball will remain unsolved.

All went well with the concert until about 10pm when the fire alarm sounded and everyone rushed outside to see the cause of the alarm. The fire was Ball's own hut, greenhouse and bathroom going up in flames. He wrote to Flora the following day:

> I rushed out and Oh! Try to picture how pleased I was when I saw my hut, greenhouse and bathroom on fire. Well I nearly had a double fit. I had taken so much trouble getting it nice, so that when I come in at night I could have a few hours real rest. The fire was caused by Lieutenant Knaggs leaving a candle on a box in his room. I have to laugh although I am really very cross.[2]

He finished the letter with the wish to be with Flora again. He would come home, *when I have made my total 40, I have only two more to get.* Again, this letter includes the comment about coming home soon, as though it was something which there was no doubt about. According to the best contemporary source on British ace scores, Ball had in fact achieved his 40 on 2 May, when he shot down the Albatros two-seater.

The loss which Ball suffered by the fire in his hut seems not to have been total and, as will be seen from letters which he wrote on 5 May, he seems by then to have got everything back in order. The list of items which were to be sent to his family after his death include not only such items as his violin, which he may well have played at the concert, but also documents which would very well have been stored in his hut, such as plans of the Austin-Ball and a draft contract. What arrangements he made for his accommodation pending the rebuilding of his hut is not clear from his letters, but tragically he did not long survive the fire.

The 3 May was also fine and Ball went over to Candas to collect his Nieuport. He flew over in A8898 and eventually returned in it that evening. Who flew the Nieuport back to Vert Galant is not known but it was certainly at Vert Galant on the 4th for Ball flew it back to Candas on that day. He now seems to have recognised the good qualities of the

2 Quoted by Bowyer p134.

SE5, having seen the demonstration of its speed and strength as well as its additional fire power over the Nieuport. He told Flora that Trenchard had given him two SE5s *so I shall be OK*. The two SEs being A4850, his original allotted machine and now A8898 which he had used on his recent patrols.

The 4 May was another good flying day. Ball led the early morning patrol in A8898, along with Maxwell and Knaggs. The three SEs patrolled the line Cambrai-Douai-Lens-Vitry, and found the area clear of all German aircraft. Heading north and climbing to 14,000ft an Albatros two-seater was seen below them and Ball led them down to attack. The German crew saw them coming and made their escape by diving eastward. Long range firing at the fleeing two-seater was fruitless and even this was cut short by gun jams. The continual frustration of not having reliable guns when a target was in sight annoyed Ball intensely and it had been a factor in many unsuccessful combats.

The pilots rectified their gun jams and climbed back to regain lost height. They had reached 12,000ft when they saw a formation of what Ball described as German 'Nieuport Type' scouts. This is taken to be a reference to the Siemens Schuckert D1 a direct copy of the Allied Nieuport 16, which had impressed the Germans by its performance in 1916. The German formation, which Ball described as coloured green did not, however, wait for the SEs to reach their level and made off to the east.

Continuing their patrol the SEs next saw two Albatros two-seaters over Vitry and went into the attack. Again the attack had hardly commenced before the guns jammed and the two German aircraft dived away. Once again the British pilots rectified their guns and climbed back to attack four more German aircraft which had appeared above them. They had no chance of reaching these new enemies before they made off to the east. The British pilots were too low on fuel to pursue and turned for home, landing at 7.30am.

Ball took out the early evening patrol, consisting of Maxwell (in A8902) and Knaggs (in A4854) at 5.30pm. Ball led the patrol to a German airfield south of Cambrai in the hope of finding hostile aircraft he could attack. The field was occupied and some Albatros scouts were just taking off. Ball did not want to sacrifice all his height by diving to attack them, nor could he wait for them to come up to him, so he flew north-west and then towards the lines.

The SEs patrolled the line Riencourt-Graincourt-Vitry at 12,000ft. They came across a formation of eight Albatros Scouts (which Ball described as similar to the one now at Candas) and climbed for a little extra height before diving into the attack. Ball's first opponent was subject to Vickers and Lewis gun fire and dived away from the formation. Ball turned to attack another, which dived away from him. He followed firing bursts from his Vickers and then secured the favoured underneath firing position, firing bursts from the Lewis which sent the Albatros down to crash near Graincourt. All the SEs were now experiencing gun trouble and Ball broke off the engagement, crossed the lines and landed at the nearest British airfield at Baizeux. The aircraft were refuelled and re-armed and the gun jams cleared. On getting ready for take off, the engine on Knagg's machine would not start, so Ball and Maxwell left him and took off and made for Douai.[3]

Ball and Maxwell climbed to 12,000ft and flew along the Arras-Douai road and noticed two Albatros two-seaters, about 8,000ft below them, working for German artillery in bombarding the British lines. These two aircraft had often been seen in this area working on artillery registration and again, without looking for any sign of fighter protection for the two-seaters Ball dived to attack. As the British machines closed they were met by four red painted Albatros scouts from *Jasta 11*. A brief dogfight ensued, but after a few minutes the Germans dived away and as the two-seaters had by now also disappeared Ball looked for Maxwell. The two then turned for the lines when suddenly they were attacked by a large number of German scouts (Maxwell estimated their number as thirty) over Beaumont. In amongst this cluster of attackers Ball also claims that there were two white two-seaters.

The two British pilots were now in a serious position. Possibly the large number of attackers helped to foil their intentions of shooting the two British aircraft down. The two SEs twisted and turned amongst their opponents, firing as a German aircraft came into their sights. The marksmanship of Albert Ball was of a high order and once on the tails of his opponents his fire forced them to dive away. Ball had no chance to follow up any advantage before he was under attack again. But eventually the expected happened and his guns jammed and he was

---

3 Bowyer, p136, says that it was Maxwell's machine which would not start. However, the report Ball submitted states that it was A4854 which refused to start and at that time Maxwell was flying A8902. It is a complicating factor that Albert Ball did not seem to use "I" to indicate his actions but used the aircraft serial number or such terms as 'the Nieuport' or 'the SE'. In referring to other pilots in his report he never gave names but only serial numbers as in this report. Maxwell had indeed flown to France in A4854 but as from the previous day he had been flying A8902. See Revell, *High in the Empty Blue* p40.

left with only the speed of the SE to escape from his opponents. This proved to be more than adequate as he put his nose down and made for the British lines, and he was soon putting distance between himself and the Germans. He saw no sign of Maxwell, made his way home alone, and was worried when he got back to Vert Galant to find that Maxwell had not returned. There was no sign of him that night and there were fears that he had been shot down, but eventually news was received that he had force landed at No.40 Squadron and spent the night there.

The 5 May saw the squadron armourers working on A8898 to try and get the gun synchronising gear to work satisfactorily. As the SE was unavailable for operations Ball switched to the Nieuport B1522 for the morning patrol. The day was fine, warm and ideal for flying but, recognising the strain which they had recently been under, Wing Headquarters ordered that the two-seater corps squadrons be given a rest. Only the scout squadrons would fly that day.

Ball and Maxwell took off at 9.45am to look for an enemy two-seater which had been reported as being near Hesdin. Arriving in the area they found nothing. Maxwell returned direct to Vert Galant and landed at 10.30am but Ball did not land until 11.15am having been on an, unsuccessful, hunting expedition. The rest of the morning and the afternoon were taken up with some test flying and the squadron did not fly another patrol until the evening.

The evening patrol saw Ball back in A8898 and he took off with a patrol consisting of Lewis, Melville, Hoidge, Broadberry and Maxwell, at 6pm. The SEs climbed for the lines but almost at once Broadberry and Maxwell had engine trouble and had to return to Vert Galant. Soon after this Ball made off on his own account towards Lens, while the rest, led by Lewis, headed for the favoured Douai area.

Ball was now at 8,000ft and clear of cloud. He saw two Albatros scouts, decorated with white wings and brown fuselages about 1,000ft higher. Ball climbed to gain height advantage but the German scouts had seen him and were coming down on him. By the time he had got to 11,000ft the first Albatros was within 200 yards. Ball turned quickly and reversed this situation and, noting that the second Albatros was too far away to be a threat, he got underneath the Albatros and fired two drums of Lewis into the belly of the German scout. He loaded the third drum, but the Albatros was diving away and Ball fastened onto its tail firing bursts from both Lewis and Vickers. The Albatros was now diving steeper and Ball considered that it was out of control. The second German had now arrived and fired at Ball. For a while the two circled as they both tried to get on the tail of the other, but neither could manage it. After this initial skirmish the two aircraft flew straight towards each other, both firing. In this traumatic moment Ball used only the Vickers gun, his Lewis ammunition being exhausted, and could see his tracers entering the enemy airplane and the German tracers coming towards him and as the distance lessened Ball thought that the German pilot meant to ram him. Ball held his course, but prepared himself for the crash and the death plunge to the ground. His engine was hit by the return fire, and his oil tank punctured, with oil blowing back towards the cockpit. His face (he never wore goggles) became smothered in oil and in this situation, with no vision from the cockpit, he pulled back on the control stick and climbed away. When he had cleared the oil from his face he looked around for the Albatros but no sign of any enemy aircraft was to be seen. His engine, though now short of oil, was running satisfactorily and he lost height towards the lines. Looking down, he saw the remains of both enemy scouts crashed within a few yards of each other on the ground. The encounter had traumatised Ball and it was fortunate that no further enemy aircraft were there to intervene. The damaged engine carried him safely back to Vert Galant, where he landed at about 7pm.

Having landed, Ball had to make out his report and he went to the office of Lieutenant Marson, the squadron recording officer When Ball came into his office it was obvious to Marson that he was in an extremely distressed and excited state:

> Flushed in face, his eyes brilliant, his hair blown and dishevelled, he came to the squadron office to make his report, but for a long time was in so overwrought a state that dictation was an impossibility to him.
>
> 'God is very good to me'. 'God must have me in His keeping'. 'I was certain he meant to ram me'. The possibility that his opponent, finding himself mortally hit, had determined to have a life for a life occurred to him. In that event his nerve failed him at the last – Ball did not flinch. But in nervous exhaustion he paid the price.[4]

Marson had been observing Ball and had realised that he was taking unnecessary chances in the air. As an older man he felt a natural concern for the young pilot and tried to warn him about this. Ball bristled at this challenge and asked what Marson knew of air fighting. Marson replied that he knew absolutely nothing, but that the principles remain the same. He had seen action in the Boer War and knew when a risk was justified and when it was not. To take unnecessary risks was tantamount to suicide. Ball's initial anger subsided and after further discussion Marson said that when a two-seater became available he would go up with Ball to wherever he wished to fly. This flight happened a couple of days later, though the type of machine was unspecified, and the two went up towards Arras. The rear cockpit was rather cramped for the more portly Marson and he was unable to fasten the safety belt. The flight lasted about an hour and included Ball diving on the German trenches but Marson was so wedged in that he was unable to reach and fire the Lewis gun! The overriding impression Marson got from the flight was that he had never been colder in his life![5]

That evening Ball wrote two letters, one to his father, the last he was to write to the parent he so loved and admired, and one to Flora. Both letters show the signs of the strain which he was under, but the light jaunty tone with which he used to write in 1916 is still there, for the benefit of his family. To his father he wrote:

Have just come down off patrol and have made my total 42.

I attacked two Albatros Scouts and crashed them killing the pilots. In the end I was brought down but am quite OK. Oh it was a good fight and the Huns were fine sports. One tried to ram me after he was hit and only missed by inches. Am indeed looked after by God but Oh I do get tired of always living to kill, and am really beginning to feel like a murderer. Shall be so pleased when I have finished.

I have got my Hut, Garden, Greenhouse and Bathroom OK again now, in fact I have just been lighting the fire to heat my bath.

Bobs. Oh she is a topper.[6]

To Flora he wrote:

4 Marson pp143/144.
5 Marson p146.
6 Ball Archives 5/5/1917.

> Well I made my total 40 last night, and General Trenchard rang up to say I am going to be presented to General Sir Douglas Haig tomorrow. Oh wont it be nice when all this beastly killing is over and we can just enjoy ourselves and not hurt anyone.

He then writes of that evening's combat:

> This makes my 42nd and the major is pleased. Re-hut and garden. Well I have got it nearly right again now; in fact I have been lighting the petrol stove in my bath tank so that I may have a bath.[7]

The following day, 6 May was a Sunday, but there was no record of Ball having left the aerodrome to go to church. In the light of the previous day's happenings, and his feelings that he had been protected by God, there is every reason that he might have done so. The day was fine but a high wind affected flying and he seems to have taken the time off to work in his garden, just the type of therapy which he must have needed. He had received the information that A4850 was now ready for collection and later in the morning he drove over to collect it and fly it back to Vert Galant. At sometime during this day the last photograph ever taken of him shows him in his SE5 with a mechanic holding the wingtip. It clearly shows the mounting of the Vickers gun above the line of the engine cowling and the long SPAD type exhaust pipes. It is not known who took the picture or where it was taken.

Having collected his SE from Candas Ball spent the afternoon working on it to see that it was in the fighting order which he required. That evening he lead a patrol, using his Nieuport as the SE5 was still not quite ready for him. He took off at 7pm leading Crowe, Lewis, Barlow and Knaggs.

In a conclusive demonstration of the superior performance of the SE5 over the Nieuport he began to drop behind the rest of the formation and over Arras he left the formation and flew towards Douai. In his favourite hunting area he saw four red Albatros scouts going towards Cambrai at 10,000ft. He dived on the nearest one and fired two and a half drums of Lewis gun ammunition into it. The Albatros formation split up and his opponent fell away to crash just south of Sancourt. The remaining three Albatros did not choose to try conclusions with him and he turned for home. At that moment the Albatros did attack him, but he easily outmanoeuvred them and they

---

7 Bowyer pp138/139.

gave up. He revelled in the superior aerobatic qualities of the Nieuport against the Albatros (which he described as 'the new type' presumably referring to the V strutted Albatros DIII rather than the DII which still equipped some units) but he did now appreciate that the superior speed of the SE5 was even more valuable. He landed back at Vert Galant at 8.40pm some ten minutes behind the rest of the formation he had left with.

That morning he had written a final letter to Lois:

Dearest Lol
Received your topping letter and cake. It is so good of you to think of me so much.

Today we drew lots for leave, and I came last, but Lol, it was a sporting chance . . .

Well, I made my forty-second Hun yesterday, so am now four in front of the French.

I am going to be presented to General Sir D.H. It will be very nice.

Was shot down yesterday, so am getting a new machine today.

Must close now,
Tons of love,
Albert[8]

This letter, as mentioned earlier, raises again the question of when Ball was to return home. If he had a definite promise, verbal or written, why was he in the draw for leave at all? Leave would only be allocated to those officers who were going to serve a full tour, which, seemingly, was not the case with Ball. He had now served a full calendar month with the squadron, though the first two weeks of it had not been operational. If this promise was made to him, and something seems to have been said from the number of references made to it by Ball and his family, why did he not say that he would be home by 8 May? Did the month run from 22 April when the squadron flew its first operational flight?

There is no doubt that Ball was stressed at this time. Although Ball had only been back a short time at the front, he had been fighting at his usual level of intensity, in conditions which were far more dangerous

8 Quoted by Briscoe & Stannard p.268. The original of this letter was recently sold at auction in 2005 and is not available for public access.

than those of 6 months before. The immediate authorities concerned, Major Blomfield, Lieutenant Colonel Newall, commanding 9th Wing, and Trenchard must have been aware of this and they would have been in a position to withdraw him from the fighting to preserve his life and the value he had to the whole Corps. Yet when Trenchard had offered him two weeks in England, which Ball declined, why had he not ordered his permanent posting to England? Blomfield seems not to have given him any information that his tour was to end, or why was he in the draw for leave?

There is one clue towards future intentions in a letter which Lieutenant Colonel Newall had written to Blomfield on 6 May. This letter asked for full details of what Ball had done since he had been with the squadron. The information was to include combat reports, evidence from other pilots as to what they had seen Ball do, the condition of his aircraft on the various occasions he returned and any other useful information. It has been concluded that this request for information was the initial stage in the recommendation of Ball for a VC. It is hard to argue with this contention. The facts called for can only have been required for such a purpose, but there is no final conclusive evidence to call this a definite objective. It is likely that Ball would have been recommended for the VC, the only additional gallantry award which could possibly have been given him, and that the announcement of the award would have been made at the same time as his withdrawal from the front.

The 7 May dawned fine, continuing the run of good weather which they had been experiencing. The forecast for later was not so promising with cloud and rain promised. Meintjes led C Flight on the early patrol at 8am. It was an eventful patrol with plenty of enemy activity. Ball was not called upon to fly and spent his morning putting the finishing touches to A4850 and the rest tending his garden plot which seemed to be growing well.

At 12.30pm Ball took off in A4850 accompanied by Knaggs and Maxwell. They were to act as close escort to the Sopwith 1½ Strutters of No.70 Squadron, which had been detailed to undertake a photo reconnaissance of German aerodromes in the vicinity of Caudry and Neuvilly. The outward trip was uneventful but on the return trip both two-seaters and scouts were seen. Ball attacked the nearest one and drove it off, but did not pursue and returned to the escort. The German formation continued to follow the Sopwith and SEs but never attempted to interfere with their progress or to engage with the escorts when they turned back towards them. The whole trip passed without serious trouble and the SEs landed back at Vert Galant at 2.30pm. This seemed likely to be the last of the day's flying as the afternoon turned cloudy and storm clouds started gathering. There seemed every prospect of rain and the cancellation of the rest of the day's flying.

There were other forces at work, however, which would affect the pilots of No.56 Squadron. It had been reported to Wing (by Major Blomfield following conversations with officers with AA batteries in the Arras area) that German fighters gathered in the Douai-Cambrai area in the evenings. It was decided to combat this German fighter activity and on 5 May Wing ordered that British fighters should patrol the area morning and evening. The forces were to comprise six Spads from No.19 Squadron, six Sopwith Triplanes from No.8 Naval Squadron and six SE5s from No.56 Squadron. This concentration of British fighters was to last from 6am to 10.30am and 6.30pm to dusk.

Looking back on the events of that day, people who were in the squadron at the time believed that a challenge had been dropped on the airfield of Richthofen's *Jasta* 11 asking them to come and meet the patrol. Unlike the earlier challenge, in which Ball had been incidentally involved, when a message was reported to have been sent for Immelmann to meet a British pilot, there is no documentary evidence remaining to support this idea. It is unlikely that such a challenge would have been given. The SE5 was superior to the Albatros DIII, as had now been proved, but the proficiency of the pilots in No.56 Squadron had not yet reached the level of those under Richthofen.

The record of the squadron since it began operational flying rested almost entirely on the successes of Albert Ball. He had destroyed thirteen aircraft in this period but only Gerald Maxwell of the other pilots had destroyed more than one, though Meintjes had six victories, including those won earlier with No.60 Squadron. Many of them were to go on to become accomplished air fighters in their own rig, but at this stage they were still learning their trade and would have found it very hard fighting against such German opposition as the events of the evening were to show.

On the afternoon of 7 May Blomfield had discussions with Major Pretyman commanding No.19 Squadron about coordinating the patrols of No.19 Squadron with those of No.56 Squadron. Pretyman agreed to send out patrols which would overlap the No.56 squadron area and Blomfield decided on a maximum strength patrol of eleven machines, even though the Wing had stated that six were to be employed. This squadron strength patrol would be under the nominal leadership of Albert Ball.

The last operational flight made by Albert Ball started from Vert Galant at about 5.30pm. Engines were started and the SEs taxied down the field to the take-off point. Lieutenant Marson was standing watching the machines as they taxied by and Ball gave him a wave as he passed. Moments later the patrol was in the air and heading for the lines.

CHAPTER TWELVE

The Last Patrol

The eleven SE5s which flew on this patrol, and Marson called it the full squadron strength at the time, were as follows:

A Flight
    Captain A. Ball, DSO, MC   A4850
    Lt. G. C. Maxwell   A8902
    Lt. K. J.Knaggs   A8904
B Flight
    Captain C. M. Crowe   A4860
    Lt. R. M. C. Musters   A4867
    Lt. A. P .F. Rhys Davids   A4868
    Lt. J. O. Leach, MC   A4856
C Flight
    Captain H. Meintjes   A8900
    Lt. R. T. C. Hoidge   A4862
    Lt C. A. Lewis, MC   A4853
    Lt. W. B. Melville   A4861

The description of this patrol setting out by Cecil Lewis is iconic and evocative of the period and the occasion:

The squadron sets out eleven strong on the evening patrol. Eleven chocolate-coloured, lean, noisy bullets, lifting, swaying, turning, rising into formation – two fours and a three – circling and climbing away steadily towards the lines. They are off to deal with Richthofen and his circus of Red Albatros's.

The May evening is heavy with masses of cumulus cloud, majestic skyscapes, solid-looking as snow mountains, fraught with caves and valleys, rifts and ravines – strange and secret pathways in the chartless continents of the sky. Below the land becomes an ordnance map, dim green and yellow, and across it go the Lines, drawn anyhow as a child might scrawl with a double pencil. The grim dividing Lines! From the air robbed of all significance.[1]

The lines were crossed at 7,000ft and the formation kept just below the clouds, heading in the direction of Cambrai. Shortly after, the gremlins, which had long haunted the Hispano engines, struck again and Melville turned away for home with a badly running engine. As they approached the lines the squadron formation split up and each flight proceeded independently. At this time Maxwell seems to have got separated from Ball and Knaggs and the two remaining SEs proceeded together into German territory at 7,000ft.

B Flight ran into a thick bank of cloud and when they emerged Chaworth-Musters was no longer with them. He had last been seen by Rhys Davids, just before they entered the cloud. Chaworth-Musters had been slightly lower and behind the rest of the formation and had dived away to attack a lone Albatros. It was not a wise thing for a relative novice, like Musters, to do and probably represented the offensive spirit of Ball, which had inculcated the younger members of the squadron. Musters, in particular, admired Ball as they both came from the Nottingham area, and this spirit possibly made him forget the rules of air fighting and to seek out a lone adversary. The Albatros which he was looking to engage was flown by Werner Voss, probably the best pilot in the German air services, and rapidly gaining a reputation to match Richthofen's. Not only did Voss fly brilliantly, he was also an excellent shot, as witnessed the damage he did to the No.56 Squadron aircraft in his final combat on 23 September 1917. Musters was not seen again and was later reported by the Germans to have been shot down and killed by Voss.

Crowe, with the remaining members of his patrol, Leach and Rhys Davids, emerged from the cloud over the Arras-Cambrai Road. They saw a lone red Albatros flying to the south of Vitry. Crowe led the attack but he misjudged his dive and overshot. Leach fired, but with no immediate effect. Crowe came in for a second attack but had a gun jam. Leach then attacked again and sent the Albatros down to crash east of Vitry.

As Rhys Davids was about to join in the attack he was attacked by

---

1 Lewis pp174/175.

another Albatros, also coloured red and with a green band round the fuselage. The first intimation which Rhys Davids had of his peril was the tracers from his attacker flying past his cockpit. It has been suggested that the pilot in the Albatros was Kurt Wolff, one the stars of the Richthofen *Jasta* and at that time with twenty-nine victories to his credit, but records show that on 6 May he had been promoted to the command of *Jasta* 29. He was not likely, therefore, to be still flying with *Jasta* 11.[2]

Whoever Rhys Davids fought, it was plain that he was an experienced pilot and held the upper hand in the combat.

The British pilot was in a serious situation, for the first burst of fire from his opponent had hit the SE5 in the engine, undercarriage and wings. Sooner or later the engine was going to stop through lack of water, as the accurate fire had smashed a hole in the cooling system. Having survived the first pass both began circling for position. The Albatros was slightly higher and dived and fired at the SE while Rhys Davids tried to gain height and get on level terms. In this situation the old problem of jammed guns happened again and Rhys-Davids had to wrestle with this as well as control his machine. Just when Rhys-Davids was wondering how he was going to get out of the situation, the Albatros dived away towards Douai and Rhys Davids turned towards the British lines. His engine finally stopped and he was unable to reach any British airfield but had to force land near La Herliére.

The aircraft of C Flight under Meintjes had destroyed a German aircraft described as a 'Nieuport Type' though it is uncertain whether this means a Siemens Schuckert D1 or the Albatros DIII with V struts and sesquiplane arrangement for the lower wing. The formation then climbed and flew north-west to the Cambrai Road. Here they came under attack by four red Albatros. These new arrivals were flown by Lothar Von Richthofen[3] (leading the *Staffel* in the absence of his brother on leave), Wilhelm Allmenroeder[4] (brother of Karl Allmenroeder[5],) Eberhardt Mohnicke[6] and either Georg Simon[7] or Leutnant Fritz Esser.[8] Meintjes was unable to shake off the Albatros on his tail and

2 See Hart *Bloody April* p338.
3 Lothar Von Richthofen had nineteen victories amassed in the period since 6 March when he joined *Jasta* 11. He was wounded three times during his combat career but survived the war with forty victories only to die in an air crash in 1922.
4 Wilhelm Allmenroeder (1894-1969) elder brother of Karl.
5 Karl Allmenroeder, killed on 27 June 1917 having by then raised his score to 30. His loss was at one time credited to Raymond Collishaw who fired at him from long range but never claimed the victory, but is more likely to have been the subject of a direct hit by anti-aircraft fire.
6 Eberhardt Mohnicke had one victory at this time out of an eventual total of nine. He survived the war.
7 George Simon (1885-1963).
8 Fritz Esser(1894-1963) A pilot in the German service since 1914.

had to spin his machine to get rid of him. This manoeuvre was successful and Meintjes climbed back to regain his height. He attacked a lone Albatros, closing to 25 yards, firing short bursts from his Vickers, and shot it down to crash at Gouy-sous-Bellone. The pilot, Wolfgang von Pluschow, was seriously injured.

Meintjes had now lost contact with his flight and while looking for them saw another lone Albatros. He dived to attack but the German pilot was fully alert and turned to meet the attack. Meintjes soon found himself out manoeuvred and his opponent was on his tail. A burst of fire from the Albatros wounded Meintjes in the wrist and damaged the control column. Under the effect of the pain of his wound Meintjes almost lost consciousness but managed to dive away and bring his plane down to land near Sains-en-Gohelle where he was lifted unconscious from his cockpit.

Crowe and Leach had become separated after the attack on the Albatros and Leach found himself under attack by another Albatros. He was wounded in the leg and fainted from the effects of his wound. He revived in time to crash land on Vimy Ridge where he was rescued by Canadian troops and taken to hospital. He was to lose his leg as a result of the wound.

Lewis and Hoidge, the remaining members of Meintjes flight, had become separated after the fight with the four red Albatros. Lewis found himself determinedly engaged by another two Albatros scouts, one of which, he noted, had a red diagonal stripe round the fuselage. Lewis turned sharply and flicked his SE over into a dive. The two Germans pursued him and things might have gone badly for Lewis if Ball and Knaggs had not arrived on the scene.

Ball and Knaggs had been patrolling together ever since Maxwell had left. They met a group of four red Albatros and Ball led the attack. Ball commenced firing at the nearest Albatros but was suddenly seen to turn away, probably because of the recurrent trouble with the Vickers gun. Knaggs continued the attack until his gun also stopped and he turned away to remedy the stoppage. It was at this moment that he saw the situation Lewis was in and went to the rescue.

Knaggs closed on the nearest Albatros firing short bursts from his Vickers. Lewis, probably unaware of the intervention of Knaggs, flew into a cloud, leaving Knaggs with the two Albatros! The trigger on his Vickers gun broke and he had to rely on the Lewis. He had secured an underneath position on one of the Albatros and emptied several rounds into the fuselage of the enemy scout. The two Albatros broke away and dived for home. Wishing to retain height, Knaggs did not pursue and began climbing again. Other British aircraft had by now got to the scene of the fighting, including Bristol Fighters and Nieuports.

Knaggs looked for Ball, but as often happened in that confused period of fighting he could not find his companion. He did find Lewis and Hoidge however and joined up with them and shortly after Ball too reappeared and the four SEs flew on together until, once again, they were split up by the gathering cloud. Lewis found Crowe and together they made an indecisive attack on a two-seater over Beaumont. The two-seater dived away from their attack and they did not pursue. Crowe found himself alone again and attacked an Albatros head on. The two kept firing until the last minute and then turned quickly to get on the tail of their opponent at which the Albatros pilot was quicker and his burst of fire almost did for Crowe, shooting off his goggles. Having survived this attack, Crowe climbed away but although he had shaken off his original opponent he was attacked by four more red Albatros. Crowe used the speed of the SE to go back towards the British lines and to outdistance the Albatros. Over Lens he met up with Ball and the two patrolled together. By this time it was beginning to get dark and the SEs were approaching the limit of their patrol time.

In this situation, with clouds and darkness gathering, Crowe and Ball flew side by side until Ball fired two red Very lights, the signal for the sighting of enemy aircraft. Crowe could see nothing, friendly or hostile, but, being aware of Ball's skill in this aspect, he continued to follow him towards Loos. Ball dived on an Albatros scout and gave it a good burst of fire before he overshot and turned away. Crowe followed Ball into the attack and also fired at the Albatros. It is almost certain that this Albatros was flown by Lothar von Richthofen, who had already had a brush with No.56 squadron earlier in the evening. Crowe also turned away ready to make another attack and saw that Ball had also re-engaged the Albatros and the two were fighting. Crowe went towards them to assist Ball, but as he approached the two opponents disappeared into a bank of cloud. In his combat report Crowe said that he followed the pair into the cloud and when he emerged there was no sign of either aircraft and he turned for home. When interviewed in the

1960s by Alex Revell he admitted that he had not gone into the cloud, thinking it both foolhardy and dangerous, and as he knew that his fuel was very low he turned for home. If he had followed Ball, history might have been different but with an endurance of 2½ hours and having taken off at 5.30pm fuel was a critical problem. Crowe was not able to get back to Vert Galant and landed at Auchel at 8.15pm. Because of the modifications made to his aircraft Ball may have had a slightly longer endurance but must still have been near the limit.

One eye witness version of what happened after Albert Ball disappeared into the cloud, is recounted by Wilhelm Allmenroeder, who must have given this account to Heinz Nowarra, before his death in 1969. The Allmenroeder account has been repeated by Peter Hart[9] in his recent work. According to Allmenroeder he came across Ball and Lothar fighting less than 100ft below him:

> I looked around and then saw, about 20 metres below me, Lothar in a wild circling dogfight with a British fighter. Both opponents circled around below me, but neither had a chance to shoot. As I was higher, I would have had a chance to fire, but I had a feeling that I had better not interfere. Besides this, I could not understand where the other aircraft had gone, and I was afraid that they might return.
>
> Each tried to better his position by wide left turns; however, no one gained an advantage and not a shot was fired. Meanwhile it became darker and darker. Off to the north-east, Douai was barely visible. The sun had just gone down. Suddenly, as if both had received an order, the two left the circle and flew straight away, Lothar to the south, his opponent to the north, I had believed that they wanted to stop the fight because of the darkness, but then both turned and rushed at each other as if they intended to ram. Lothar dipped under the other and then both turned and rushed again at each other, only a few shots being fired. At the third frontal attack, Lothar came from the south, and his opponent from the north – I waited. The machine guns peppered again. This time Lothar's opponent did not give way sideways but dived down to the ground. I had wanted to see where the plane crashed, but I became anxious because Lothar also went down in a rather steep turn and disappeared in the

9 Hart *Bloody April* pp340/341.

mist. I flew back to our airfield to order that a search be made for Lothar. As I jumped out of the plane it was almost night. I was immediately informed that Lothar had made an emergency landing because his engine was hit. He himself was not injured.

This is the only account we have of the last combat of Albert Ball and we have to see it as one version of how the British ace came to his death. It seems to have been a fight which lasted for some minutes, much longer than the average dog fight. Even in the gathering darkness each pilot must have been able to see his opponent clearly particularly when they were flying towards each other head on. The question arises therefore why Lothar should claim the victory over Ball and say that his opponent was flying a Sopwith Triplane? There could be no mistaking the two machines in the air at close quarters.

There is one other account, quoted by Bowyer[10], but he does not say from whom it came. This claims that in the combat between Lothar and Ball they came down to a low level, flying west, with Ball pursuing the Albatros towards Annoeullin. The efforts of the younger Richthofen to get Ball off his tail were unavailing and finally, with his petrol tank riddled, he crash landed but was unhurt. Ball then climbed away into the cloud. This account can only have come from an eyewitness on the ground. Was it Hailer? The time of these sightings on the German side seems to have been between 8.15 and 8.30pm, but this was in German time, one hour ahead of British time.

It can be accepted that Ball and Lothar did engage in combat and that Lothar suffered enough engine damage to force him to land. Whether this was in the combat with Ball cannot be known for certain but it looks likely. Whether this combat was the one recounted by Allmenroeder is another question. Did Allmenroeder see the same combat that Crowe saw, ie before Ball and Lothar entered the cloud? Or did he see them again after they had emerged from the cloud presumably into a patch of clear sky?

The question of what happened to Albert Ball is more difficult to decide. If Allmenroeder's account is correct he was seen going down, 'dived down to the ground' as he described. We know from later evidence that Ball was neither killed nor injured in aerial combat. We also know that he was becoming low on fuel and that this could have forced him to try and land on the German side of the lines or, more

---

10 Bowyer p150.

likely, to make a dash to try and reach the lines, having decided that his fuel state did not enable him to continue the combat. Finally we have to consider that his SE suffered sufficient damage to the engine to force him to come down. Some German officers, however, who later inspected the wreckage of the SE agreed that it did not appear to have suffered any damage from combat. This judgement must be treated with some reservations as the machine was a wreck and such damage might not have been obvious.

The final sighting of Ball's aircraft was by four German officers, Franz and Carl Hailer, who were brothers, and two companions, all from *Flieger Abteilung* A292. Franz Hailer's account was given to Nowarra also in the 1960s. They heard the sound of aircraft engines and through binoculars saw Ball's aircraft emerge from low cloud:

> The aircraft was upside down with the wheels 'sticking up'. It was leaving a cloud of black smoke and this I considered was caused by oil leaking into the cylinders.[11]

The officers watched as the SE5 continued in a shallow dive, disappearing behind a line of trees and they heard the sound of a crash. The aircraft had crashed into slightly rising ground near a farmhouse called Fashoda about a mile from Annoeullin. When Hailer and his companions reached the site they found that Ball had already been lifted from the wreckage by a local French girl, Mademoiselle Cecile Deloffre. He was still breathing when he was brought out but lived only a few seconds and opened his eyes just once. When Hailer got there Ball was already dead:

> We examined the wreckage and we all came to the conclusion that the aircraft had not been either shot down in an air fight or anti-aircraft fire as the dead pilot had no marks or scratches and had not been wounded. I looked through his papers and found it was Captain Ball. We called him the English Richthofen. We were very disturbed by it all. I took his dead body to the field hospital. The doctor couldn't find any bullet wounds on the body, although the back and one leg were broken.[12]

From that time to now supposition has been rife as to how Ball died. This remains a mystery which will never now be solved. When

11 Hart *Bloody April* p342.
12 Ibid.

Lieutenant Charles was asked by Alex Revell how the Hispano engine would behave in this situation, ie flying in an inverted position. Charles stated positively that the design of the carburettor did not allow inverted flying and that fuel would flood the air intake and stop the engine.

When Ball entered the thundercloud he must have become disoriented and got his plane in an inverted position. I am informed, by an experienced pilot that, without modern instrumentation, it was perfectly possible for a pilot to be upside down in a cloud and not realise it. In this position, Ball emerged from the cloud, with the engine stopped and only 200ft of height to get the plane back to a normal flying position. This was not possible and the aircraft crashed upside down, accounting for the injuries which Ball received in the crash.

In his interview Hailer gave his opinion on what he thought might have happened:

My own opinion, and you will appreciate I was not in the air at the time, covers just two possibilities: 1) The odd chance that Lothar Von Richthofen, in exchanging shots with Captain Ball's SE5, hit the aircraft with a stray shot – the breech of the Vickers gun carried a bullet hole. 2) I have thought that Captain Ball, flying into a cloud, turned the aircraft over and was unaware of this until he broke cloud, then so low that he could do nothing and the aircraft flew into the ground. Again, when the SE5 crashed, it did not fire, and he must have been very low on fuel.[13]

This last statement is significant. Ball was very probably down to his last dregs of fuel and might not have had enough to get back to the British lines.

In establishing Ball's identity Hailer and his companions had searched the body and collected some personal belongings; a gold identity bracelet, a white initialled handkerchief, a small prayer book given to him by Flora, a penknife, a fountain pen, pencils, a £1 banknote, a small damaged cigarette case and a compass. From his uniform the RFC wings and the medal ribbons were cut off. Hailer retained the handkerchief and prayer book as his own mementos.

There was no mention of any firearm being recovered from the wreckage or from Ball's body. According to Marson, Ball had told him that he would never surrender even if he was forced to land behind the

11 Hart *Bloody April* p342.
12 Ibid.
13 Hart *Bloody April* p343.

German lines, meaning that he intended to fight to the death rather than be made a prisoner and to do this he must carry a revolver with him. This, Marson said, made him accept that Ball was dead when he failed to return on 7 May, even before the official news of his death was received. Such a statement seems unlike Ball. He did not hate the Germans and had already reached the stage that he regretted the killing he had to do. I believe that, if he had survived the crash behind the German lines, his attitude would have been that he had done his best and that he would not want to bring further sadness to those he loved by needlessly giving up his life when he had been spared in the crash.

That evening Ball's body was taken from the field hospital to a specially prepared 'chapel' to lie there prior to the funeral. In a chivalrous gesture Hailer suggested to his unit commander that Ball's body be wrapped in a flag and dropped by parachute behind the British lines so that Ball could be honoured by his comrades. This generous idea was not accepted and preparations went ahead for a funeral to be held in the local village cemetery. This took place on 9 May with full military honours and in attendance were German military officers from local units, some British Prisoners of War and a crowd of local French civilians. It is not recorded if Lothar Von Richthofen attended. There is solid evidence that the photograph showing this occasion does not, in fact, show the funeral of Ball.

The Germans were now pushing forward with their procedures for claiming the victory for Lothar von Richthofen. In his 1960's interview Hailer claimed that revolver bullets had been fired into the wreckage of the SE5, apparently to simulate combat damage and strengthen Lothar's claim. Hailer also stated that *Jasta* 11 phoned his airfield on the evening of 7th and asked if they could confirm a British machine had been shot down in the area that evening. Hailer, who answered the phone, confirmed that a British machine had been shot down and that it was Captain Ball, but that it had not been brought down by aerial combat. At this point his commanding officer took over the phone and Hailer did not hear the rest of the conversation.

Lothar made out his combat report for the fighting on 7 May stating that he had had a combat with many triplanes and one 'attacked me in a very determined manner'. This triplane he claimed to have shot down although he too was forced to land. He quoted the engine number of the Hispano Suiza engine of Ball's SE5 but not the serial number of the SE. It is said that on the impact with the ground that the tail unit broke completely off and was not recovered by the Germans. This might explain Lothar's inability to quote this number.

Under German air force regulations Lothar had to produce at least three witnesses to vouch for his claim. These were forthcoming; apart from Leutnant Hailer already mentioned, Leutnant Hepner of Kite Balloon *Abteilung Nr* 1 witnessed a triplane fall out of control, an anti-aircraft battery saw a triplane shot down and another kite balloon section saw a British aircraft crash near Fashoda. It should be noted that British records do not show any triplane lost on that day. However, this confirmation was enough for the authorities to award the victory to Lothar.

The wreckage of Ball's SE5 was scavenged by the Germans and items presented to Lothar as souvenirs, including the Vickers gun and some dashboard instruments. These items were kept at the Richthofen home, along with the similar souvenirs of Manfred until the Russians arrived in the area in 1944.

At Vert Galant, Major Blomfield the pilots, and the ground crew of the squadron waited for the patrol to return. By 8.30pm, of the eleven SEs that had left on the patrol only five had returned, Maxwell and Melville being the first and Lewis, Hoidge and Knaggs later. News later trickled in that Crowe and Rhys Davids were safely down behind the British lines. Later in the evening news came that Leach was in hospital seriously wounded and then that Meintjes was also down wounded. No news had been received of Ball or Musters and the squadron went to bed in a sad mood. Most chose to believe that Ball could not be dead, that he must be a prisoner. Those who had seen him in action were convinced that he ran too many risks to last long and that while they hoped he was a prisoner some accepted that he might very well be dead.

The various members of the squadron remembered their thoughts at the time of Ball going missing, thus Cecil Lewis:

> The Mess was very quiet that night. The Adjutant remained in his office, hoping against hope to have news of the six missing pilots, and, later, news did come through that two had been forced down, shot in the engine, and that two others had been wounded.

But Ball never returned. I believe I was the last to see him in his red-nosed SE going east at 8,000ft. He flew straight into the white face of an enormous cloud. I followed. But when I came out on the other side he was nowhere to be seen. All next day a feeling of depression hung over the squadron. We mooned about the sheds still hoping for news. The day after that hope was given up. I flew his Nieuport back to the Aircraft Depot.

It was decided to go over to Douai and drop message bags containing requests, written in German, for news of his fate. We crossed the lines at 13,000ft. Douai was renowned for its anti-aircraft. They were not to know the squadron was in mourning, and made it hot for us . . . Over the town the message bags were dropped, and the formation returned without encountering a single enemy machine.[14]

Rhys Davids added a PS to a letter on the 8th May:

The result of our show was that we got four certain, perhaps more, and have lost two plus 2 other pilots including Leach wounded. I am terribly afraid the wonderful little man is one of the missing – you know who. All the best huns were up against us.[15]

Maxwell wrote on 8 May to his family:

We had the most awful scrap yesterday and Ball and another man are missing. Eleven of us in the squadron went out at 5pm and only three of us arrived back at the aerodrome (I being one of them) all the rest have turned up though now except Ball and the other fellow. They are probably killed . . .

It is absolutely awful about Ball. He is the bravest and best man in the whole of the British Army and it is a terrific thing for the Germans getting him as it will buck up the whole German Flying Corps.

I wonder if they will make much fuss in the papers about Ball. Send me all the pictures and cuttings you can. I hope he gets the VC. He was to have been presented to Haig in a day or two and after that he was going home for good as soon he had got fifty Huns. I think his total is forty-six. Our Squadron has now got thirty-three since being out.[16]

---

14 Lewis pp178/179.
15 Revell Brief Glory p101.
16 Quoted in Revell High in the Empty Blue p49.

Maurice Baring wrote in his Diary:

> We got news that Ball is missing. This has cast a gloom through the whole Flying Corps. He was not only perhaps the most inspiring pilot we have ever had, but the most modest and engaging character. His squadron, and indeed all the squadrons, will feel this terribly.[17]

Trenchard sent a telegram to the squadron on 8 May regretting the loss of Ball and describing him as 'one of the most daring, skilful and successful pilots the Flying Corps has ever had' and that his loss would be felt not only by the squadron but by the whole Flying Corps.[18]

Those who took part in that patrol must, on reflection, have thought that things had not gone well for them. In the conditions prevailing, of large cloud masses, the patrol had got fragmented and remained that way. Occasionally, two or three SEs would get together and then become separated again. Flight discipline should have ensured that even if the eleven SEs did not remain together, at least the flights should have done so. The action of Musters of leaving the formation to attack an Albatros on his own initiative was foolish. It might have been the practice of Albert Ball but it was not the way for a relative novice to behave. There was only one Albert Ball, and he relied on skills which Musters did not have, in addition to which you needed luck, which for Ball ran out that night. If Musters had stayed with the formation he might very well have returned alive to fight again another day. Individuals had fought well, particularly Rhys Davids, but they had lost two killed and two injured, forty per cent of the total force. The patrol had not been a success: they had met some of the best pilots in the German Air Service and acquitted themselves well, as individuals, but the future of air fighting lay more in larger formations than two or three SEs getting together. It must also be said that the Germans too were frustrated by the conditions and did not patrol in large numbers.

By 9 May the mindset was that Ball was a prisoner and would not be back with the squadron. That day Lewis flew Ball's Nieuport back to the Aircraft Depot where it was refurbished and reissued to No.1 Squadron on 7 June.

The appeals to the Germans for information on Ball did not produce immediate results and it was not till the end of the month that they

---

17 Baring p221.
18 NA AIR1/1905/204/229/5.

dropped various messages which confirmed his death and his burial in Annoeullin. The messages, as passed to Headquarters 9th Wing, contained news of Musters. As recorded by 9th Wing Ball was assumed to be 'probably dead'. It is difficult to understand why the Germans were so late in confirming the death of Ball. From a point of propaganda or an humanitarian view it made sense to release the news as early as possible. According to an early biography of Ball[19] two reports were issued by the Germans but he does not date them: one report by German radio said Lothar Von Richthofen had shot Ball down in a triplane and the other, by the Wolff News Agency, said that Ball had been shot down in 'the newest English solo fighting machine' without specifying the type.

Major Blomfield, who had written to the family on 9 May, received a letter from Ball's father dated 12 May:

> I very much regret that you have lost the services of my boy, Captain Albert Ball, who I am sure has done all he possibly could to uphold the reputation of your noble Corps. I sincerely hope that he has made a good landing and that nothing more serious than being a prisoner in Germany is his fate.
>
> He was always such a topping sport and one of the best sons any man ever had.[20]

His father, like many in the squadron, still hoped that Ball had landed safely and was no worse than a prisoner for the remainder of the war. He asked for his son's possessions to be sent over to him. Preparations were made for this and a list made of all his possessions, amongst the items listed were two plans of aeroplanes, one draft agreement, one violin and one harp[21]. The plans presumably related to the Austin-Ball Scout.

A couple of days later Ball's father wrote again:

> Mrs Ball and myself more than appreciate your kindness in sending us your letter of 9th. I have received a letter from General Trenchard and we are proud to think that our boy has done what he could to uphold the reputation of the splendid Corps to which he belonged. It was at least some satisfaction to us to know that he had earned 'well done' from his Commanding Officer. As a son he was as good as he was a soldier. If he was

19 Briscoe & Stannard pp280/281.
20 Ibid.
21 NA AIR1/1908/204/229/10.

killed the loss to us at home will be terrible but we must face it like thousands of parents have done in similar circumstances and thank God that our son has been so useful in his short day. We have the feeling, however, that he is not killed but only wounded and a prisoner.[22]

The final traces of Ball's time with the squadron were cleared up during the month, when the belongings taken from his hut were sent on to his family. At one point some items, including Ball's diary, seem to have gone missing, though they later all turned up. It would be fascinating to see this diary but it is no longer with the Ball papers in the Nottingham Record Office.

The news of Ball's death was finally broken at the end of May. The news received from the Germans of Ball's death was passed to the War Office. The task of breaking the news to Ball's family fell to Arthur Richardson, the local Member of Parliament. The news shattered his mother and she never really recovered from it and was unable to face the memorial service held in Nottingham for her son. Her life was changed for ever, she shunned social occasions, and lived the rest of her life, still grieving for her son, until she died in 1931.

On 8 June the award of the Victoria Cross to Albert Ball was announced in the *London Gazette.* At the same time the President of France announced that Ball was to be made a Chevalier of the Legion d'Honneur. Two days later there was a Memorial Service in St. Mary's Church, Nottingham, attended by senior Army and RFC Officers. The service was attended by both his father and his brother, Cyril, but his mother was still so grief stricken that she was unable to attend.

Nottingham City Council held a meeting as soon as news of Ball's death was confirmed and paid tribute to Ball. The same meeting agreed to open a fund for the purpose of erecting a statue to Ball to be raised in a prominent place in Nottingham. The fund was well subscribed to from all sorts of people, from local schoolboys to local business leaders. The progress towards the completion of the memorial proceeded slowly and the sculptor was not appointed until January 1919. The debate as to where to place the statue was finally decided in favour of the grounds of Nottingham Castle though it was once proposed, by Albert Ball senior, that it should be in the city square, but this idea was not acceptable to others. By the end of 1919, the statue and plinth were

---

22 Ibid.

completed, and at this stage the council found that they did not have enough money to completely fund the project and had overspent to the tune of £1,000. Private appeals were again made to the local business leaders and the balance of the money was raised.

The Prince of Wales had been invited, and accepted, the invitation to unveil the statue, but later found he was unable to do so and Trenchard took his place. Trenchard was happy to come and pay honour to a pilot he regarded as the personification of the spirit of the old RFC but he asked for less emphasis to be laid on his attendance and more on Ball. The statue was finally unveiled on 8 September 1921 in the presence of Ball's family and large crowd of local citizens.

While Ball was honoured in his home town, his father journeyed to France to see the site where his son had crashed. He purchased the field in which his son's plane had crashed and put up a memorial stone as near as possible to the spot where the crash had happened as far as he could establish the place from local people. He also arranged for the wooden cross, which had been placed on the grave by the RAF, to be replaced by a more permanent memorial in stone. He established a fund for the permanent maintenance of the grave. The body was to remain in Annoeullin Cemetery and not put in one of the British War Cemeteries, which were now being established in France and Flanders. Later, he insisted, against the suggestion of the Imperial War Graves Commission, and the local Member of Parliament, that the body be brought back home and buried in Nottingham, but that it should remain in Annouellin. There it remains to this day, the only British grave among those of his former foes.

What of those people whom Ball had known and loved and were close to him throughout his career? As remarked earlier his mother never recovered from the shock of losing her beloved eldest son and died heartbroken in 1931.

His father continued his political career in Nottingham and defended his son against a perceived attack when the biography of R. H. Kiernan came out in 1933. His resentment subsided after, it is assumed, actually reading the book and finding it laudatory, rather than otherwise, of his son. He died in 1946.

Lois married in 1918 and had two children by George Anderson, an army officer. Her son, also called Albert, was killed in September 1943 in the Mediterranean when his Spitfire's engine failed and he baled out at too low an altitude for his parachute to operate. Lois died in 1984.

Cyril came out to France in December 1917. He was posted to No.60 Squadron to fly SE5as. He felt a certain urge to 'live up to' his brother and perhaps took some unnecessary risks. On 5 February 1918, while over German territory, his engine was hit by anti-aircraft fire and he set out to glide back to the British lines. He came under attack by an Albatros scout and was forced to land and spend the rest of the War as a prisoner. The fact that another of her sons had gone missing was a further blow to Harriet Ball and she was inconsolable until the news of his being a prisoner came through. Cyril died in 1958.

Flora Young married William Thornhill in 1925 and died in Essex in 1985. She and Lois remained friends and cooperated with Chaz Bowyer in the biography of Ball in the 1970s.

Thelma married William White in 1921. According to her daughter, she and Ball had known each other since childhood and the relationship ended when Thelma met somebody else. Thelma died in Leicester in 1986.

The loss of Ball was a blow to the whole of the British flying services. Those who were perceptive were anxious about his style of fighting and knew that such good fortune as he had enjoyed could not last forever. He was a unique force in the RFC. His methods were peculiar to himself and in the changing world of 1917/18 became less and less applicable in the fighting which went on that period. Bishop and Voss remained the last of the individualists (though it is probably the case that Billy Barker was the very last) but air fighting was following the model set by Boelcke and expanded by Richthofen that of developing tactics and employing larger forces. The legacy of Albert Ball to the RFC was one of an example of sheer courage. It could be said that Ball continued the maxim of Lanoe Hawker which the latter had pinned on the notice board of No.24 Squadron, 'Attack Everything!' Unlike Richthofen the example of Ball did not leave a legacy, of changes to the methods of air fighting, but an equally important personal example which inspired those who came after him. Many years ago in correspondence with Air Vice Marshal Collishaw, I asked him for his comments on the proposition which had been put forward in a recent book, that the deeds of Ball and his influence had been exaggerated by the British authorities to counter the effect of von Richthofen. He replied:

In respect to Captain Ball, anyone familiar with his activities cannot but be enthralled at his enterprise and gallantry. It is just silly for armchair critics to indulge in criticism 50 years after the event.[23]

This comment, coming from probably the best pilot, in the British services, not to get a VC, says all that needs to be said about Albert Ball.

---

23 Collishaw to the Author 12/8/1965.

'The Wonderful Machine'

One of the mysteries of Albert Ball's life is what was the 'wonderful machine' that he was referring to in his letter to his father on 14 April 1916?

The first question that naturally comes to mind is how and why the plans for this machine should have been in the possession of Ball. He was not at that time the famous celebrity that he was later to become. In fact he had only about two months experience at the front and none in single seaters. His combat experience was limited and he would not have seemed to be a natural choice for anyone wishing to get their ideas accepted by the RFC except for one factor: his family connection with the Austin Motor Company. Only the Austin Company would have listened to any proposal from Ball for the design and production of an aeroplane. Other manufacturers would have taken note that the person making the proposal was of limited operational experience and had no success in aerial combat to his name.

It must have been known that Ball, through his father, had connections with the Austin Company. It must also have been known that Austin's were going to expand their business activities to include the construction of aircraft, initially in the role of sub-contractor. Therefore, anyone who might have had ideas for a fighting aeroplane and wished to get them considered by a manufacturer might very well have thought of Ball as a useful point of entry to the aviation industry. It would have been a far more direct route than putting them forward through the channels of the Headquarters RFC in France.

It is obvious that Ball had not drawn up the plans himself for he talks of 'managing' to get the plans and his expertise did not extend beyond basic mechanical engineering. On the same basis it is obvious that the plans had not been sent to Ball by his father, but from some third party, asking for his opinion. Ball was telling his father something of which the latter was unaware. The most reasonable assumption must be, therefore, that the plans were drawn up by someone in the squadron and then handed to Ball for him to try and get the machine built by Austin's.

We will never know who in the squadron it was, for no clue is given in any of Ball's correspondence. In the same letter that he mentioned the plans to his father he also talks of Lieutenant Villiers, who was his best friend in the squadron and often flew as his Observer, as leaving to take a pilots' course and he described Villiers as 'clever' and 'knowing a lot about flying'. Ball also asked his father to see if he could get Villiers a job at Austin's after the War. Villiers might be a candidate for the production of the plans and he was certainly close to Ball and would have known his family background. However, it is reasonable to suppose that if these plans had been drawn up by his best friend Ball would surely have said so in his letter home.

Also, what did Ball mean by 'plans'. Surely not full production drawings which, even for the relatively simple machines of 1916, would still have been a weighty pack. I am certain that he must have been in possession of an outline drawing possibly supplemented by some technical information. This seems to have been the sort of information which he himself later supplied to the Austin Company and which was translated by the company into the Austin-Ball. Ball planned to send the plans home to his father, but found that he could not send them through the post. He therefore planned to bring them with him when he next came home on leave.

Another mystery is why anyone should look to produce an answer to the Fokker monoplane when by April 1916 it was obvious that the DH2, the FE2 and the early examples of the Nieuport Scout were the answer which the Allies were seeking.

Appendix 2

The Austin-Ball Scout

Unlike 'the wonderful machine' mentioned in Appendix 1 the Austin-Ball was a design arising from the ideas of Albert Ball. It seems to have sprung from thoughts jotted down by Ball during the summer of 1916 as his experience of air fighting grew and his ideas of what he wanted formed in his mind. In his biography of Ball[1], R.H. Kiernan accepts that the earlier plans, which Ball had spoken of in April 1916, were drawn up by Ball and that, over the summer, they gestated into the Austin-Ball. As stated in Appendix 1, I do not accept this scenario. The words of Ball in his letter to his father *I have managed to get the plans* indicate that he had no direct hand in preparing them. At that time, as has been previously stated, Ball was a comparative novice and had yet to fly a single-seat scout or have a combat in the air.

As with the previous design that he had had in mind, Ball thought immediately of putting his ideas to the Austin Motor Company, (of which he was a shareholder as well as his father being one of the directors). The company had an aviation division, engaged in work producing aircraft engines as well as the BE2c and RE7 aircraft under sub-contract. Herbert Austin had taken on John North as the manager of this aircraft side of the business.

Ball sent the documents, containing his ideas, to his father, who then showed them to North. When Ball returned home in October 1916 he was able to get in touch with the Austin Company personally and explain his ideas in more detail. The sanction of the head of the company, Herbert Austin, was obtained, but only if the idea was discussed with the War Office and they gave agreement for the construction of a prototype to go ahead. Not only did Ball approach Austin's, he had also gone to see Sir David Henderson, the Director

---

1 *Captain Albert Ball VC DSO* by R. H. Kiernan (John Hamilton 1933) p114.

General of Military Aeronautics, and explained his ideas to him. Henderson had, it seems, given him the encouragement to proceed and had told Sefton Brancker that Ball had spoken to him about the ideas for a new scout.

Lieutenant-Colonel Beatty, Assistant Director of Aircraft Equipment, had written to Austin's on 17 November saying that they understood that the firm was preparing to produce an aeroplane based on the ideas of Ball. Austin's replied on 20 November that they were proposing to prepare a design for a fighting aeroplane on these lines and they confirmed that they were prepared to undertake the manufacture of fighting aeroplanes on this basis, but at the present time they had no knowledge of the quantities required or details of the type but, 'precise particulars of the machine could doubtless be agreed upon at a conference, when it is decided how many machines are required'. Plainly, by this time, the details of the machine were not fully finalised and the initial ideas of Ball were still the only specification available. Based on these ideas and later discussions, a specification for the aircraft was produced in late November 1916 and copies sent to both Austin's and Ball.

By 27 November 1916 Austin's had written to the War Office confirming the arrangements concerning the 'special type of aeroplane to be built to the details furnished by Captain Ball'. On 1 December the War Office formally wrote to Austin's enclosing the specification asking them to provide general arrangement drawings and to fill in a technical data form. Only when these had been received would the proposal be considered by the appropriate committee and possible modifications suggested. When the design was finally approved two prototypes would be ordered. Further orders would depend on the success of the first two machines. The specification for the machine stated that it was to be fitted with the 150 hp Hispano Suiza, and fuel capacity was to allow for two hours' flight. The armament was to consist of both Vickers and Lewis machine guns. The Vickers gun was to fire through a hollow airscrew shaft (an idea for which Herbert Austin had taken out a patent, and which was also being experimented with by the Spad designer) with the rear of the gun being easily accessible. A belt of 500 rounds was to be provided and there was even talk of these belts being replaced by the pilot while in flight, a procedure which one would think would require more attention than a pilot flying in hostile skies might be willing to give it.[2]

A Lewis gun was to be provided on the top wing with stowage for four double drums of ninety-seven rounds apiece. Albert Ball added his own thoughts at the end of the specification; that the stability of the machine should be as near neutral as possible. This remark is signed and dated 8 December 1916. By the end of 1916 the detailed requirements for the machine were largely agreed, except for the layout of the wings. In his discussions with Austin's, Ball had, based on his experience of the Nieuport Scout, proposed the idea of a slight sweep-back on the wings. This point left open for further discussion later and in the end a normal straight edge wing was used.

Ball took an intense interest in the aircraft and he was soon involved in the detail of the design and the performance of the prototype. He wrote to the Technical Committee of the War Office asking for details of the performance of the Hispano Engine and for an example of the Foster Mounting as he had been unable to obtain drawings.

Others too were taking a keen interest in the design and were not too happy with what they saw. A memo, dated 25 January 1917, to General Pitcher from his deputy, Beatty, states the uneasiness which was felt about some aspects of the project and the doubts that it could achieve a sufficient performance to make it suitable for substantial production orders:

> The performance quoted is not impossible in view of the horse power of the engine and the weight of the machine. Its performance, however, has been attained in some measure by curtailing the fuel capacity – which is only for two hours at full speed – while no gravity tank is provided. If so small a capacity is accepted – and it is a ready means of attaining performance – then the design can be regarded within the requirements.
>
> It should be noted, however, that the machine has, what may be termed, a distinct German appearance, by virtue of the 'swept back' wings and the 'fish' tail. In other respects and general points it resembles in no small degree the French Spad (also added here in ink 'and the Nieuport').[3]

---

2 Previous accounts of the Austin-Ball, which I have been able to find have always stated that a Lewis Gun was to fire through the airscrew shaft (eg see the entry on the Austin-Ball in J.M. Bruce's *British Aeroplanes 1914-1918*) but the original specification is quite clear that a Vickers Gun was originally envisaged for this position. It may be that this may have been found impracticable when tried and the Lewis substituted but I have yet to find proof of this having taken place.

3 NA AIR2/11 *Specification for Austin-Ball*.

The writer went on to note that the wing loading at 7lb per sq. ft. was high for a fighter and hoped that this would lead to a higher speed for he considered that such a loading would adversely effect its manoeuvrability. He also doubted that the machine could reach its claimed ceiling of 18,000ft under service conditions.

The design of the fuselage did not meet his approval either, considering it 'exceptionally deep' and that it tapered off too much towards the tail for a high speed machine and that'it will have a rather low resistance to torsional stresses which are likely to be particularly high with the large rudder fitted above the body'. Finally the observation was made that the tailplane was not adjustable in flight, which could be accepted if a two-hour endurance was acceptable; and the view from the cockpit would be obstructed by the exhaust pipes which ran alongside the fuselage and discharged aft of the pilot. The general feeling within the Department was, however, that the design could be proceeded with, if the 2 hours endurance was acceptable but noted that extra capacity would involve additional weight and reduce the performance. The memo was endorsed at the top, 'Captain Ball to see General Brancker'.

In a letter to his mother Ball spoke of his meeting with Brancker:

> ... Saw Branker and got order to complete first two machines at once. If they are found to be any better than any others we get big order. That is left for me.
>
> I told Austin's I was surprised at their calling the machine the Austin and forgetting it was to be called the A.B. or Austin-Ball. So much for that. I saw Lord Northcliffe and he is going to put in a word for me and my machine.
>
> I want a bit of cash from Austin's or they will not have the big job when it comes and come it will.[4]

Ball was generally unhappy with the slow rate of progress between Austin's and the War Office and thought his personal interventions would help to spur things along. It is not known what 'cash' Ball is referring to in this letter. It would be interesting to know more, but this is the only mention of the matter which I have been able to trace. The sanction of the Air Board was obtained and the design and construction of the prototype could go ahead under Contract No

4 Ball Archives 10/2/1917.

87/A/1524. This was for the production of two prototypes but it is doubtful if the second was ever completed as no photograph or other record of it exists.

On 13 February, Austin's, aware of the meeting between Ball and Brancker wrote to say that they understood that it had been agreed to proceed with construction and they asked Brancker to let them have the formal contract. Brancker forwarded the letter to Pitcher noting that the matter referred to was the proposed order for two experimental prototypes 'of a type designed by Captain Ball'. He noted, 'the designer has much experience in aerial fighting and in view of this and his being <u>encouraged</u> I recommend that two machines be produced'. Pitcher agreed and the formal contract was issued soon after. It is plain from these comments that Ball was looked on as the designer of the type rather than Charles Brookes and John North of Austin.

John North, remarked on the genesis of the Austin-Ball to the Westland test pilot, Harald Penrose, many years later:

> . . . Young Ball's idea was basically a water cooled Hispano powered Nieuport with two upward firing guns located on a low centre-section for easy changing of magazine drums. We structured and detailed the general arrangement to more practical form.[5]

Apart from the Lewis gun the final design, as stated above, carried a Vickers gun firing through the propeller shaft. This type of mounting was not one envisaged by Ball in his original specification, but he may well have thought, once he learnt of it, that it might have been preferable to the early CC synchronising gear which had been fitted to the SE5 and which later gave him so much trouble.

The first British machine to go to France fitted with an interrupter gear was a Bristol Scout D No 5313 which was issued to No.12 Squadron in March 1916 but later was on the charge of No.11 Squadron where Albert Ball had used it to drive down an Albatros two-seater on 15 May. Apart from this brief experience Ball had fought predominantly with the Nieuport with the over-wing mounted Lewis, so it is not to be wondered at that his specification included this armament.

---

5 British Aviation. *The Great War and Armistice* by Harald Penrose (Putnam 1969)p.185.

Another point with regard to the reported comments of John North is the type of engine specified, the Hispano Suiza. This was the engine intended by Austin's, but the original requirement laid out by Ball, now unfortunately missing along with the aviation records of the Austin Company, might have called for a rotary engine.

Once Ball had returned to France his direct input on the matter ceased. It became a matter of discussion between Austin's and the War Office. However, given Ball's disappointment with the SE5 he still pinned hopes, unrealistically it must be said, of Austin's producing a machine for him to take to France. He wrote to his father on 18 March, from London Colney, that General Henderson had been to visit the squadron and Ball seems to have taken the opportunity to discuss the Austin Scout. Ball said that 'the WO is mad on my machine being finished at once' and that he intended to visit Austin's the following week to try and hasten completion.[6]

Just two weeks before the squadron was to leave for France he wrote to his father again:

> The Hun RFC is far ahead of us this time, in fact about 30 mph. Oh I do wish I had got a Nieuport and above all I wish I had my own machine.
>
> The SE5 has turned out a dud . . . It is a great shame for everyone thinks they are so good and expect such a lot from them.
>
> Well I am making the best of a bad job. If Austin's will not buck up and finish a machine for me I shall have to go out on the SE5 and do my best . . . It is a rotten machine and if the Austin's machine is not finished I am afraid that things will not go very OK.[7]

By the date of Ball's death the construction of the machine was still not complete. The Hispano Suiza engines had been delivered in the middle of March but it wasn't until 22 May that Austin's reported the machine as nearly completed and asked whether the War Office wished to send an officer along to inspect the machine before it went to the research and testing station at Martlesham Heath. A Captain Rowell was sent up to look at the machine and orders were given to Austin's that the machine was to go to Martlesham Heath by train on

---

6 Ball Archives 18/3/1917.
7 Ball Archives 23/3/1917.

26 May. The official serial number B9909 had been given to the prototype prior to the departure for Martlesham Heath.

The machine seems to have spent some two months before there was a first recorded flight. At some stage it was decided to change the existing propeller for an SE5 propeller and one was sent to Martlesham Heath for the purpose. The first flight recorded in the machine's logbook is on 27 July when Lieutenant K.P. Henderson took it up for twelve minutes. Between then and the time that it left Martlesham Heath the Austin-Ball was flown for a total of 27 hours and 25 minutes. Amongst those who flew the machine was Captain Henry Tizard.[8]

Austin's wrote on 26 July asking for a copy of the Test Report and a summary of this went to them on 28 July. It is not precisely certain therefore when the assessment of the machine was carried out but it most probably would have been in the second half of July.

On test the Austin-Ball performed well in comparison with the SE5 and was conventionally manoeuvrable. Fitted with the 200 hp Hispano Suiza engine it produced figures as good as other contemporary scouts, but the aircraft did not offer sufficient advantage over existing service types such as the SE5a and the Sopwith Camel, to make it worthwhile interfering with the production orders for these types. The comparative performance figures for the Austin-Ball , SE5/5A and Camel are shown below:

	Austin-Ball 150 Hispano	SE5 150 Hispano	SE5A 200 Hispano	Camel 130 Clerget
Speed mph:				
10,000ft	126.5	114	128	113
15,000ft	120.5	98	115.5	106.5
Climb:				
6,500ft	8 mins	6 mins	6 mins	
10,000ft	8 mins 55 sec	14mins 10sec	11mins 2sec	10mins 35sec
14,000ft	14 mins 30 sec	-	-	-
15,000ft	-	29mins 30sec	22mins 30sec	20mins 40sec
Ceiling	22,000ft	17,000ft	19,000ft	19,000ft
Endurance	2¼ hrs	2½ hrs	2¼ hrs	2 ½ hrs

The aircraft remained at Martlesham Heath for another couple of months. In that period the wing layout was changed and a Spad type

8 Later Sir Henry Tizard (1885-1959). A distinguished scientist who served in various government posts as an advisor. He championed the development of radar as Chairman of the Aeronautical Research Committee. During the early part of the Second World War he pressed the case on the government of sharing our scientific knowledge with the USA in order that their production facilities would be available to help meet the demand for the new equipment.

arrangement was fitted with straight wings with negative stagger and double bay strutting. The reason for this change in layout is not given in existing records and one visitor on seeing the additional struts considered them crude and heavy and called it a 'retrograde step'. Some correspondence went on for some time on the strength of the new wings, but there was no way forward for the type. Well as it had performed it did not offer sufficient an advantage over the existing types to warrant an order. It too would have been another aircraft requiring the 200 hp Hispano engine and there were already insufficient of that type of engine to meet requirements. Perhaps progress had been retarded by the loss of Ball's personal interest when he returned to France and his later death. He became reconciled to the SE5 and the requirement for an 'improved Nieuport' lessened in his mind.

At the end of October, Martlesham Heath was ordered to send the machine to Ascot but to take out the engine before doing so. They reported on 30 October that this had been done and the machine was on its way to Ascot by train. This was the end of the official interest in the machine and it never appeared again.

Appendix 3

List of No.56 Squadron Pilots
up to 7 May 1917

Pilots who flew to France on 7 April 1917

Name	Date Posted	Date Left	Reason
A. Ball	26/2/17	7/5/17	KIA
L.M. Barlow	9/2/17	21/10/17	HE
R.M. Chaworth-Musters	4/3/17	7/5/17	KIA
R.T.C. Hoidge	5/1/17	19/11/17	HE
M. Kay	13/3/17	30/4/17	KIA
K.J. Knaggs	16/2/17	16/6/17	Wounded
C.R.W. Knight	3/1/17	9/5/17	2 ASD
J.O. Leach	16/3/17	7/5/17	Wounded
H.M.T. Lehmann	5/3/17	7/5/17	HE
C. A. Lewis	20/3/17	13/7/17	HE
G. J. C. Maxwell	12/3/17	21/10/17	HE
H. Meintjes	4/4/17	7/5/17	Wounded
W. B. Melville	14/2/17	7/5/17	Wounded
A. P. F. Rhys Davids	3/3/17	27/10/17	KIA

Replacement pilots

Name	Date Posted	Date Left	Reason
H. F. W. Bailey	8/4/17	9/4/17	Hospital
E. W.Broadberry	20/4/17	12/7/17	Wounded
C. M. Crowe	19/4/17	13/7/17	Hospital
J. H. Flynn	30/4/17	8/5/17	Hospital
C. E. French	20/4/17	20/5/17	POW
A. J. Jessop	20/4/17	12/5/17	KIA
E. Lloyd	22/4/17	27/5/17	POW
J. Toogood	20/4/17	22/4/17	2 ASD
G.M. Wilkinson	20/4/17	28/5/17	Wounded

Pilots attached to No.56 Squadron but did not proceed to France on 7 April 1917

Name	Date Posted	Date Left	Reason
M. H. Coote	23/2/17	13/3/17	To No.49 Squadron
E. L. Foot	10/3/17	6/4/17	Car Accident
I. H. Henderson	24/2/17	30/4/17	To Eastern Command
J. E. Hunt	14/2/17	?	?
W. J. Potts	22/3/17	?	Injured in crash
W. O. Russell	9/3/17	?	To No.60 Squadron
S. A. Villiers	15/3/17	?	?

KIA = Killed in Action
HE = Home Establishment
POW = Prisoner of War
2ASD = 2nd Aircraft Supply Depot

APPENDIX 4

Victories List

No.	Date	E A Type	Aircraft	Sqdn	Remarks
1916					
1	16 May	Albatros.C	Bristol 5312	11	OOC
2	29 May	LVG C	Nieuport 5173	11	OOC
3	29 May	LVG C	5173	11	FTL
4	1 June	Fokker E	5173	11	FTL
5	25 June	Balloon	5173	11	DES
6	2 July	Roland CII	Nieuport A134	11	DES
7	2 July	Aviatik C	A134	11	DES
8	16 August	Roland CII	A201	11	FTL
9	22 August	Roland CII	Nieuport A201	11	DES
10	22 August	Roland CII	A201	11	DES(F)
11[1]	22 August	Roland CII	A201	11	DES
12	25 August	Roland CII	A201	60	OOC
13[2]	28 August	Roland CII	A201	60	FTL
14	28 August	Roland CII	A201	60	DES
15	28 August	C	A201	60	FTL
16	31 August	Roland CII	A201	60	DES
17	31 August	Roland CII	A201	60	FTL
18	15 September	Fokker DII	A200	60	DES
19[3]	15 September	Roland CII	Nieuport A212	60	DES
20	21 September	Roland D	Nieuport A213	60	FTL
21	21 September	Roland D	A213	60	DES
22	21September	Roland CII	A213	60	DES
23[4]	22 September	Fokker D	A213	60	DES
24[5]	23 September	Roland CII	A213	60	DES(F)
25[6]	25 September	Albatros C	A213	60	DES(F)
26	28 September	Albatros C	A213	60	DES
27	28 September	Albatros C	A213	60	FTL
28	28 September	Albatros C	A213	60	FTL
29[7]	30 September	Albatros C	A201	60	DES(F)
30	30 September	Roland CII	A213	60	OOC
31[8]	30 September	Roland C	A213	60	OOC

1917					
32[9]	23 April	Albatros C	Nieuport B1522	56	DES
33	23 April	Albatros DIII	SE5 A4850	56	DES(F)
34	26 April	Albatros DIII	A4850	56	DES
35[10]	26 April	S.S. DI	A4850	56	DES(F)
36	28 April	Albatros C	A4850	56	DES
37	1 May	Albatros C	A8898	56	DES
38	1 May	Albatros C	A8898	56	OOC
39	2 May	Albatros DIII	A4855	56	DES
40[11]	2 May	Albatros C	A4855	56	DES
41	4 May	Albatros DIII	A8898	56	DES
42	5 May	Albatros DIII	A8898	56	DES
43	5 May	Albatros DIII	A8898	56	DES
44[12]	6 May	Albatros DIII	Nieuport B1522	56	DES

OOC = Out of Control; FTL = Forced to Land; DES = Destroyed; DES(F) = Destroyed in Flames

Notes

1 Flown by Offz. Cymera (wounded) and Lt. Becker (died of wounds) of *Kampstaffel* 1.
2 Flown by Lt. Von Arnim(killed) and Lt Bohne.
3 Flown by Uffz. Carstens(wounded) and Oblt. du Cornu(died of wounds).
4 Lt Grafe of *Jasta* 2 (Killed).
5 Believed to be Lt Kliche & Oblt Miner (Both Killed).
6 Flieger Tewes (Wounded) and Lt. Hoffman (Killed) of FA(A) 237.
7 Shared with FE2b of No. 11 Squadron flown by Lt. Roberts and Lt. Collins.
8 One of either Victory 30 or 31 was believed to be Lt. Diener of *Jasta* 2 who was killed.
9 Believed to be Lt. Siebel.
10 Believed to be Vzfw Eisenhuth of Jasta 3 (Killed).
11 Originally believed to be Lt. Prill & Lt. Reichl but this seems to be incorrect as Reichl was killed 27 September 1916.
12 Vzfw Jager of *Jasta* 20 (wounded).

Bibliography

Andrews, C.F., *The Nieuport 17* (Profile Publications)

Barker, Ralph, *The Royal Flying Corps in France. From Mons to the Somme* (Constable 1995)

Bishop, William Arthur, *The Courage of the Early Morning* (McKay 1965)

Bowyer, Chaz. *Albert Ball VC* (Kimber 1977)

Boyle, Andrew, *Trenchard. Man of Vision* (Collins 1962)

Briscoe W.A. & H.R., Stannard *Captain Ball VC* (Jenkins 1918)

Brown, Malcolm, *The Imperial War Museum Book of 1914* (Pan 2005)

Bruce, J. M. *British Aeroplanes 1914-1918* (Putnam 1957)
   The Aeroplanes of the Royal Flying Corps (Military Wing) (Putnam 1982)
   The Sopwith Pup; The Sopwith Triplane); The DH2 (Profile Publications)

Cole, Christopher, *McCudden VC* (William Kimber 1967)
   Royal Flying Corps Communiques 1915-1916 (William Kimber 1969)

Cross & Cockade, Various Journals

Duffy, Christopher, *Through German Eyes: the British on the Somme 1916* (Weidenfeld & Nicholson 2006)

Fry, Wing Commander William, *Air of Battle* (Kimber 1974)

Gray, Peter, *The Albatros DI-DIII* (Profile Publications)

Hart, Peter, *Somme Success. The Royal Flying Corps and the Battle of the Somme, 1916.* (Pen & Sword 2001)
   Bloody April. Slaughter in the skies over Arras, 1917 (Cassell 2006)

Insall, A.J., *Observer* (Kimber 1970)

Jones, H.A., *War in the Air Vol. II & Vol. III* (OUP 1928)

Kiernan, R.H., *Albert Ball VC DSO* (Hamilton 1933)

Lewis, Cecil, *Sagittarius Rising* (Greenhill 2006)

Libby, Frederick, *Horses Don't Fly* (Arcade Publishing 2000)

Malinovska, Anna and Mauriel Joslyn, *Voices in Flight* (Pen and Sword 2006)

Marson, T.B., *Scarlet & Khaki* (Jonothan Cape 1930)

Morris, Alan, *Bloody April* (Jarrolds 1967)

Penrose, Harald, *British Aviation. The Great War and Armistice* (Putnam 1969)

Revell, Alex, *Brief Glory* (Kimber 1984) (Pen & Sword 2010)
   High in the Empty Blue (Grub Street 1997)

Russell, D.A. with W. M. Lamberton etc *Fighter Aircraft of the 1914-18 War* (Harleyford 1960)

Shores, Christopher, Norman Franks & Russell Guest, *Above the Trenches* (Grub Street 1990)

Weir, Chris, *Nottingham a History* (Phillimore 2002)

Index

Adinfer 164
Air Board 62, 143, 163, 212
Allbourne, Dorothy ('Dot')
24-26, 31
Allmenroeder, Ltn. Karl 191
Allmenroeder, Ltn. Wilhelm
191, 194-5
Althaus, Ltn. Ernst 47
Anderson, Lt. G 79
Andrews, Captain J.O. 113
Annoeullin 6, 11, 202, 204
Arnim, Ltn. Joachim von
109
Arras 10, 55,165
Aubigny 66, 91
Auchel 194
Austin Ball 132, 137, 141,
161, 178, 209-216
Austin, Sir Herbert 209-210
Austin Motor Company 25,
132, 137, 139-140
Avesnes les Bapaume 126

Bailleulmont 123
Balcombe-Brown, Captain,
E 84
Ball, Albert (father) 12-16,
24, 26, 30, 55, 57, 77, 87,
96, 133, 135, 202, 204, 209
Ball, Captain Albert
Early Life: 12, 14-20
Volunteers for the Army: 21
Army training: 22-31 Flying
Training: 9, 27- Transfers to
the RFC: 32-34 Commercial
Ventures: 19-20, 27, 30, 61,
135-136, 155 Relations with
women: 30-32, 38 Religious
beliefs: 7, 53, 55, 82, 112
Gains R.Ae.C Certificate: 34
RFC Flying Training: 34 First
Solo: 36 At CFS 38-41 Gains
'Wings': 41 Leaves for France:
42 With 13 Sqdn.: 43-61
With 11 Sqdn: 62-90 First
flight on Nieuports: Awarded
the MC: 77-78 Comparison
with von Richthofen: 83

Noticed in the press: 83
Request for a rest from
operations: 89-91 Service in
8 Sqdn.: 91-100 Spy Mission:
95 Tests BE12: 99 With 60
Sqdn.: 106-130 Fits red
spinner to Nieuport: 107
Keeps record of his victories:
110 Account of exploits in the
French Press: 110 Publicity
in the British Press: 110-111
Personal feelings on his
victories: 112, 127 Awarded
the DSO: 113 Made Flight
Commander in 60 Sqdn: 117
Awarded Bars to the DSO:
Promoted Captain: Leaves 60
Sqdn: Last home leave: 132-
137-145 In Home
Establishment: 137
Volunteers to return to France:
138 and the Austin Ball: 132,
137, 139, 141, 209-216
Dislike of the SE5: 141, 142,
155, 161 Made Freeman of
Nottingham: 144-145
Presentation of silver bowl:
Joins 56 Sqdn.: 146 Meets
Flora Young: 156 Returns to
France: 159-160 Given
Nieuport: 160, 161 Leads
first patrol: 164 Reconciled to
the SE5: 168 Evidence for VC
recommendation: 119 Last
Patrol: 189-196 Death:
195-196 Award of VC: 203
Monument: 204
Ball, Lt. Cyril 12, 15-16, 25-
26, 30, 55, 63, 67, 73, 106,
125, 152-153, 205
Ball, Frederick 22, 27
Ball, Harriet 12, 52, 55, 204
Ball, Lois 12, 25, 27, 33, 39,
52, 55, 67, 85, 110, 170,
185, 204
Bapaume 105, 109, 118, 120
Baring, Captain Maurice
160, 161, 201

Barlow, Lt. L.M 149-151,
160, 164-167, 172, 184
Barnwell, Frank 46
Baumann. Edward 9, 27, 33
Beatty, Lt. Colonel 210-211
Beaumont 71, 193
Bell, Geoffrey 17
Bell-Irving, Lt. A 127
Bellevue 91, 95
Bernert, Ltn. Otto 117
Berr, Oblt. Hans 117
Beugny 99
Bishop, Major William
Avery 9, 69, 111, 120
Blomfield, Major, Richard
148, 151, 157, 160, 161-
162, 172, 177, 186-188,
199, 202
Boelcke, Oswald 8, 47, 62,
109, 115, 117, 120, 149,
169, 205
Bowyer, Chaz 6, 7, 32
Brancker, Lt. General Sir S
79, 210, 212-213
Broadbery. Lt. E 181
Brookes, Charles 213
Buddecke, Oblt. Hans 117

Caldwell, 2/Lt. K.L. 96
Cambrai-Bapaume Road
109, 112, 122, 170
Candas Aircraft Depot 53,
58, 60, 61, 87, 161, 162,
172, 184
Caudry 186
Central Flying School 9
Chantilly Conference 79
Charlton, Brigadier L.E.O
145
Charles, Lt. H.N 151-154,
160, 164, 197
Chaworth-Musters, 2/Lt. R
150, 160, 164, 189-190,
201-202
Colincamp 113
Collishaw, Air Vice Marshal,
Raymond 205-206
Cooper, Captain H.A. 75

Croiselles 164
Crook, Captain 84
Crowe, Captain, Cyril 148-149, 165, 170, 172-173, 184, 189-190, 192-195, 199
Cruickshank, Captain G.L. 117

Davids, Lt. Arthur Rhys 8, 150-152, 160, 189-190, 191, 199-201
Dawes, Major 63
Deloffre, Cecile 196
De Havilland, Geoffrey 44, 48
'Dollie' 139
Dore, Major, A.S.W 61
Douai 72, 165-166, 175, 191, 200
Doullens 160
Dowding, Colonel (later ACM Lord) Hugh 10, 89

Esser, Ltn. Fritz 191

Falkenhayn, General Erich von 80
Fokker, Anthony 8
'Fokker Fodder' 45
Folland, Henry 141
Foster, Sergeant R.G. 69
Foot, Captain, E.L 75, 107, 119, 126, 130-131, 148, 150-151, 153, 159
Fry, Lt. William 101-103
Fullard, Phillip Fletcher, Captain (later Air Commodore) 6, 69

Gallop, Major Clive 148
Garros, Roland 47
Gavrelle 55
Gilchrist, 2/Lt. E 118
Givenchy 54, 167
Glew, Lt. A.E 113
Goodden, Major Frank 141-142, 144
Gossage, Major Ernest 147
Gosport 41
Grantham Grammar School 15
Green, Lt. 49

Gregory, Lt. R 50, 52, 55
Grevillers 120
Griffiths, 2/Lt 79
Guynemer. Capitaine, Georges 82, 112, 156, 169-170

Haig, Field Marshal Sir Douglas 10, 80. 185, 200
Hailer, Ltn. Carl 196
Hailer, Ltn. Fritz 196-199
Hamlincourt 129
Haplincourt 125
Hardy, Theodore 15
Harvey-Kelly, Major H.D 147
Hawker, Major Lanoe 9, 46, 48, 81, 142, 205
Heinkel, Ernst 48
Henderson, General Sir David 140, 209, 214
Henderson, Captain, Ian 148
Henderson, Corporal J 107
Henderson, Lt. K.P 215
Hendon 27
Hepner, Ltn 199
Herbert, Captain P.L.W 43
Hervey. Lt. H.E. 96-98
Higgins, Brigadier General J.F.A 61, 71, 73, 77, 82, 89, 95, 97, 106, 130
Hill, Lt. Roderic 142-143
Hoffman, Ltn. M 124
Hoidge, Lt. R.T.C 154, 160, 165, 181, 189, 192, 199
Hubbard, Major T.O'B 61, 63, 70, 72, 75-76, 79, 85, 89-90, 99, 101, 103, 107
Hythe 66, 138-140

Immelmann, Max 8, 41, 47, 62, 74
Insall, Lt. Algernon 52, 63, 65
Insall, Lt. Geoffrey 65
Izel le Hameau 51-52, 106, 113, 160

Jagdstaffeln 1: 113, 120
  2: 109, 113, 117, 127, 129
  3: 117
  4: 117
  5: 117
  6: 117
  7: 117
  11: 187
Joel, Lt. W 51-52, 61
Jones, Captain, Ira 9

Kay, 2/Lt. M.A 153, 164-165, 170, 172-173
Kenworthy, John 141
Kings Lynn 145
Kitchener, Field Marshal Lord 21
Knaggs, Lt. K.J 160, 164-165, 171-172, 175, 178-180, 184, 186, 189-190, 192-193, 199
Knight, 2/Lt. C.R.W 160, 165-166, 171-172, 175-176

Lagnicourt 127
Lang, Sergeant, Frederick 66
Leach, Lt. J.O 151, 156-157, 160, 165-166, 170, 172-173, 189, 190, 192
Lehmann, Lt. H.M.T 160, 165-167, 175-176
Lenoir, Adjutant, Maxine 111
Le Prieur Rockets 66, 84, 120
Lewis, Lt. Cecil 149-151, 158, 160, 171, 181, 184, 189, 192, 199
Libby, Lt. Frederick 75-76
Lievin 164
Lloyd George, David 137
London Colney 146-147, 150
Lucas, Captain, G 67

Mannock, Major Edward 9, 97, 101
Marieux 44
Marsh, Major A.C.E 45, 53, 55, 57-58, 60-61, 63
Marson, 2/Lt. T.B 148, 158, 182, 183, 188, 197-198
Martlesham Heath 214-216
Marquion 175
Maxwell, Lt. G.C 149-151,

160, 162, 164-165, 170-172, 179-181, 186-187, 189, 199-200
McCubbin, Lt. Alan 74
McCudden, Major James 11, 14, 26, 66, 69, 86, 97, 145, 148, 151, 164, 168, 175
Meintjes, Captain, H 148-149, 158, 161, 186, 189, 191-182, 199
Mellenthin, Ltn. Ewald von 117
Melville, Lt. W.B 160, 165-167, 181, 187, 199
Mercatel 81
Mohnicke, Ltn. Eberhardt 191
Morgan Cars 136
Morris, 2/Lt. L.B.F 104
Mulcahy-Morgan, Captain T.W. 93
Muspratt, Lt. Keith 150, 151

Neuvilly 186
Newall, Lt. Colonel, Cyril 186
NMDCC 23, 33
North, John 209, 213
Northcliffe, Lord 145-146
Nottingham Evening News 133
Nottingham High School 15

Orfordness 137-138
Oxford 138

Palmer, Lt. A.M. 97
Parker, Captain, G.A 91, 98
Pelves 84
Pemberton-Billing, Noel 45
Pitcher, General 144, 211, 213
Playfair, Captain, Patrick 63, 90, 94, 98, 130
Pluschow, Ltn. Wolfgang 192
Pretyman, Major 187
Price, Captain 76

Reffell, Sergeant 79
Rees, Lt. 104
Richardson, A 140, 203
Richthofen, Ltn. Lothar von 191, 193-195, 197-199, 202

Richthofen, Hauptman Manfred von 41, 83, 86, 109, 113, 142, 147, 187, 189-190, 205
Royal Aircraft Factory 44, 141, 144
Rouvroy 58
Ruffi (Ruffy), Aime 27
Ruffi, Felix 27

St. Leger 96, 103, 120
St. Omer 160
Salmond, Major General (later MRAF) Sir John 10, 151
Saulnier-Peyret Interrupter Gear 47
Savy 52, 60, 75, 113
Schafer, Lt. Karl 41
Selous, Lt. F.H.B 142-143
Senlis 106
Sherwood Foresters Regiment 22, 32
Simon, Ltn. Georg 191
Smith-Barry, Major Robert 41, 89, 107, 111-112, 114, 119-121, 125, 129-130
Somme, Battle of 10, 63, 76, 81, 86
Squadrons:
No. 9 Reserve Squadron 34, 37
No. 8 89, 91-100
No. 8 Naval 187
No. 11 11, 35, 62-90, 91, 95, 99, 101-106, 117, 127
No. 13 43-61, 93
No. 18 35
No. 19 160, 187-188
No. 20 41, 176
No. 22 41, 43
No. 24 48-49, 113
No. 25 74
No. 48 176
No. 56 146-206
No. 60 10, 41, 96, 104, 106-130, 187
No. 66 160, 176
No. 70 186
No. 74 97
Starr, Thelma 31, 37-38, 52, 74, 78, 85-88, 96, 100, 106,

114, 124, 132, 139, 152, 156, 205
Summers, Captain, A 118-19

Tewes, Flieger 124
Thompson, Major A 147
Tizard, Captain Henry 215
Tower, Captain, H.C 120
Transloy 109
Trenchard, Major General (later MRAF), Hugh 10, 76-77, 79, 82, 89, 95, 118, 143, 151, 160, 163, 170, 177, 179, 186, 201, 204
Trent College 8, 14-19

Upavon 38

Vaughan, Major, R.M 147
Verdun, battle of 80
Vert Galant 43, 158, 160, 166, 169, 171-172, 176, 178, 181, 184-185, 187-188, 194, 199
Vickers-Challenger Gear 46, 60
Victor, Mons. 95
Villiers,2/Lt. S.A 51-59, 61, 152
Vimy 54, 192
Vincent, Lt. S.F. 107-108
Vitry-en-Artois 172
Voss, Werner 97, 190

Waldron, Captain F 44
Waller, Corporal, J 74
Walters, Lt. A.M 118, 127
Weir, Sir William 144
White, Mr 136-137, 155-156
Winchester, Clarence 29
Wolff, Ltn. Kurt 191
Wright, Lt. F.C.W. 67

Young, Bill 160
Young, Flora 21, 32, 139, 156-160, 164-165, 169, 178-179, 183, 197, 205

Zander, Hauptman, Martin 117
Zeppelin Raids 32